Praise for *Powerful Leadership Through Coaching*

"A great coach helps people understand how they can grow, improve, and achieve excellence in every aspect of their life. This is how I coached my players and staff at Notre Dame. I recommend you read Michael's great book, *Powerful Leadership Through Coaching*, as it will teach any leader or manager how to better motivate and improve success both professionally and personally."

Lou Holtz, Former Notre Dame Football Coach,
Southbend, IN

"Finally, a book that makes a clear distinction between professional coaching and managerial/leadership coaching. Michael makes it clear that great leaders and effective managers, coach their people and the organization. Unlike many who position the 'so-called manager-as-coach' as simply managers using coaching skills, *Powerful Leadership Through Coaching* is written for organizational leaders and managers by providing a practical coaching process (diagnose, design, and deliver) combined with the skills and wealth of supporting resources needed to thrive in today's complex and competitive business environment."

Dr. Terrence E. Maltbia, Associate Professor of Practice &
Faculty Director, Columbia Coaching Programs, Department of
Organization and Leadership, Teachers College,
Columbia University, New York City, NY

"The difference between a good and a great leader is the ability to coach and develop others. This is a practical playbook packed with tons of powerful and provocative questions—a good coach's primary tool! This is an essential coach's companion that I will use in my coaching practice and to teach others how to be effective coaches."

Natalie Painchaud, Director of Learning,
Innosight Corporation, Boston, MA

"I have invested in hundreds of companies throughout China and Southeast Asia. One key skill needed with each of my investment companies is how leaders can better align, engage, and motivate people through the skill of coaching! Michael Simpson has provided me and my partners with a coaching framework and set of tools in how to ask more effective questions. This book will help to engage people on their path to greater focus, clarity, and business results."

Mr. Yang Qing, CEO and President, Shang Jing,
Fund of Funds Investment Group, Beijing, China

"I wish I had this coaching resource many years ago. Its genius lies in its simplicity and yet it strikes at the core of leadership, to effectively drive what every leader and manager at every level is continuously striving for—lasting behavioral change and results. This book is practical, motivating, and has some splendidly crafted tools that can literally be used 'the next day at work.' I would highly recommend this book to all leaders."

Rajan Kaicker, Executive Chairman and Managing Director,
FranklinCovey India and SouthAsia, Delhi, India

"Michael Simpson has written another excellent coaching guide for today's leaders. *Powerful Leadership Through Coaching* teaches the skill-set required for organizations to be successful at all levels to over-achieve. Similar to what is taught in coaching athletic competition, you'll learn a powerful coaching methodology and the skills needed to finish first in business, government, or education."

Peter E. Pilling, Athletic Director of Intercollegiate Athletes,
Columbia University, New York City, NY

"Michael has not only written a coaching book. Michael has collated his years of client experience into a how-to guide that is more of a coaching toolbox than a book. He does not only state the coaching theory, he translates it into implementable action steps. This book walks the talk. Bravo, Michael!"

Dr. Naif Al-Mutawa, MA, MBA, Ph.D., LH.D., New York State,
Kuwait, Dubai, Bahrain, and Qatar Licensed Clinical Psychologist;
Assistant Professor of Clinical Psychology,
Kuwait University, Faculty of Medicine, Kuwait

"Michael K. Simpson wrote a masterfully brilliant leadership and coaching book. With clear vision and direction, Michael expertly 'Diagnoses' coaching challenges, 'Designs' prescriptive, easy-to-access approaches for great coaching, and 'Delivers' a how-to guide for personal and professional success. Informational, educational, and inspirational, *Powerful Leadership Through Coaching* is a coach's playbook, written by an elite coach, and is a MUST READ for anyone aspiring to be a great leader!"

Bob Kulhan, Founder and CEO, Business Improv;
Author of *Getting to "Yes And":*
The Art of Business Improv, Chicago, IL

"I could not put this book down—Michael's book is a must read and a great playbook that simplifies coaching, teaching, and leadership. Coaching is every leaders' responsibility to achieve extraordinary results, whether it's with C-level leaders in an 8,000-person organization, or a manager leading eight people. This book will help every leader coach their team members to achieve to their fullest potential and help their organization exceed its goals and objectives."

Walter Levy, CEO and President,
NCH Corporation, Dallas, TX

"This book will change your paradigm about coaching and help you to understand the principles and practices of coaching in a very systematic, logical, and practical way to become a great coach. This is a great book for every new and seasoned leader who wants to unleash the true potential of their people through coaching."

Ms. Porntip Iyimapun, Founder and CEO, PacRim Consulting
Group, Bangkok, Thailand

"In *Powerful Leadership Through Coaching,* Michael has put his finger on one of the most critical elements for any leader or manager as we move into the age of the artificial intelligence. In my consulting practice, I am finding that skillful listening, asking powerful questions, and the art of developing others offers critical competencies for all great leadership and great teams in this new world of work. Michael has taken a deep dive into helping leaders develop the mindset, mastery, and skill of coaching."

Dr. Tony C. Daloisio, Ph.D., Founding Partner,
Charter Oak Consulting Group, Atlanta, GA

"This coaching book is a definitive and high-quality guide for any leader who aspires to be great. *Powerful Leadership Through Coaching* is a must-read book for leaders at all levels. Michael's book is ideal for any and all organizations that desire to develop coaching skills for their leaders, managers, and teams. I highly recommend this amazing book!"

Lavleen Raheja, Chairman and CEO, FranklinCovey India
and SouthAsia, Delhi, India

"Coaching is more than a skillset, it's a mindset and a way of being. Michael's book captures the essence of what it means to be a great coach and offers the skills on how to be a more effective leader. This is a must-have book for any company wanting to develop great coaching skills."

David Dai, Founder and CEO, Blue Oaks Capital Group,
Guangzhou, China

"Over many years of work and conversations with Michael, we have discussed how the present-day workforce cannot simply be managed but needs to be better led. True leadership must take a coaching approach, as opposed to directing, telling, or micro-managing. So, in a real sense, all of us need to become coaches. Michael's book helps leaders focus on the need to listen more empathically, to ask better questions, to solicit the wisdom from others, rather than providing our own answers and advice. Michael's book is terrific in helping leaders develop the right mind-set and skill-set and to become more authentic and better business partners with their people—whether at work or at home."

Mr. V.S. Pandian, Chairman and CEO,
Leadership Resources, Kuala Lumpur, Malaysia

"Everyone wants to succeed in life. A huge engagement factor and recipe for success is through coaching others. Unfortunately, very few leaders or managers choose to play. Michael's book offers great coaching insights and tools to help aid in the path towards success with others both personally and professionally."

Sheila D. Humphrey, Product Line Manager,
Strategy Execution Leader, John Deere Turf Care,
Fuquay-Varina, NC

"In order to be a great leader, you need to be a great coach! By applying the principles, practices, and skills Michael outlines in his book, you can find your passion and truly contribute to something larger than yourself—and empower those you lead to do likewise!"

Curt Allen, CEO, Agilix Online Learning, Provo, UT

"I have known Michael Simpson for 35 years. If you spend five minutes with him, you'll sense his character and genuine belief in the goodness of people and their potential to become 'better' and achieve great success, peace, or happiness. If you spend 30 minutes or more with Michael, you'll discover what is most important to you, why, and develop a detailed path forward—to overcome difficult things and to reach your highest potential. Take time to read his book. He offers powerful insights and tools that will engage any leader, manager, or coach to become better."

W. Brent Mason, Executive Leadership and Talent Management
Advisor, Saudi Aramco, the Kingdom of Saudi Arabia

"Michael beautifully illustrates powerful coaching principles and practices with real-life examples. It's easy for me to endorse *Powerful Leadership Through Coaching*, as it resonates so strongly with my experiences as a leadership coach and consultant. Coaching is about creating a safe environment and open dialogue to help people discover and develop their potential. Any leader who reads Michael's book will clearly understand the power they have to significantly enable others' whole-person effectiveness, as well as how to unlock and increase their own personal potential."

Dr. Walter L. Ross, Former MSOD Program Direction,
Pepperdine University's Masters of Science of Organizational
Development, Irvine, CA

"Michael Simpson masterfully illustrates the art of executive coaching as a core leadership skill. Leaders at all levels will find this book engaging, accessible, and practical --a game-changer in their development as a leader!"

Alan Hyatt, Director, Workforce Transformation,
PricewaterhouseCoopers, Salt Lake City, UT

"If you want to unleash the talent of your team, then becoming a great coach has become less complicated with Michael Simpson's book in hand."

Mr. Satyo Fatwan, Managing Partner, Dunamis
Organizational Consulting Services, Jakarta, Indonesia

"Michael makes a compelling case for the transformative power of coaching. His passion for developing leaders shines through in this practical guide that will empower managers and leaders at any organizational level to engage and develop their people. This is a must read for anyone who truly wants to make a positive impact at work and in life."

Dr. Mark Horney, Assistant Dean, Career Management Center,
Columbia Business School, New York City, NY

POWERFUL
LEADERSHIP
THROUGH
COACHING

FOREWORD BY **Dr. Marshall Goldsmith**

POWERFUL
LEADERSHIP

THROUGH

COACHING

Principles, Practices, and Tools
for Leaders and Managers
at Every Level

MICHAEL K. SIMPSON

WILEY

Library of Congress Cataloging-in-Publication Data:
Names: Simpson, Michael K. (Leadership coach) author.
Title: Powerful leadership through coaching : principles, practices, and
   tools for managers at every level / Michael K. Simpson.
Description: First edition. | Hoboken : Wiley, 2019. | Includes index.
Identifiers: LCCN 2019037259 (print) | LCCN 2019037260 (ebook) | ISBN
   9781119529026 (hardback) | ISBN 9781119529033 (adobe pdf) | ISBN
   9781119529040 (epub)
Subjects: LCSH: Executive coaching. | Mentoring in business.
Classification: LCC HF5385 .S66 2019 (print) | LCC HF5385 (ebook) | DDC
   658.4/07--dc23
LC record available at https://lccn.loc.gov/2019037259
LC ebook record available at https://lccn.loc.gov/2019037260

Cover design: Wiley

Printed in the United States of America

V10015575_111319

The best way to change the world is to become a great coach! Life can be hard and full of challenges and difficulties. It can also be an abundant, ongoing blessing and adventure. There are those leaders and managers who constantly inspire each of us to reach for new heights, to build upon our talents and strengths, and who challenge us to make a difference in the world. This book is dedicated to those powerful leaders and coaches in my life — my wife Cynthia Reeves-Simpson and my children Zachary, Luke, Jacob, and McKay. My family has shown love and encouragement to me throughout my life. They have been a constant inspiration and support with everything I have chosen to do. It is my hope to develop every leader and manager as a coach. My intent is for all coaches to help others dream big, achieve their goals, make good decisions, positively impact change in behavior through accountability, in order to connect with and inspire others. My hope is to add some effective tools to your coaching toolbox so that you will continue to impact the success of your life and the lives of those you lead. Enjoy the journey!

Contents

Foreword

Michael is one of the top global coaches to executive leaders and teams that I know. His vast experience in global coaching and in his latest coaching book, *Powerful Leadership Through Coaching,* offers a set of practical and timeless tools, powerful coaching questions, and examples that will help any leader or manager become a great coach.

This book balances Michael's real-world, practical coaching experience, as well as his global thought leadership in working with teams in over 35 countries. I know you will enjoy using these essential coaching tools that will equip any leader, manager, and team to increase clarity, focus, engagement, and improved results.

Dr. Marshall Goldsmith,
Keynote Speaker, Global Leadership and Executive
Coach, Bestselling Author or Co-author of
Stakeholder-Centered Coaching, MoJo, Triggers,
How Women Rise, and *What Got You Here, Won't Get You There*

Introduction: A Coach's Journey

I'm a coach. Not an athletic coach—I coach leaders in business, government, and education. And I love it. Why?

Because coaching transforms people more than anything else I have experienced in 30 years as an executive coach in 35 or so countries to many of the world's top companies, including:

- ExxonMobil
- Chevron Phillips
- Shell Oil
- PETRONAS
- General Electric
- Samsung
- Ericsson
- TE Connectivity
- Laird Connectivity
- Hewlett-Packard
- IBM
- Marriott
- Hilton
- PepsiCo

- Frito Lay
- John Deere
- Sabre
- Baxter
- Amgen
- Eli Lilly
- Johnson & Johnson
- Nike
- HSBC
- OCBC Bank
- Bank of Islam
- US Department of Defense
- US Army, Navy, Air Force, Marines, and Coast Guard

And many, many more. Every company wants success on the same measures: profitability, vision, budget compliance, strategy, goals, effective execution, culture change, and simple but powerful leadership development processes. Leaders want to overcome barriers, change mindsets, and grow trust. As an executive coach, I've seen small changes in leaders turn into massive increases in profits and other key success measures.

I have personally witnessed how a simple coaching process and tools can unlock individual talents and organizational strengths to achieve what matters most with the people I coach.

That's why coaching is my career purpose and passion!

The Realities of Being a Coach

Everybody in business, government, or education has hard issues to face. We face plenty of challenges and suffer a lot of stress no matter what our jobs are. Sometimes we feel defeated and don't know where to turn. We've all worked for that difficult boss or on a team that is divided and unproductive. Everybody is constantly distracted by the noise of everyday life. Sometimes we feel tossed around as if by waves in the ocean or pulled along on strong currents we can't control, yanked away from achieving the goals that really matter to us.

A leader I admire, Henry B. Eyring, was given this advice by a friend: "Hal, when you meet someone, treat them as if they were in serious trouble, and you will be right more than half the time." Not only was he right, but I have learned over the years that he was too low in his estimate. Leaders who don't know this about people will eventually see problems fester and human potential go untapped.

Skilled coaches honestly confront the big issues and the personal behaviors that affect results. Of course, coaches might have some advanced financial, technical, or operational skills, but those usually are not called for. The primary work of a coach is to help people develop the right mindset for achieving their goals—whether those goals are about sales, marketing, operational performance, customer service, or technology. Equally important is building the right culture —one that is customer and market focused, performance based, accountable, respectful, responsible, and trustworthy.

That's why this book aims to help you coach individuals first and then teams and organizations. Both skillsets are crucial. A great coach helps individuals leverage their own gifts, talents, and strengths to bless society, improve change, and achieve results. A great coach helps a person overcome triggers, fears, resentments, and obstacles. A great coach helps people change "from the inside-out"—they come to know themselves better and to live according to the principles that get great results.

A great coach also helps teams and organizations find the right focus: clear vision and strategy, customer loyalty, positive shareholder value, goal clarity, and flawless execution. A great coach helps organizations leverage diversity, succeed across cultures, resolve conflicts constructively, and communicate across functional and globally diverse boundaries. And a great coach helps team leaders in turn to coach their teams to higher levels of performance.! Remember, to be a great coach you do not have to have the right answers, but you must ask the right questions.

Making a Small Dent

Where did I gain a love for coaching and a desire to coach executives? The late Steve Jobs was famous for wanting to "make a little dent in the universe" (Sheff 1985). In a speech to Stanford University graduates, he added, "Your work is going to fill a large part of your life, and the only to be truly fulfilled is to do what you believe is great work. And the only way to do great work is to love what you do" (Jobs 2005). I truly believe that my coaching work has made, and continues to make, a little "dent." I have found real joy in helping people go from where they are now to where they want to be. My professional mission is to "influence the influential, in people, teams, and organizations worldwide."

It's been a real journey. My work is mostly with executive leaders and teams, helping them design and live by their missions, values, 5–10 year visions, 2–5 year corporate strategies, and shorter-term 1 year goals. In this 30-year journey, I am more than 3 million miles on Delta Airlines. I'm on the road about 150 days per year. I have been privileged to coach thousands of leaders in teams and one on one. I've worked in some 35 countries. I've loved making my "little dent," as Steve Jobs would say. This dent in the world has been fulfilling and purposeful, and has hopefully made as significant an impact on my clients as they have made on me during our coaching engagements.

For about a year, I coached the president and leadership team of a division of Chiquita Brands. One day the president called me and said he wanted to make a career change and asked me to help him explore how to make his next leadership move from a whole-person perspective. So I went to his new office near Grand Rapids, Michigan, and we mapped out the engagement.

I partnered with him and his team as they worked out their company goals with clarity and focus on improving profitable growth across the Americas. We also helped operationalize clear values and built a high-trust culture focused on customer service. Sometime later, at a leadership meeting in Maui, Hawaii, the president of this now $40 billion consumer products company and I wandered out into the Pacific Ocean for a private coaching/swimming session. We floated on the breaking waves and talked about where we had been and what was left to do. It felt like the world had stopped, with the sun on our faces, the warm water, and sounds of the breaking surf—it was like a small slice of heaven.

We talked things back and forth, from professional to personal. No notes, no time limits, no distractions—just a safe, confidential, human connection. I had found the ideal coaching relationship, far more than just a transaction between a consultant and a client. It felt like my entire career as a coach had led to this enlightened, nirvana moment in the Pacific. Ocean, connecting with that incredible human being.

My Personal Coaching Journey

I reflected on the life experiences that had led me here.

I looked back on my years with Covey Leadership Center, beginning in 1987 as the 35th employee, under the mentorship of the legendary Dr. Stephen Covey. His principle-centered approach to life and work inspired me, and I saw how I could use it to unleash my own potential and dramatically impact many of the Fortune 500 companies. I helped train leaders at Robert Redford's Sundance Ski Resort in the 7 Habits Principle-Centered Leadership. We worked with executives on their 360-degree feedback to pinpoint how to improve their effectiveness, and then used a blended model of training, coaching, and certification to facilitate their personal and organizational development.

In August 1995, I left Covey Leadership Center to teach business at South China University of Technology in Guangzhou and consult with Nike Corporation on building high-potential Chinese leaders. There I learned even more how central coaching can be to changing mindsets, to adapting to rapid change, and to building high-performance teams.

Returning to the United States, I entered the graduate school in Organizational Behavior at Columbia University in New York City. I was excited to bring my decade of practical work experience to research projects on organizational change and high-performance team building. As I applied different human-performance theories and change models to leaders at the United Nations and Ernst & Young, I was brought back again and again to the importance of leadership mindset.

At Columbia, I met Dr. Terry Maltbia, director of the university's professional-coaching certification program. A world leader in the study and practice of business coaching, he has allowed me to partner with him in certifying many effective coaches around the world. Terry is not only an expert in the various coaching models and tools, but also a wonderful model of empathic listening and provocative questioning—essential coaching skills.

After Columbia, I joined the Strategic and Organizational Change Practice at PricewaterhouseCoopers in New York, helping them develop their partners through a program called "PwC Leadership and Teamwork in Action." In my role as regional Knowledge Management practice leader, I met quarterly with PwC thought leaders across the United States, Europe, and Asia to share client experiences and research results.

As it became more and more clear to me that executive coaching had tremendous influence on organizational results, I dove deeply into it, becoming certified as an executive coach by Columbia University, the University of Maryland, and Inside-Out Coaching.

These influences and others have helped me immeasurably in my leadership development and international coaching practice. As I have sought to "influence the influence in people, teams, and organization's everywhere." My career in coaching has offered the incredible privilege of working directly with thousands of leaders and organizations worldwide.

I've also enjoyed writing seven books on leadership and coaching to leverage my professional work and amazing journey around the world. These writings have helped to synthesize and highlight practical experience over the years engaging with many diverse and inspiring leaders, teams, and organizations.

I tell you these things not to simply provide you my experiences, but to outline my global journey and the deep corporate and government experiences I've had in coaching and leadership development, so you can read this book with confidence that I know whereof I speak.

That's enough about my fun and enjoyable journey around the world. Now, let's talk about why you as a leader or manager should want to become a great coach.

References

Jobs, Steve. (2005). *Commencement address*. Stanford University.
Sheff, David. (1985). Playboy interview: Steve Jobs. http://reprints.longform.org/playboy-interview-steve-jobs.

The Realities of Being a Great Coach

1

Why Every Leader and Manager Should Be a Great Coach

Fulfillment is a right and not a privilege. Every single one of us is entitled to feel fulfilled by the work we do, to wake up feeling inspired to go to work, to feel safe when we're there and to return home with a sense that we contributed to something larger than ourselves.
—*Simon Sinek, British American author, keynote speaker, and organizational consultant*

What's the difference between a good leader and a great leader? All leaders are expected to improve performance and achieve great business results. Some leaders are lucky and succeed in spite of themselves. Some get mediocre results. Others succeed in the short term but in ways that don't build trust or sustain results.

I submit that the difference between good and great leaders is the ability to coach and develop people.

Damon was a vice president of operations within his organization, a firm plagued by low levels of trust. He knew that to move forward in this firm, he should make a serious effort to build trust with his boss and colleagues. I was asked to coach him.

But I found that Damon was unwilling to put in the work to actualize that goal. He was disorganized, an inefficient planner, and poor at prioritizing tasks. Though he worked very hard and was quite brilliant, he was also a chronic micromanager and often got lost in the weeds, taking his team with him. Essentially, Damon "got a lot done," but he was a horrible leader. He failed to define a clear strategy, set focused goals, and empower and engage his team around those goals.

Furthermore, Damon was less a leader than a cop. A favorite pastime was to catch his team members doing things wrong—"gotcha!"

games. He tried to make up for his lack of performance by blaming his team. When the time came for Damon's boss to move on, he naturally expected to get the open job. Neither his peers nor his team trusted him to do the job that needed to be done, so it went to someone else.

"Quit and Leave" or "Quit and Stay" Syndrome

There might have been a time when aggressive behaviors paid off for leaders like Damon, but that time is about over. Faced with untrustworthy managers, employees take one of two actions: they quit and leave or they quit and stay.

We all know what it means to quit and leave, but what does it look like to "quit and stay"?

Consider Scott Adams, who created the cartoon *Dilbert*. Adams began cartooning while he was working at an unmotivating job for managers who were utterly uninterested in him. How could he do a full-time job and still produce his famous workplace cartoons? He basically quit and stayed. He explained it himself: "The day you realize that your efforts and rewards are not related, it really frees up your calendar. . . . I had time for hobbies." His day job gave him plenty of practical and fun material to work with.

Leaders who try to drive, insult, or micromanage people will end up with team members who quit and leave or quit and stay. It's a natural consequence. The inevitable result is mediocre business performance or worse.

Coaching—the right kind of coaching—is the antidote to poor leadership.

Coaching by Definition

If you want to lead, not drive or micromanage, you need to become a coach!

According to the International Coach Federation, the body that sets standards for professional coaching worldwide, coaching is "a partnership that is formed to inspire others to maximize their personal and professional potential."

That's powerful. It means that a leader-coach honors team members as experts on their own lives. "The person who is currently doing a job is in the best position to know how to do it better," Dr. Ben Nelson observes. Coaches honor this expertise. They believe in the team and the employee. They know that the people they lead are creative, resourceful, and whole. They take responsibility to discover, clarify, and align each person's goals with the goals of the organization, producing a "win" for everyone. Coaching is the practice of getting people from where they are now to where they really want to be.

How does coaching work? Coaches listen, observe, and adjust their influence based on the needs, talents, and strengths of the team and the individual employee. By asking powerful coaching questions, the coach elicits solutions and strategies directly from the employee to help achieve the aims of the organization as well as those of the individual. Thus, coaching is also the art of building an effective culture and work environment.

Obviously, coaching executives and coaching athletes are alike in some ways, and the two kinds of coaches can learn from each other. One of the greatest coaches I have ever had, whether in a sports or corporate arena, was my sophomore high school basketball coach, Ron Burnside.

Coach Burnside was a short guard with a peculiar appearance and a distinct, high-pitched speaking voice. But he knew people, cared about his players, and had a strong commitment to coaching. He built into 16 boys a team mindset so we learned to care about each other, play for each other, and play to win. He understood purpose, vision, values, and high-performance expectations. He coached from the bottom up— through fundamentals and hard work to skill development. Although he was known for his challenging practice sessions, he kept things fun and entertaining. We knew he cared about each one of us as individuals first and players second. He showed trust and respect with each of us.

Under Coach Burnside's leadership, our team won 16 of 20 games, beating teams with far superior athletic talent and size. We did this because our coach believed in us as individuals, challenged us to be our best as a team, and set high expectations in our practices and game performance. He would often say, "You will play in games the same way you play in practice."

So you've never been a "coach" before? It doesn't matter. Coach Burnside was young. He had played college basketball but had very little coaching experience. As I've reflected over the years why Coach

Burnside was such an inspiring and motivating coach, these qualities come to mind:

- He inspired us with a clear vision, purpose, and values.
- He put each of us in positions to play to our unique gifts, strengths, and talents. We were very clear on our individual roles, but we were trusted and empowered to shoot the ball when open.
- He was demanding but never demeaning, disrespectful, or abusive. He treated all of us with respect, honesty, and loyalty.
- He understood how to build both a player's skills and basketball IQ and knew how to unleash the potential in each of his players.
- He demanded that each player achieve personal mastery though hard work and discipline.
- He communicated very well and connected personally with each player.
- He helped us form great relationships and build our confidence in each other.
- He put in the time needed to prepare his players well for every game.
- We had fun!

Coach Burnside took us from being young, immature kids to being confident, focused, and skilled champions.

Can you re-create that in your life and in your business? Can you create a great team by discovering individual strengths and potential, communicating effectively, actively forming relationships of trust, and putting in the time necessary to help develop the talents, skills, and capabilities of those around you?

If you cannot say, "Yes!" to this now, you will be able to by the end of this book. You'll be prepared to lead and effectively influence others around you. Fortunately, if you're amazing to work with and for, the consequence is natural: people will stay and give you their best work. You will retain and fully engage your talent, you will build up new leaders, and you will continue to grow in your career and in life.

Unfortunately, in too many organizations, the exact opposite is happening.

A business executive told me recently that in the next five years, 65% of his employees not only *could* but *would* retire. The statistics were devastating to him. "Michael," he explained, "I don't have anyone in-house to replace them. We have not developed the next generation of talented leaders that are prepared to take over. We have a huge talent gap!"

This executive is not alone. All too often, organizations are unprepared with their leadership and talent pipeline. This lack of preparation poses a real strategic threat to any team or organization. What's the solution? Coaching and development of your people. Coaches understand what is important for customers and the business. They understand how each business unit and team supports a shared leadership responsibility for vision, strategy, goal execution, and delegation. They also understand what is involved for employees to grow their skills; increase their decision-making; expand their roles and responsibilities; and increase their motivation, productivity, and engagement.

Your top talent, and often your middle talent, will have multiple career choices and options outside of your organization. Some may feel like their job is a dead end. Others will have a bad relationship with the boss or other team members. Others find no significant purpose or excitement in their current roles.

That's why it's urgent that you become the kind of coach I've defined here: a true partner who inspires others to maximize their personal and professional potential.

Coaching: What It Is and What It Isn't

Coaching is unlocking a person's potential to maximize their own performance. It's helping them to learn rather than teaching them.
—Sir John Whitmore, founder of GROW Coaching Model and co-founder of Performance Consultants International

I've known many leaders who tried to become trained as coaches but found their training didn't work. It was too simplistic, boring, overly theoretical, not practical, or too academic. Others felt their coach training was from a different planet, taking them on a New Age–filled psychological journey loaded with mystical lingo with no relation to reality.

In contrast, the coaching skills and tools in this book are practical and easy to use. They are based on years of testing, trial, and practice. My purpose is not to bore or mystify you, but to help you understand the basic elements of how to become a great coach.

Coaching is not consulting or counseling. This is a surprise to many people who do not understand the foundations of coaching. A coach does not walk in, tell you how to succeed, and solve your problems for you. Neither does a coach probe your childhood traumas while you lie on a soft couch in a dark room.

A real coach:

- Takes a collaborative and supportive approach by partnering with others
- Asks powerful and provocative open-ended questions at the right time, in the right way
- Focuses on the client's agenda and what is most important to them
- Focuses more on solutions and opportunities than on past problems
- Helps identify and overcome obstacles to success
- Shows courage by asking honest questions *and* consideration by showing respect
- Helps clarify a client's vision, strategies, goals, and objectives
- Helps clients improve their mindsets, behaviors, and ability to change
- Encourages clients to make their own informed choices
- Holds clients accountable for their choices

A real coach does not:

- Provide consulting services, which usually entails giving expert advice
- Provide counseling or therapy
- Hold open-ended conversations that go nowhere
- Figure out why people are broken and what needs to be "fixed"
- Tell people what to do and how to do it

Now I hope you realize that you don't have to be a pro at counseling or consulting to be a great coach.

Coaching Can Be a Game Changer!

Never doubt that a small group of thoughtful, committed citizens can change the world. Indeed, it is the only thing that ever has.
      —*Margaret Mead, American cultural anthropologist*

Everyone has the potential to be a great leader and coach. Within every human soul is the capacity to develop natural gifts, talent, and strengths. It starts with focusing less on self and more on building, developing, and empowering people around us.

My first introduction to professional executive coaching occurred back in the 1990s when I was working for PricewaterhouseCoopers as a management consultant. I saw a coaching course advertised at the University of Maryland, and I was instantly intrigued. The title was "The Art and Practice of Coaching Leaders."

Coaching leaders. Not athletes. Not All-Americans, but leaders in a business context. I went to the course, and as I sat there, I was instantly hooked. I saw at once that coaching in the workplace could become a critical part of an effective leader's toolbox.

After that, I knew I could walk into my family room, my favorite automobile repair shop, or the corner executive office of a Fortune 500 company as a coach. I knew I could bring about a significant, productive change in thinking no matter where, no matter with whom.

Since then, research data show my instincts were good. According to a study published in *The Manchester Review*, the right kind of coaching can improve productivity by 53%, quality of work by 48%, working relationships by 71%, teamwork by 67%, and job satisfaction by 61%.

I strongly believe that everyone can be a great coach and that coaching is needed everywhere. In fact, I've built an entire business around the belief that coaches are not born: coaches can be developed. All it takes is learning a few new skills and turning those skills into a natural competency.

This is my coaching promise: as you read this book and put these tools to work, you will increase your skills and capabilities as a coach. You will gain the ability and confidence to better engage and unleash the passion and talent of your team toward their highest goals and priorities.

An Example of a Highly Effective Coach

Early in my career, I had a leader who was great because he was a highly effective coach. His name is Stephen M.R. Covey, the son of Dr. Stephen R. Covey. Over the three years he led and managed me and our consulting team of 20 people, I came to recognize that he had strong business acumen. He worked at understanding our customers, the industry, and the market. He was sound in his judgment and in strategic thinking. He was a very competent business person.

But his true greatness as a leader was in his highly effective coaching. He was highly emotionally intelligent.

Stephen M.R. had ongoing coaching conversations with me about my job performance, my future, my learning and development, and even my personal and family goals. His coaching was both personal and professional. He knew me, cared about me, and brought out the best in me. He evaluated my performance against a "win-win agreement"—a plan by which both the firm and I would benefit in concrete ways.

Instead of handing out directives, Stephen M.R. asked questions. He empathically listened to the answers—from customers and from his own people. He sought our input and feedback and validated our views. He took a deep interest in us, treating us as whole-people and not just cogs in an organizational machine. He recognized and rewarded our contributions. I was impressed by how open he was and how much he trusted everyone on our team.

Stephen M.R.'s coaching was open, honest, humble, positive, and focused on solutions. He was interested in *our* success, not in finding fault, judging, blaming, or shaming. He was fully invested in the art of coaching others to become successful leaders themselves.

I firmly believe every leader can be a great coach, like Stephen M.R. Covey. That's why I've written this book. In my view, coaching is the central skillset of a great leader. As you read this book, consider the many, many leadership challenges that can be solved through great coaching. Here are just a few such challenges to ponder:

- Do team members buy in to the organizational strategy? How can you help them get aligned with organizational and team goals?
- Are team members fully aware of the performance standards they are expected to meet?
- Do they get effective feedback? Do they know what needs to be improved and by when?
- Do they have "skill issues" or "will issues"?
- Do they know what their strengths are and how to consistently leverage their gifts and talents?
- Do they have clear action plans with defined accountability and support?
- When they fall short, are they dealing with issues within or beyond their control?
- What training, resources, or mentoring do they need to improve their performance?

- What options do they have for overcoming obstacles?
- Are you clearing the path for them so they can overcome obstacles outside of their control?
- Do they know what the consequences are for falling short of goals?
- What kind of recognition and reward do they really need when they succeed?

As you contemplate these challenges, ask yourself what kind of skills you need as a leader to help your team meet them. I guarantee that the most effective skillset you need right now is the skillset of an effective coach. In this book, you will learn how to:

- Hold effective coaching conversations—whether long or short, planned or in the moment
- Listen empathically
- Influence the mindset of your team members through questioning rather than dictating
- Help clarify strategic direction, goals, and objectives
- Discover and use each team member's natural gifts and strengths
- Offer feedback that is helpful rather than hurtful
- Help members develop personal awareness and devise their own plans for improvement

Now see yourself as a great coach. You'll have a team that is crystal clear on strategic direction and clear performance goals. You'll elicit the best from your team by asking good questions and exhibiting great listening skills with empathic accuracy. You'll create a high-trust culture by treating people as partners and capable assets rather than underlings. You'll identify the unique skills, strengths, and talents of your team members. You'll position people in the right roles. When confronted with weak performance, you'll give honest, respectful feedback that will strengthen people rather than tear them down. And you'll be affirming and supportive, and celebrate their achievements along with them.

That is the promise of this book. Now let's get started.

2

The Simpson 3Ds Coaching Model: The "How to" of Coaching

Often it only takes small changes in the behavior or viewpoint of a manager to create amazing changes in a team's performance.
—Alan Sockwell, private and public board of directors advisor

The skillset of an effective coach starts with an effective coaching model. Like the One Ring in J.R.R. Tolkien's *Lord of the Rings*, you need "one coaching model to rule them all."

There are as many coaching models as there are coaches, of course, but most are structured according to the same basic process. You want a step-by-step approach to any coaching opportunity—a performance challenge, a career-path opportunity, mindset or behavior change, a human relations issue—because much of your success as a coach will come from mastering the coaching process. Great coaching requires the coach to ask the right question, the right way, at the right time.

Over the years, I've studied many influential models that coaches use to unleash great performance and potential.[1] To paraphrase Tolkien, all coaching models have their worth, and each contributes to the worth of the others. From the many models I've studied, I've sought to simplify coaching into a very basic framework I call the *Simpson 3Ds Coaching Model*: a simple, interrelated process anyone can use to coach people no matter what issue they face. In this chapter, I provide

---

[1] Those models include Columbia's 3 Cs Coaching Model, the Co-Active Coaching Model, Sir John Whitmore's GROW Model, Gallup's strengths-based coaching model, Marshall Goldsmith's stakeholder-centered coaching model, John Maxwell's Professional Coaching model, the NLP model, the Action Learning model, the evidence-based coaching model, the Herrmann Brain Dominance Instrument (HBDI), the 70:20:10 model, the EQ Coaching model, ASPIRE, FUEL, OSKAR, CINERGY, SOAR, CLEAR, ARROW, and many others.

an overview of the 3Ds Coaching Model and associated tools, which you can access or download online at www.simpsonexecutivecoaching.com.

Here are the 3Ds:

1. Diagnose: What is the coaching agenda?
2. Design: What matters most?
3. Deliver: What actions will be done?

Let me explain them and provide powerful coaching questions that are useful at each phase.

1. Diagnose: What Is the Coaching Agenda?

If I had an hour to solve a problem and my life depended on the solution, I would spend the first 55 minutes determining the proper question to ask, for once I know the proper question, I could solve the problem in less than five minutes.
—Albert Einstein, German-born scientist and theoretical physicist

In the diagnose phase, you're finding out what is happening and why. You empathically diagnose the current and past state to understand the employee better: their strengths, their perspective, and their influence on others. You're learning historical context, listening to their story, figuring out their mindset. You're defining the agenda of your coaching experience.

Suppose you have Morgan on your sales team. It's close to year end, and Morgan is not delivering the expected sales results. You don't know why. You ask Morgan to meet with you and find a quiet room for a coaching conversation. You explain to Morgan that you want to understand what is happening in the sales process and get a better idea of where clients are in the sales pipeline. You might ask these diagnostic questions:

- "Can you tell me more about how you and your team are doing on sales goals?"

- "What is your current sales goal target?"
- "How do you currently measure success?"
- "Are you currently on track to hit your sales number?"
- "What does success look like for you?"
- "Where do you need to be successful in the future?"
- "When you consider your sales pipeline, what accounts are closest to close?"
- "What seems to be getting in the way of achieving your overall sales goal?"
- "What activities have you tried, to move clients along in the sales process?"
- "What appears to be the biggest challenge with closing sales?"

Morgan says there are several deals in the pipeline, but nothing is closing this quarter because the market is slowing.

You might drill deeper:

- "Tell me more about the client's average sales cycle."
- "Tell me more about why clients are having such a hard time making a timely decision."
- "Who are the key influencers at your client site who could possibly help influence sales decisions?"
- "What aspects of the sales pipeline are in your direct area of influence or control?"
- "What areas of the sales pipeline are completely out of your influence or control?"
- "Focusing on that which you can directly influence, what do you think are the most critical actions to pursue to influence a sales decision?"
- "Have we developed a solid business case for clients to act on?"
- "Do they understand the value of what we are offering?"
- "How do they know that what we have to offers adds the most value?"
- "In what areas are they most likely to want [product/service/value]?"
- "In a barrier-free world, how would you like things to be different in the coming weeks/months?"
- "Considering your current pipeline, which accounts do you believe would be closest to making a decision?"

- "Are there any client decision-makers we should schedule a meeting with by phone or in 'person'?"
- "How do you believe I can best help you in advancing your clients in the pipeline?"
- "How can our team or the organization help you with those clients closest to closing?"
- "Are there any clients who would be willing to meet in person in the coming days?"
- "Which accounts do you believe would be most likely to meet and close in the near term?"
- "On a scale from 1 to 5, 1 = low and 5 = very high, where are you in your motivation to pursue these clients in your pipeline?"
- "What would help make them a 4 or 5 for your motivation to seek to close them?"
- "What are your biggest sales opportunities that excite and motivate you to focus on right now?"

In diagnosing, the emphasis is on discovery and learning about conditions, setting, context, history, background, issues, current state, barriers, and obstacles. When you diagnose, you explore personal awareness, gaps, capacities and strengths, current mindset and paradigms, current behaviors, as well as the employee's perspective on their personal story.

When you ask questions during the diagnostic phase, you are establishing the scope of Morgan's work, clearing up expectations, determining what to focus on, finding out what's holding them back, articulating the business case or benefits, exploring inner innovation, and building the foundation for an effective, high-trust coaching relationship. You are a guide on the side to help them curiously explore reality and context.

Following are some excellent coaching questions that can be asked during the diagnostic phase of any generic coaching conversation:

- "What brings you to coaching? Where do you want to start? What's your agenda?"
- "What would you like to achieve in this session?"
- "What are the issues, challenges, or big opportunities you would like to discuss/explore?"
- "What seems to be the *main* issue?"
- "What concerns you most about [topic]?"
- "What current goals do you want to accomplish? What do you want to change about yourself/your team/the organization?"

- "What are your future goals? What are your choices? What is possible? What excites you?"
- "What is happening now? What are the performance challenges?"
- "Can you give me some history and context of what is happening now?"
- "What data, observations, or experiences would suggest there is a problem/opportunity?"
- "Will you tell me more about that? What else has taken place? How did you feel about [topic]?"
- "What led up to this? What happened? What caused this? Can you tell me more?"
- "How are things going? What's new? What is the latest news?"
- "What are the benefits of this course of action? What are the costs of not doing this?"
- "What barriers or challenges are currently getting in your way?"
- "What barriers would you need to overcome?"
- "How do you feel about overcoming this barrier? Can you say more?"
- "Are there any required shifts or changes in mindset, behaviors, actions, or resources?"
- "Where are you now on the road to the goal? Where do you want to be [the gap]?"
- "What specific changes would you like to make?"
- "Can you state where you are now and what you would like to accomplish in one sentence?"
- "What headline would describe what you want to focus on and your biggest challenges or opportunities?"
- "On a scale from 1 to 5, 1 = low and 5 = very high, where are you in your motivation to accomplish your goal?"
- "If your ideal situation or desired state of success is a 5 on the scale, where are you now?"
- "In a barrier-free world, what would you like to be different in the coming weeks/months/year?"
- "How will you know when you have arrived and been successful? Any measures of success? Any desired state outcomes?"
- "If you had a magic wand and could change anything to ensure your success right now, what would that be?"
- "What big opportunities excite and motivate you to focus on right now?"
- "What do you want to or hope to accomplish? What else?"

- "What would you summarize that you want to focus on going forward?"
- "As a result of our conversation today, what one or two things would you like to focus on before our next meeting?"
- "What actions will you take? By when?"
- "How can I/the team best support you going forward?"

In summary, the diagnosis phase is about helping clients, team members, or colleagues understand their past and current mindset, barriers, faulty assumptions, and beliefs. Coaching in the diagnosis phase helps to summarize their learnings so they can clearly define their issues, challenges, and opportunities for growth and success. In diagnosis, the key is to clarify the gap or goal and summarize why they need to change, what is most important, and the scope of the pain, gain, or opportunity. They prioritize and narrow the focus on a few key areas and discuss their targeted areas for behavior change, performance improvement, development, or goal setting.

2. Design: What Matters Most?

Your ability to divert your attention from activities of lower value to activities of higher value is central to everything you accomplish in life.
—*Brian Tracy, Canadian American motivational public speaker and self-development author*

In the second phase of coaching, you are helping clients design solutions for themselves, their teams, or their organizational context. You consider what's working and what isn't and begin creatively brainstorming what could work. When you diagnose, you discover what is happening and clarify key priorities and objectives. When you design, you test assumptions, creatively and innovatively brainstorm, imagine desired future states, and explore various options for going forward.

In the design phase, you may want to ask Morgan:

- "What has worked in the past to help close sales?"
- "What new or creative actions could you take to help advance and close your pipeline?"

- "What areas of your sales pipeline do you believe you should focus on right now?"
- "What opportunities to close business have you not explored or considered?"
- "What can be done to help you test, try, or pilot any of these options now?"
- "What seems like the most practical or best option to pursue?"
- "What resources, help, or support do you need from me or the team?"
- "How would you prioritize from 1 to 5 the most critical sales areas to work on in your pipeline?"
- "What are you most excited about trying to close right now?"
- "What would those actions be?"

Perhaps Morgan has been communicating with customers via text and phone but believes a site visit in person would be more engaging and helpful. Morgan may also say, "I've been working with just one or two people internally, but I am having problems accessing the real decision-maker."

With the design of a plan in place, now is the time to develop that plan further, by asking:

- "How can we help you do that as soon as possible?"
- "Who are their internal buyers and decision-maker(s)?"
- "Do we have any other internal relationships that can help influence them to action?"
- "What do you believe would add the most value to them [product, service, value]?"
- "What do you think would be the best way to contact their other key internal influencers?"
- "Are there any additional sales influencers we would need, to help influence the decision-makers prior to an onsite meeting?"
- "When do you think you could get a meeting scheduled onsite with them?"
- "What do you need from our organization to help you?"
- "What do you need from me or your team to make this happen?"
- "What resources can we make available to help you present/close an effective sales meeting to their key decision-maker(s)?"

Following are some excellent coaching questions that can be asked during the design phase:

- "What [coaching topic] do you want to address today?"
- "How would you describe and summarize the situation?"
- "What are you most motivated and excited about focusing on? Why?"
- "What are your key takeaways from this situation?"
- "What insights emerged for you from feedback, the data, observations, or evidence?"
- "How are you feeling or reacting to the [data/situation]?"
- "Did you gain any new insights? Can you say more?"
- "What was the key lesson or insight for you?"
- "What do you think this situation amounts to? How would you summarize this situation?"
- "What key data points, key issues or big opportunities, or key relationships have you highlighted?"
- "Did any aspect of the conversation or data confuse you? Seem unclear? Not make sense?"
- "What does this situation tell you about yourself?"
- "How do you feel you can be most proactive and responsible in responding to this situation/information?"
- "Have you noticed any opportunities to improve relationships with key people or stakeholders?"
- "Who are the important people, key relationships, or important stakeholders who have specific needs for you to effectively improve?"
- "Are there any team, organizational, or customer relationships or performance opportunities that you need to strengthen and improve?"
- "What are your current strengths and weaknesses in this area?"
- "What are your options in addressing this [relationship/situation]?"
- "What are your important lessons from this?"
- "What would that solution look like? Will you give me an example?"
- "As you brainstorm creative options, what kinds of ideas come to mind?"

- "Which targeted areas excite you the most or are you most motivated to improve?"
- "What anticipated benefits are there for acting on those options?"
- "If you had to do it all over again, what would you do differently?"
- "What are the downfalls, pitfalls, or watch-outs going forward?"
- "Has anything worked in the past? How might it apply to this situation?"
- "Given the available options, which areas would you like to pursue?"
- "What seem to be the most important priorities for you to pursue?"
- "If you were to focus on your natural strengths and talents, what are you motivated to go after?"
- "What resources do you need in order to be successful?"
- "If you were to prioritize the top one to three most important areas for action, what would those be?"
- "How do you suppose you can improve the situation?"
- "What are the possible solutions?"
- "Considering all of your choices and options, what would you like to pursue or go after?"
- "What are you most excited to focus on going forward?"
- "What actions will you take? By when?"
- "How can I/the team best support you going forward?"
- "Because of our conversation today, what one or two things would you like to focus on before our next meeting?"

In summary, the design phase is focused on helping clients, team members, or colleagues design innovative solutions for themselves, their teams, and their organizational context. Coaching in the design phase helps them consider what's working and what isn't and begin clarifying and sifting through various solutions and desired future scenarios. There is exploration of how they can best prioritize and impact key performance areas, important stakeholder relationships, and organizational and customer needs. The design phase is about exploration, brainstorming, and creatively discussing various options and plans that will be most motivating and successful prior to putting plans into action. During the design phase, coaches can add tremendous value by helping others clarify priorities, explore options, choices, tap into creativity, inner innovation, strengths, excitement, and exciting new and better options going forward.

3. Deliver: What Actions Will Be Done?

Clear, simple goals don't mean much if nobody takes them seriously. The failure to follow through is widespread in business, and a major cause of poor execution. You need robust dialogue to surface the realities of the business. You need accountability for results—discussed openly and agreed to by those responsible—to get things done and reward the best performers. You need follow-through to ensure the plans are on track.
—Ram Charan and Larry Bossidy, Execution: The
Discipline of Getting Things Done

Peter Drucker once said something like this: "All grand strategies eventually boil down to work." In the delivery stage, detailed plans and accountability processes for execution are put in place to make it real. This is the area of focused goals, desired results, milestones and success measures, execution plans, accountability, ongoing communication, and action-learning.

In the delivery phase, the detailed steps of accountability are mapped out. You determine how and when to put the plans into action to improve performance, achieve results, and build trust by ongoing engagement with all key stakeholders.

Coaches can help advance the delivery phase by asking questions like these:

- "Why is this issue [topic] so important to you? What's the mission, purpose, or big picture?"
- "What is your strategy, your path, and your game plan going forward?"
- "What are your key goals, outcomes, objectives, and measures? What does success look like?"
- "What goals [topic areas] would you like to put into action?"
- "What measures or key milestones need to be achieved to determine your success?"
- "Who needs to be involved or reported to in order to ensure support and success?"
- "How are you going to get this done? What are your defined actions and behaviors?"

- "When will you plan on carrying out these key actions? When will you get started with the daily/weekly actions?"
- "What action plans do you need to develop over the next 30, 60, 90 days?"
- "What barriers do you see to achieving these goals and objectives? What steps will you need to take to avoid or overcome those barriers?"
- "How can I/the team offer support and provide needed resources for your future success?"
- "Whom do you have to engage to get this done?"
- "What people, teams, divisions, leadership, key stakeholders, or organizational support must you effectively engage to execute your goals and objectives?"
- "What actions will you take? By when?"

Back to our case study with Morgan. In helping Morgan in delivery phase, a coach might say, "Morgan, what are the first steps you need to take to best execute your plan?"

Morgan may decide to call client contacts and schedule an onsite meeting with the key decision-maker(s).

You may then ask, "Morgan, what are other barriers may be in your way?" Morgan may then share that there's a technology component to his presentation that he needs help with. It will be critical and beneficial to the presentation if someone from leadership comes to the presentation to influence decision-makers.

"Morgan, that's a great plan. When can you schedule this? How can I support you? What will offer the most value to the client and this upcoming meeting? After your meeting, how will you measure success? How can I follow up with you? Is there anything else you need from me, the team, or the organization? What's the best way to hold yourself accountable for your plan?" Close by expressing support, confidence, and affirmation. "I am confident that things will go very well. I think this is a terrific plan. I'm excited to support this effort."

Following are some excellent coaching questions to ask during the deliver phase:

- "What issue, challenge, or opportunity [topic area] are you most excited about executing?"
- "What energizes you and excites you the most to focus on and improve?"

- "Why is this [topic area] so important for your time, focus, effort, and energy?"
- "What is ultimately the most strategic thing for you to do going forward?"
- "What are the one or two most important [topic areas] to focus on?"
- "Have you mapped out an overall game plan? Tell me more about it."
- "Who would you need to engage to ensure success? Your plan? By when?"
- "What role models, supporters, sponsors, or mentors are available for help?"
- "Who else could help?"
- "On a scale from 1 to 5, how committed are you/your team/your stakeholders to this [topic area]?"
- "What else might you do to gain more commitment?"
- "Where do you go from here?"
- "What is the best way to hold accountability for success going forward?"
- "How would you define success with your plans going forward?"
- "Ok, let's summarize your game plan. What are you committing to do?"
- "Is there anything you need to do before that?"
- "Is that action a stretch for you?"
- "When will you do it?"
- "Who will you talk to?"
- "How can I/the team best support you going forward?"
- "Where would you like to focus your actions?"
- "What actions can you commit to? By when?"
- "How can I/the team best support you?"
- "Within the next 30, 60, or 90 days, what do you want to commit to and have happen before our follow-up meeting?"
- "Because of our conversation today, what one or two things would you like to focus on before our next meeting?"

In summary, the delivery phase is focused on helping clients, team members, or colleagues move from designing innovative and creative solutions into detailed steps of accountability. Concrete actions are mapped out. Clear, focused mindsets, styles, behaviors, and performance goals and objectives are clearly identified. Clear expectations are agreed to for reporting. Future action steps and success with relationships, partners, team members, and key stakeholders are mapped out for execution.

Coaching in Action: Rebecca's Story

Rebecca was facing a challenge: she was brought into an international organization to help strengthen relationships with customers and local distributors. Studying the data, she broke the current distributors into three general categories based on their performance and ease of doing business with them: top performing, middle performing, and low performing. Her goal was to address the low-performing distributors, but when she examined the situation closely, she discovered that they were "protected" through their friendship with the CEO.

In a coaching session with Rebecca, we utilized the Simpson 3Ds Coaching Model: 1. diagnose, 2. design, 3. deliver.

1. Diagnose: What Is the Coaching Agenda?

Rebecca explained to me, "Michael, there's a serious problem here. We have some low-performing distributors who are losing customers and losing their own employees. But they know that they are protected by their longtime friendship with the CEO. I can't address the problem with them without them complaining to the CEO, which may get me fired. I have no power here. How do I influence upward when there are serious political consequences, and the CEO has the power to get rid of my job?"

As the children's story reminds us, it's very hard to tell the emperor that he has no clothes.

I restated the situation to make sure I understood it. "Rebecca, this is a difficult and sensitive situation. The distributors seem to be old school buddies, protecting themselves in ways that are not adding value and making this a political situation."

I then introduced to Rebecca the mindset of "courage and consideration" (more on this later). When coaching upward, it's crucial to lead with absolute consideration—start with loyalty and respect, expressing a desire to hold a hard conversation about improving the situation.

Then balance consideration with courage—lay out your data and feedback and your perceptions of the risks. Assure the boss that you are being fully transparent. Focus on customer value and objectives, organizational benefits, and shared opportunities for the customer and the business.

2. Design: What Matters Most?

"Rebecca, right now you're alone on this problem, and if you attack it alone, how will you be perceived? As a whiner, a complainer, and not being loyal to the boss, she responded. "Can you attack his ego straight on?" I asked. She realized that she would lose that battle, and that she needed internal political and business support.

"Who else is impacted by this situation?" I asked. "Which stakeholders are also paying the cost for this? Where else can you turn to get support? Tell me more about whom you need to influence and who might offer political support internally."

Rebecca shared that the chief operating officer was approachable and would be a good ally. Rebecca understood that she also needed to influence members of the board of directors. She began to brainstorm a plan that was inclusive and solution-oriented rather than problem- or person-focused.

"What messages will appeal to the COO? To the board of directors? What business data do you need to compile, and what fact-based message will you need to prepare for them? How can the data speak to customer needs, customer value, and to the best interests of the business?"

"Michael, the data clearly show that we are losing good employees and good customers," she replied. "Both losses are very costly and risky to the business and to our future viability and sustainability. That means our opportunities for growth are being hurt, and the culture of our corporation is suffering. I need to show the CEO that protecting a few nonperforming friends who are modeling the wrong values and behaviors is backfiring in a big way. I need to talk about turnover, low productivity, nonperformance issues, misalignment to values, and poor customer feedback. In the end, the CEO is a logical man and wants what is best for the business and to look good in eyes of his board of directors. With the COO's help and the board's support, I think he'll listen to logic, facts, data, and customer needs."

3. Deliver: What Will Be Done?

To wrap up our coaching conversation, I asked Rebecca, "We've talked about a lot today. What is your plan for getting it done? What issues are you motivated to go after based on our conversation? What do you feel that you need to do first?" Rebecca then developed a plan. She decided to start by forming a coalition with her COO and members of the board of directors. She would test their support and get feedback to make sure the messaging was accurate and would be well received by the CEO.

She needed to recruit support that could back her up in a professional, respectful, and loyal way, not in an emotional or judgmental manner. She needed to be both highly considerate and at the same time highly courageous in her feedback and messaging. Otherwise, the message would not be heard, or her job would be at risk.

"What tools do you need? What resources do you need?" She felt that she needed to assemble a persuasive package of data based on customer needs, market needs, turnover reports, exit interviews, and profit/loss statements. She had to connect the dots for the CEO and ensure that he did not feel attacked. That meant presenting hard facts: customer data, customer loyalty feedback, employee turnover, exit interview data, and so on.

"What are you committed to doing in the next 30, 60, and 90 days?" I asked, Rebecca committed to scheduling a meeting first with her COO, then a key influencer with whom she had credibility on the board, and then with her CEO.

"How can I support you and help hold you accountable to this plan?" I asked. We agreed that I could call her every two weeks to check in and see how things were progressing. We also agreed that she could email or call me anytime if anything unforeseen happened or if she needed additional support.

PRACTICE: YOUR COACHING PLAYBOOK

Consider an issue that has become a challenge in your team or organization. Either alone or with your team, take the time to practice the following coaching phases with their interrelated powerful coaching questions:

1. *Diagnose:* What is the coaching agenda?
2. *Design:* What matters most?
3. *Deliver:* What actions will be done?

3 Coaching from the Inside-Out

Coaching starts within us. Before can we help others, we need to examine ourselves and our motives and seek to model the change we seek in them. It is hard to get others to do something unless we are willing to do it first. It's called having real street credibility.

The key question for a coach is, "How well do I connect with others?" Dr. Brené Brown says in her book *Daring Greatly*, "Connection [is] the energy that exists between people when they feel seen, heard, and valued; when they can give and receive without judgment; and when they derive sustenance and strength from the relationship" (Brown 2012).

The heart of leadership is inspiring trust and connection with others. Leadership is not so much about what we say—it is more about what people hear and feel. As a leader, you are first a model of trustworthiness. Great leaders focus on their own good win-win intent and credibility first.

Nothing lacks real credibility more than someone who doesn't walk their talk. That's why effective coaches always start "from the inside-out." To be a great coach, you must drill down to your own inner motivations, ambitions, goals, and feelings. You must understand your own mindset. Why do you have this mindset? What is the "back story" of your approach to leadership?

To get answers to these questions, we need to ask some basic fundamental questions: Why are you, you? What makes you tick? What are your real motives and most important influences?

What brings you joy? What helps you calm down? How easy is it for you to get angry, impatient, and frustrated? When faced with a challenge, do you dig in, do you effectively engage? Or do you disconnect and walk away before you have to invest too much? Do you strongly believe in yourself and your abilities, or do you hear a constant message in your head that convinces you that you're a failure? What's your story?

Framing Your Personal Story

Don't underestimate the power of your mindset and vision to change the world. Whether that world is your business, your community, your government, an industry or a global movement, you need to have a core belief that what you contribute can fundamentally change the paradigm or way of thinking about problems.

—Leroy Hood, American biologist and developer of scientific instruments

Your personal story is your mindset based on your life's experience. It's your personal narrative, your inner dialogue; and when you're ready to analyze a problem, decide, or act, it's there to tell you to who you are, whether to move forward with success, or to stop because you will fail. Henry Ford said, "Whether you think you can, or you think you can't—you're right." Your mindset is a powerful driver for most of your decisions, motivations, and actions. When you get to the core of how someone thinks and what motivates them, you can begin to influence new perspectives, new ways of seeing the world, and new forms of innovation. A coach starts the discovery process with assessing and understanding mindset.

Dr. Carol S. Dweck, author of the book *Mindset,* describes a study of children trying to solve puzzles. As the puzzles got harder, she was amazed by two students who reveled in the difficulty. One boy expressed his joy that he was finally given a challenging puzzle. The other was excited that he was going to learn something informative that day. Dweck wrote that as she watched them, she thought, "What's wrong with them?" (Dweck 2006).

It was their mindset. These children loved challenges and knew if they put in the effort, they could solve whatever problems came their way and learn from it!

Mindset is how you look at the world around you. According to Dr. Dweck, your mindset profoundly affects the way you lead your life.

By the way, like individuals, teams also have mindsets. As you discover the collective mindset that drives a team's vision, values, and goals, you can effectively test assumptions, tap into their strengths, and improve their decision-making and innovation.

Examine your own personal mindset. Some mindsets can be realistic, some can be limiting, and others can be flat-out distorted, false, and wrong. It is your mindset asking questions like, "Why am I so smart?" Or "Why am I so stupid?" "Why is everyone around me smarter (or more stupid)?" These inner conversations are the most important conversations you will ever have. Your conversation with yourself will determine the outcome of your life and dramatically influence all of those around you.

Coaches can offer great insights into what motivates and influences mindset just by framing the right questions.

Overcoming a Fixed Mindset

We generally categorize mindsets as either *fixed* or *growth* mindsets.

If you have a fixed mindset, you believe that you cannot grow, improve, or change. You also believe you were born with a certain level of intelligence and certain personality traits. And that's it. It's fixed—it's determined.

By contrast, if you have a growth mindset, you believe that you can keep growing and learning with time, effort, and help. The sky is literally the limit. People with a growth mindset agree with the former American Major League baseball pitcher Roger Clemens: "I think anything is possible if you have the mindset and the will and desire to do it and put the time in."

One of your primary tasks as a coach is to help your clients discover *inner innovation* within themselves: a growth mindset rather than a fixed mindset (see Figure 3.1). With a fixed mindset, they cannot make much progress because they don't think it's possible. This is doubly true for you as the coach: you are not likely to help others if you are encumbered with a fixed, judgmental, or pessimistic mindset.

Besides, mindsets can and do change. Those with a fixed mindset actually believe in an illusion—that nothing can ever change them.

Fixed or Growth Mindset

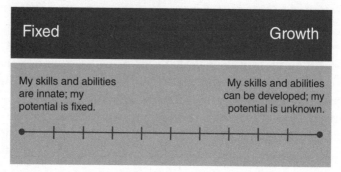

Figure 3.1. The spectrum of fixed mindset to growth mindset.
Source: Dweck 2006.

This is false. Mindsets are often very changeable, dynamic, progressing, and evolving.

For example, after my acquaintance Carter injured his spine serving in the military, he found a job in a community that looked to be a good fit for him and his family. As luck would have it, his boss was also former military. They understood each other and communicated well with each other based on similar life experiences. Carter felt a strong camaraderie with his boss. When a new colleague, Mallory, came on, Carter told her that the boss was one of the best people he had ever worked for over his long career.

Unfortunately, Carter's boss one day made a promise to him—and broke it. (At least, that was how Carter perceived it.) Nearly overnight, Carter's boss went from best in the world to a horrible person and a liar. Carter's job went from being ideal to an ordeal.

What had happened? Carter's mindset had shifted in a negative, poisonous direction.

Ideally, Carter's boss might have stepped in and addressed the situation but did not. Carter's peer, Mallory, saw her co-worker begin to spiral downward and disengage, doing only the minimum to maintain his job. It was a bad situation for everyone. Although she was his peer, Mallory decided to try coaching Carter. To begin with, she needed to discover the reasons for his mindset shift: How did he go from loving his job to hating it so quickly? What could be salvaged in this situation? Let's watch Mallory practice two of the 3Ds Coaching phases with Carter:

1. **Diagnose Phase: What Is the Coaching Agenda?**
   Finding some time at lunch away from the office, Mallory asked Carter, "I'm curious. Why have your feelings about your job changed so quickly? You used to be satisfied. Give me some context to your current situation. What has happened over the past few months?" She empathically listened closely to his story without interrupting him, agreeing with him, or trying to fix or defend the boss.
   Instead, she offered support. "It sounds like you've experienced a betrayal of trust and lack of clear expectations in your job."
2. **Design Phase: What Matters Most?**
   Mallory then started the design process by reframing the situation: "Is there a positive reason to stay? Going forward, what benefits and creative opportunities excite you? In a barrier-free world, what innovative and creative things could you do to best impact the boss and the current situation? If you do leave, what positive things will you take with you to your future job?"

One of the most gratifying things about coaching is helping someone challenge false, limiting, or ineffective mindsets—to help them reframe the situation and overcome pessimism or lack of hope. Many people find themselves in a place of despair or self-defeating behaviors; I love witnessing the transformation when the person I am coaching begins to use natural resources of creativity, skill, and hope to find new strategies and approaches. Reframing limiting or false mindsets; helping people overcome mental roadblocks; liberating them to increase their self-awareness, expanded responsibility and choices, and confidence—these are a few of the intrinsic rewards of effective coaching.

What is your inner narrative? What story of yourself has influenced your mindset? As author Patrick Rothfuss states in his book *The Name of the Wind*, "Everyone tells a story about themselves inside their own head. Always. All the time. That story makes you what you are. We build ourselves out of that story" (Rothfuss 2007).

Our inner narrative can also distract, distort, or deceive us. It can tell us that we're dumb, that we are not enough, or we lack the power to influence our situation in life. It can tell us that we add no value. If so, we hide in shame, self-pity, self-doubt, or fear. We avoid situations where we might fail, because our mindset tells us that we are always failing—that we are failures. In his book *Working with Emotional*

Intelligence, Daniel Goleman says, "If we lack the belief that we can handle [life's] challenges, we can start to act in ways that doom us. The thought 'I can't do this' is crippling" (Goleman 1998). We get stuck. We disengage.

How do we overcome this negative, fearful inner narrative?

We find our personal power. We find our truth and begin to live it.

Dr. Mark Goulston, author of *Get Out of Your Own Way at Work*, shares the story of how he became chronically carsick. He wrote that when he was a young boy he read a comic book in the backseat of the family car, got sick, and then threw up.

His mom explained that he was prone to being carsick and he would get carsick every time he read in the car. And he was! Dr. Goulston admitted that every time he tried to read in the car he would get sick. He did not have a similar problem on a plane or a train because his mother never warned him about being sick in those environments. But the time came when he really wanted to read in the car. So, he started reading! He immediately felt nauseated, but he pushed through until the queasiness passed. "And I have been able to read in a car ever since without being sick. The mind and the will to persist is an amazing thing, isn't it?" (Goulston 2005).

Dr. Goulston points out how easily we can get stuck inside a limiting narrative—and break through it! If he could read in the car, what else could he do? And why didn't he realize it sooner? Our inner narrative tells us what we can and cannot do, and we listen to it! We work within the limitations. Many self-imposed limitations can become self-fulfilling prophesies. If you think you can or you cannot, you are right.

Perhaps you got scared by a dog when you were little and grew up convinced that all dogs are aggressive and mean. Perhaps you watched your dad revel in his new Ford, which he hand-washed every Saturday morning, and you grew up thinking that Ford was the best brand of car and the only one you would consider purchasing. Perhaps you think you're the smartest person in nearly every room you ever enter. Or perhaps you think you're dumb and if you open your mouth in a staff meeting everyone will confirm it.

What are the consequences of having a limiting or fixed mindset? As fitness and wellness author Kelli Calabrese stated, "There is nothing on the outside that is going to make you happy, unless you have peace and joy on the inside" (Calabrese 2015).

Recently I had an opportunity to coach Maria, a very smart and ambitious engineer in a very successful firm. She was also the only female engineer at her executive level. Although she stood out at work, she would try to disappear in staff meetings.

I asked her, "Maria, what is happening in these meetings? What triggering event or circumstance happens where you would say to yourself—I add no value in our meetings and must stay quiet?"

"Michael," she said, "when I'm in these meetings, I am sitting there with all these bright, intelligent engineers. I know they have more experience and are smarter than I am. Nothing I say can say will sound intelligent to them. So I don't say anything at all. I sit there in silence knowing that my voice and contribution in our meetings won't matter."

"Maria," I responded, "why don't you think your perspective matters? Why do you believe this voice that tells you you're not smart enough? How can you silence that inner critic that says you are not smart enough, your voice and opinion doesn't matter, and that you're stupid compared to everyone else? How can you reframe this situation so these negative thoughts stop influencing your behavior?"

Maria determined that when these negative thoughts or feelings surfaced in moments of insecurity, she wanted to be more assertive and to amplify her voice.

"I do have an inner critic that sabotages my voice and silences me," she shared. "And it diminishes my voice and my value at work and in other key relationships that are important to me. We explored two key strategies that she could do when these negative triggers appear: 1. Focus on her gifts, strengths, and talents and how she could best add value to the group. 2. Get curious and ask questions in areas where the team may struggle, need to solve problems, or need to focus on customer value, partner support, and market opportunity."

Recognizing that coaching is not counseling or therapy, how would you coach someone like Maria to help her reframe her inner narrative? Here are some questions that might help a client, a partner, or a direct report overcome a limiting mindset:

- Can you think of a time when you might act or respond negatively or reactively?
- What triggering event influences you to go negative or pessimistic, or to be reactive?

- Do you recognize times when you are responding from a place of fear or self-judgment?
- What negative thoughts sabotage you? How would you like your response to be different? What would an ideal response look like?
- How could you respond in a more effective way?
- What would be the benefits of responding in this new and better way? What would be the costs or downside if you do not respond differently in the future?
- How can you begin to share your natural gifts, talents, and strengths?
- What strengths do you bring to the team, and how can you best use them for the overall benefit of the team?

Remember, coaching is not intended to be therapy. I did not need to psychoanalyze, evaluate, fix or advise Maria. I did not need to discover if there was a fifth-grade teacher or negative parent in her past who told Maria that she was never going to be as smart as the boys. That's not coaching. The need to be the expert in the room, or to add value or advise, can be challenging for most coaches. It's also very hard not to do! We want to help and tell people what to do. Many times our nature is to fix, solve, and make everything better.

In an article for *Forbes.com*, Susanne Biro discussed how often the lines between coaching and counseling are blurred (Biro 2017):

> *Many leaders believe they understand how to coach well. However, when I teach coaching to leaders and put them into their first coaching conversation, I inevitably find the leader giving their advice, telling people what to do, and telling them how to do it. Those well intended strategies can often get in the way of the performer, direct report, or coachee from discovery and doing the heavy lifting and thinking.*

It's a natural response, Biro argues. "We want to help! But telling someone what to do is not helpful." As a boss, remember if you continually tell people what to do, and it doesn't work, whose fault is it?

A great coach asks questions to enable people to own their own problems, to resolve their own issues, and to explore creative ways to improve their situations. Coaching does not mean we have to check all our wisdom, judgement, advice, and experience at the door. We can use it as needed. But our competencies and experiences often get in the way of helping others develop their own competencies and learn from their own experiences. The person being coached should always do the heavy thinking and lifting.

Once Maria saw that her inner narrative was self-deceiving and false, I asked her to tell me about a time when she felt smart and what it was like when she added significant value in a staff meeting. She told me of a previous work situation where she felt valued because of her ability to see the big picture without getting lost in the tactical weeds, as many managers often do. "I am really good at creating a vision that is attainable, but despite being a good engineer, I do not like staying in the nitty-gritty details. I also feel that I am good at drawing connections with customers, partners, and market input while gaining needed buy-in and support for our products and services."

As I continued to coach Maria, we explored ways to use her "big picture" perspective and involvement with key stakeholders. "When your inner critic goes negative, how can you best reframe this trigger into a move positive response? What is true about your gifts, strengths, and talents during your staff meetings? How can you best connect the team to customer needs, interrelated systems, and stakeholder buy-in during your team discussions? Is it true that you do not add value in your meetings and should remain silent? Is your team making sound engineering decisions without your key insights and perspectives?" The obvious answer was no.

I asked Maria to set a goal to make at least three comments in her upcoming staff meeting. We role-played what she could do and what key questions she could ask. "When you show up and stay silent, you are living from a place of distortion and deception," I reminded her.

Eventually, Maria's boss noticed a change in her. "I really appreciate your contributions and input in our meetings," he told her. "We are now asking more connected and more aligned questions about our products and services to our customers." Maria has more confidence. She still struggles to speak up, but she is aware of the negative impact of holding back. She knows she has silenced herself for too long, and she is excited to live a life free of shame and fear.

Coaching helped Maria break out of her negative mindset and play more fully to her natural gifts and strengths.

Great research from experts such as Peter Drucker, David Cooperrider, Dr. Martin Seligman, Don Clifton, Marcus Buckingham, Tom Rath, and many others points toward a strengths-based approach to gaining more productivity, motivation, retention, engagement, performance, and results. In truth, our people's strengths are our greatest asset in coaching.

As financial motivational speaker T. Harv Eker says, "Do it. Get in the game. One step in the right direction is worth a hundred years of thinking about it. There is no right time. Right now is the time to be courageous" (Eker 2009).

Avoiding Your Inner Saboteur

> *Turn down the volume of your negative inner voice and create a nurturing inner voice to take its place. When you make a mistake, forgive yourself, learn from it, and move on instead of obsessing about it. Equally important, don't allow anyone else to dwell on your mistakes or shortcomings or to expect perfection from you.*
>
> —Beverly Engel, addiction recovery author, counselor, and therapist (2008)

Do you have an "inner saboteur"—a voice that constantly nags you about your limitations, your mistakes, and your incompetence? A voice that continuously reminds you of your failures?

Just about everyone has unproductive inner conversations like these at least occasionally. They sabotage our best efforts and sap our energies. We often say things about ourselves we would never say about others.

Your inner saboteur might also be reminding you about impossible barriers, challenges, or circumstances—you'll never succeed against the obstacles that are ahead. Yet life is 1% what happens to us and 99% how we choose to react.

It's easy enough to point these things out to others. As a coach, you'll encounter this kind of inner sabotage in the lives of your clients. But also as a coach, you'll want to be deeply aware of your own story—those aspects of your personal narrative that sabotage you. Is the story true? Is it valid? How does your inner story or dialogue impact the results you get? How would you like things to be different or better?

Mindset is a daily choice. Answer the following key coaching questions to further assess your self-view and mindset:

- What story about myself am I telling myself today?
- In what ways am I sabotaging myself?
- How do I improve my view of myself?
- What are my true strengths, gifts, and talents?
- How do I view and connect with those around me?
- How do I view their true potential and strengths?

When we intentionally focus on our own personal mindset, we amplify our self-awareness. We choose to be responsible for our mindset. Instead of interacting with the world as a victim or a martyr, we gain control of our emotions and our choices. We cannot control our circumstances, but we can completely control our responses to what happens to us, and our choices. Jim Collins stated it best in his book *Good to Great*: "Greatness is never a function of luck, circumstance, or environment, it is always a matter of disciplined thought, disciplined choice, and disciplined actions" (Collins 2001).

Owning Your Own Story

In you must go.

– Yoda

Bad things happen. Life is unfair. People disappoint. Setbacks and failures occur. But these things do not have to define your own inner story.

In the 1980 film *The Empire Strikes Back*, the main character is full of potential but kind of whiny and tends to give up when things get hard. His name is Luke Skywalker. As part of his Jedi training, he is required to face his fears in a dark cave. He is scared. But his teacher, Yoda, explains, "In you must go." Inside the cave, he fights his enemy, Darth Vader; and when Luke cuts off Vader's head, Luke sees his own decapitated head staring back at him.

Author and psychologist Dr. Brené Brown, in her book *Rising Strong*, observes that we must all face the inner narratives that hurt us. It can be frightening. But, as Brown explains, "Owning our stories means acknowledging our feelings and wrestling with the hard emotions—our fear, anger, aggression, shame, and blame. . . . To harness

the Force, we must own our stories and live our truth. In we must go."
As author and motivational speaker Les Brown stated, "Life is for living. As you make your goals and your dreams, make your move before
you're ready" (Brown 1992). Find your power within and design your
story—one that you want to focus on and live!

Reframing Your Own Story

Reframing the internal narrative has been called "the most powerful
tool in the everyday coaching toolbox" (Stubblebine 2016). The underlying principle is that, by necessity, our brains can hold only so much
information, which means we must be selective. "What you feed your
mind, will lead your life," says professional coach Kemi Sogunle.

To illustrate this point, once there were two able, hardworking,
qualified shoe salespeople. They were both given a new territory on a
Pacific Island. Immediately upon arrival, the first salesperson placed
an urgent call back to the home office: "Get me out of here. It is hot,
dirty, and no one on this island is wearing shoes. This area is a waste
of time!" The second salesperson also called the home office: "You
would not believe my area. Put me in contact with our manufacturing and shipping departments immediately. Our prospects are very
good. There are so many people here, and no one on this island has
shoes." The way we frame the situation is more critical than our circumstances, education, money, or talent.

Another coach was talking with a CEO about a troubling employee
(Stubblebine 2016). The employee was gifted and had come into the
job with very strong recommendations. The CEO was excited about
the employee's potential contribution—except the employee hadn't
contributed a thing. All this time, the CEO was telling himself the
story "I have this amazingly talented employee!" until a coach came
along and asked one question: "What is this employee contributing
to you and the organization?" The CEO quickly answered, "Nothing."
Only then did the CEO know what to do: he had to let this employee
go and wish him well. The CEO was able to reframe his perspective
and act.

Through simple questions, coaching can reveal why we think the
way we do, why we act or react to certain triggers, and how to explore
possible responses to difficult situations. When we recognize what we

are doing and why, when we become self-aware of the stories we are telling ourselves, we can stop, reflect, and have the power to change our course of action.

Becoming a Confident Coach

It's what I've looked for and tried to build in every executive who has ever worked with me. Confidence gives you courage and extends your reach. It lets you take greater risks and achieve far more than you ever thought possible. Building self-confidence in others is a huge part of leadership. It comes from providing opportunities and challenges for people to do things they never imagined they could do—rewarding them after each success in every way possible.

—*Jack Welch (2001)*

Jack Welch, one of the great businessmen of our time, grew up with a speech impediment. As he explains in his book *Straight from the Gut*, his stammer embarrassed him from a very young age. Then his mother helped reframe his limitation for him. "It's because you're so smart," she told her son. "No one's tongue could keep up with an intelligent brain like yours!"

Welch believed his mother: that his mind worked faster than his mouth, and that's why he had a stammer. So, he stopped worrying about it.

Decades later, Welch saw some pictures of himself as a child and was shocked by his appearance. He was small! "Yet I never knew it or felt it," Welch wrote. "It's just ridiculous that I wasn't more conscious of my size. . . . My mother convinced me that I could be anyone I wanted to be. It was really up to me" (Welch 2001). Instead of limiting him, his mindset drove his success as a business leader.

An effective coach enables clients to develop mindsets that are engaged, productive, adaptive, and innovative. That's why leaders need to be effective coaches. As leadership expert and author Fred A. Manske Jr. observes, "The ultimate leader is one who is willing to develop people to the point that they eventually surpass him or her in knowledge and ability" (Manske 1999).

Choosing Your Story ═══════════════

> You can't stop the onslaught of the pounding waves, but you
> can learn to surf.
> —Jon Kabat-Zinn, American professor emeritus of medicine
> and teacher of mindfulness

Like Jack Welch, we can tell ourselves a different story about our challenges and surmount them. A great coach continually urges clients toward a mindset that makes the most of any situation. When the client's story isn't working, the coach helps them reframe, rewrite, and choose a different story.

When I coached Ethan, the company he worked for was expanding internationally. Ethan had been good at setting price points for new products domestically, but the international markets were much trickier. Meanwhile, Ethan's peer was a true expert at pricing. "And, truthfully, he thinks he should have my job," Ethan admitted to me. "His passive aggressiveness is overwhelming at times."

I asked Ethan if he thought his own response to his peer was within his control. Of course it was, he said. No matter how difficult the situation, we can always choose our response to it. We have no control over how others behave, whether they are passive-aggressive, toxic, or openly hostile, but we can frame our own response. Someone else's anger, hostility, ego, dominance, and diminishing behaviors have nothing to do with us, so why should we allow them to control our behaviors and possibly ruin our lives?

I asked Ethan, "When you encounter this passive-aggressive behavior, what is a productive way to respond? What are the opportunities for improving this situation? How can you influence the situation in a more positive way? Who are your allies? Who are your advocates when someone is being destructive or diminishing you?"

Unfortunately, the antagonizing peer did not become his best friend—there are no fairytale endings here—but through ongoing coaching Ethan thrived. As his coach, I was able to help him reframe his story of bitter helplessness and victimization. He found new resources and allies at work. He developed some practical tools to help handle this difficult situation.

"When you're going through a hard time, there's a part of you that doesn't understand that it's going to be all right, that you're going to come through to the other side," Ethan told me later. "It was hard for me to keep moving forward when I just wanted to give up. I was so focused on the negative, I did not leave enough room for the positive to sink in. Knowing I could control my response and that I had rational options helped me see the situation through a different lens. I started looking through a positive lens instead of a negative doom-and-gloom lens."

Fundamental to coaching success is this ability to help people reframe unproductive mindsets. As a coach, you start by discovering the client's mindset and whether it accurate or not. What in that mindset is blocking the client from seeing a whole world of possibility? That's the most crucial discovery you can make as a coach because it governs everything you do from then on. In addition to mindset, it is also important to examine their results and see if those results offer them outcomes that give them success.

PRACTICE: YOUR COACHING PLAYBOOK

Based on what you've learned in this chapter, grade your own mindset. On a scale from 1 (low) to 10 (high), how positive and optimistic is your mindset? Where do you fall short? Are you a victim of what fate or circumstance has dealt you, or fixed in an unproductive narrative? Do you have it within yourself to grow, improve, and change your narrative? Can you help others discover their own effective stories? As a leader, in what ways can you begin to improve your mindset and your team's mindset? Check yourself against the following questions.

Mindset Check List

1. Do you have positive inner thoughts and messages for yourself with good intent or motive?
2. Are you acting with integrity and in alignment with your deepest motives, values, and beliefs?
3. Are you assuming and looking for good intentions in others?
4. Are you acting toward others with genuine care, respect, and mutual benefit?
5. How can you catch others doing something right?
6. How will you make time to connect with others in honest and open communication?
7. How will you actively listen, show respect, and fully understand the viewpoints of others?

References

Biro, Susanne. (2017). The four foundations of exceptional coaching. Forbes .com. https://www.forbes.com/sites/forbescoachescouncil/2017/01/04 /the-four-foundations-of-exceptional-coaching/#3bafed2c7c7b.

Brown, Brené. (2012). *Daring Greatly: How the Courage to Be Vulnerable Transforms the Way We Live, Love, Parent, and Lead.* Avery.

Brown, Brené. (2015). *Rising Strong: The Reckoning. The Rumble. The Revolution.* Spiegel & Grau.

Brown, Les. (1992). *Live Your Dreams.* HarperCollins.

Calabrese, Kelli. (2015). Creating new habits. Quoted on Josh Trent's Wellness Force Radio podcast. https://radiopublic.com/wellness-force-radio-WzYLBp.

Collins, Jim. (2001). *Good to Great: Why Some Companies Make the Leap and Others Don't.* HarperBusiness.

Dweck, Carol. (2006). *Mindset: The New Psychology of Success.* Random House.

Eker, T. Harv. (2009). In *The Compass* by Tammy Kling and John Spencer Ellis. Harper Element.

Engel, Beverly. (2008). *The Nice Girl Syndrome: Stop Being Manipulated and Abused—and Start Standing Up for Yourself.* Wiley.

Goleman, Daniel. (1998). *Working with Emotional Intelligence.* Bantam.

Goulston, Mark. (2005). *Get Out of Your Own Way at Work.* Putnam Adult.

Manske, Fred A., Jr. (1999). *Secrets of Effective Leadership: A Practical Guide to Success.* Leadership Education & Development.

Rothfuss, Patrick. (2007). *The Name of the Wind.* DAW.

Stubblebine, Tony. (2016). The complete guide to reframing for coaches and people who care about smarter decisions. BetterHumans. https:// betterhumans.coach.me/the-complete-guide-to-reframing-for-coaches -and-people-who-care-about-smarter-decisions-29a3656d21be.

Welch, Jack. (2001). *Straight from the Gut.* Business Plus.

4 Coaching with a Mindset of Abundance

Once I was attending a family party where a young boy was fanatically guarding cupcakes that had been set out by an aunt. When the boy saw his younger sister coming toward him, the hope of eating a cupcake written all over her little face, he loudly announced, "Each cupcake is five dollars!" and stretched out his hand for payment.

His little sister was incensed! He didn't make those cupcakes! He had nothing to do with the cupcakes! He had no right to ask for this outrageous sum! It wasn't fair!

Just as the boy's little sister was about to lose her mind, their even smaller cousin walked up, pretended to take five dollars out of her back pocket, slapped the boy's hand with an imaginary bill, and announced, "There's more where that came from!" as she took a cupcake.

She had a mindset of abundance.

A mindset of abundance doesn't get lost in what is right or fair. Abundance knows that there's always more. Choosing to be an abundant leader means there are always more resources, credit, recognition, opportunities, possibilities, and acknowledgment to go around. You don't have to watch your back. You don't always have to protect your selfish interests. You don't have to be wary of someone you think is proverbially getting in your lane at work. Abundance is choosing to be the leader who is ready to rise together with everyone else. There is a saying: "High tides raise all boats." Abundance allows others to rise, to get credit, to be recognized, and to be valued. Nothing is lost when this happens—there are only gains, and enough for everyone.

I believe people respond better when treated abundantly. Imagine a world where most people could wake up each day inspired to go to work with a winning team where they are valued and trusted—and then go home feeling confident, happy, engaged, and fulfilled.

As a coach, a peer team member, or as a direct report, it is critical to ask: Is everyone coachable? I had the opportunity several years ago to work for a man I'll call Micah. He was a savvy business operator. He talked a good game and had been blessed with much financial success in his career.

But in working for him, I realized that his success came at a cost. He was the consummate blamer. He would not take responsibility for his mistakes. He couldn't recognize the contributions of others because he was so insecure. He truly believed he was better and more successful than everyone else. He saw himself on top of the world, and when his promises went undelivered, when business deals and invoices were protested, he always found a way to blame, shame, and judge everyone else and stay on top. He had no vulnerability or authenticity, could show no weaknesses, and had to remain in control and protect his image at all costs. As an internal or external coach, it is important to assess the readiness of the person on a team to be open to change, self-reflection, improvement, and getting better.

Micah could be smart, charismatic, and witty, but he could flip a switch and just as quickly become vicious, insulting, and cruel. He would often badmouth others behind their backs. He would act as though he trusted people, but then micromanage them. He would gladly throw people under the bus, manipulate data, and distort facts just to look good and to survive another day as the manager.

I worked for Micah for two years. I wondered if he would ever be open to a coaching conversation, and whether he would ever be self-aware to ask: how am I showing up with my leadership team? What derailing behaviors might be getting in the way? Working in such a toxic culture was discouraging. Every day I asked, "Why am I still here? Is my paycheck worth this? Do I really have influence with this key manager and the management team?"

For me, it was just a job. When I realized life was more than growing sales, hitting targets, and making money, I left. Although creating a safe environment for coaching can add great performance improvement opportunities, unfortunately, not all people, teams, or organizations encourage a coaching culture. Some people may not be coachable or ready for coaching.

There is a universal law of Karma believed by many: "What comes around, goes around"—how you act with others will eventually return to you, whether positive or negative. Micah's behavior came back to haunt him. He was eventually fired by the company's board of directors. Many people he thought were loyal to him had been acting out of fear and self-preservation. Unfortunately, the way this leader modeled and created a toxic environment, with an appearance of being polished and successful to others, had led to a fake culture of distrust, shame, fear, resentment, and disloyalty. Ultimately, this mirage evaporated as he torched himself with his board and his management team. His lack of good intent came full circle when he was asked to leave the organization.

Personal greatness does not come from wealth and status, but from seeking to effectively influence and build up others. Not all organizations will embrace a culture of openness, leadership development, and coaching. Many myopically focus on everything else—money, title, position, control—which should be secondary.

Former US President Dwight D. Eisenhower said, "You do not lead by hitting people over the head—that's assault, not leadership." An effective leader is abundant, generous, and civil as they seek to influence the lives of others for mutual benefit.

One of my clients, Ashley, switched jobs in 2002 during in a down economy. She had taken a pay cut for something a little more stable but still ripe with opportunity. "I thought that I found a really good fit for me," Ashley admitted. As a mid-level executive, she was promised everything from the opportunity to lead high-level negotiations to fun trips.

"What I was promised in that interview back in 2002 is almost laughable now," Ashley said. "I rarely saw anything outside of the four walls of my office. Luckily I had a great view from the window!"

What happened? According to Ashley, her employer, Scott, viewed relationships as "win-lose." If Ashley made a great contact, Scott saw it as a blow to himself. Ashley found herself left out of important meetings. So, she became isolated until Scott was ready to move on.

Scott was smart and expedient. He was friendly. He was outgoing. If you asked him how he was "showing up" among his employees every day, he would probably say that he was loyal, fun, and got a lot done. But he lacked the emotional intelligence (more on this later) to understand what he was doing to those around him. He did not realize he was managing from a place of scarcity and insecurity, rather than a place of abundance.

As a result, Scott only profited from a small portion of the talent Ashely had to give to the company. Her talents and gifts were underutilized.

Adopting a Learner Mindset

*Asking a question is the simplest way of focusing thinking
. . . asking the right question may be the most important part
of thinking.*
— *Edward de Bono, pioneer in brain training*

A coach with an abundance mindset will be insatiably curious, always
wanting to learn more.

Dr. Terrence E. Maltbia, the director of our Columbia University
Executive Coaching Certification Program, would often remind us,
"When you are coaching others, be as curious as a 10-year-old child.
If you are doing most of the talking, you are not being a good coach."
Curiosity is the hallmark of an abundance-minded person. In her
book *Change Your Questions, Change Your Life,* my close friend Dr.
Marilee Adams suggests there are two kinds of mindsets for peo-
ple: Judger and Learner (Adams 2016). To oversimplify, those with a
Judger mindset try to direct and control the world around them, while
those with a Learner mindset seek out new opportunities for learning,
exploration, and innovative solutions. Some of the Judger and Learner
mindset characteristics are listed here:

Judger mindset
- Fixed/closed
- Problem-focused
- Afraid of change
- Inflexible/controlling
- Reactive/victim
- Directs/tells/advises
- Excludes/defends
- Blames/shames/judges
- Knows all the answers
- Self-important/entitled
- Pessimistic/diminishes
- Win-lose
- Ego-driven/fearful
- Scarcity
- Yes, but . . .

Learner mindset
- Inquiry/learner
- Solution-seeking
- Embraces change
- Active listener/empathic
- Proactive/responsible
- Explores possibilities/ curiously explores
- Accepts/open to ideas
- Includes/values differences
- Opportunities/discovery
- Optimistic/multiplier
- Win-win
- Humble/vulnerable
- Creative/innovative
- Yes, and . . .

People with a Judger mindset are scarcity minded, while people with
a Learner mindset are abundance minded. Now, nobody is entirely the
one or the other, but ask yourself, "What happens if I show up 80% of

the time as a Judger? How do I speak and behave with self and others? What results will I get? On the other hand, what happens if I show up as a Learner 80% of the time in my relationships?" How do I speak and behave with self and others? What results will I get?

To dramatically transform the way people solve problems, they need to shift their mindsets. If you have a Learner mindset, you are open to what is possible. You do not focus on the problem, you focus on your responsibility, your creative choices, and on new and better solutions. An effective leader starts with a Learner mindset and coaches others toward a Learner mindset.

On the other hand, Judgers live out of fear and defensiveness. They are close-minded. Blame and shame others and hold them hostage to the past. They think they know all the answers and seek to control and micromanage others.

I was recently leading a large-scale coaching engagement with General Dorothy Hogg, who is the surgeon general and leader for the US Air Force Medical Services Corps. in Washington, D.C. Among her executive teams were a number of very experienced major generals, brigadier generals, and colonels. This was an exciting engagement where I was able to personally offer both team and one-on-one coaching over a six-month period with each of these leaders. They were going through a number of monumental changes with military healthcare reform, an internal transformation and reorganization effort with their military health system, and many budget allocation and resource changes. Having a Judger or reactionary mindset and culture is common in organizations with changes of this magnitude that were this disruptive. The coaching engagement required a number of shifts in thinking and behavioral changes for the leadership team, as well as for the organizational system as a whole. Certainly, any such change takes time and requires tremendous effort and support at all levels. That said, I was very impressed with how well the overall team was able to adapt and establish trust as they led this change effort by building a common language, a common learner mindset, and a common set of communication tools to help influence high-trust conversations with all of their key stakeholders. Developing a more proactive, Learner mindset helped establish General Hogg and her leadership team to focus on those things they could directly influence and control, versus getting stuck or reactionary about the many things they could not control during very turbulent and distrusting circumstances.

How do you see yourself? As a Learner or a Judger? Answer the following questions and decide for yourself:

- Are you being judgmental of yourself and others?
- Are you reactive, close-minded, defensive, and protective?
- Are you showing up as a Judger 80% of the time?
- How can you be more self-aware when you fall into the role of victim or Judger, or have a closed mindset?
- When have you recently been a Judger? What was the triggering event? What was the impact? How would you like your response to be different in the future?
- What are the negative impacts of being a Judger and being closed, inflexible, and intolerant of others' viewpoints?
- Are you showing up as a Learner 80% of the time?
- When have you recently been a Learner? What were you curious about? What was the impact? In what ways can you continually seek to receive the benefits of being a Learner with others?
- What would be the benefits in your relationships of being a Learner versus a Judger?
- What are the benefits of practicing being a Learner, seeking common understanding and common purposes?
- How can you reframe situations and become more flexible, adaptable, open-minded, and encouraging of diverse and challenging perspectives?
- How are you being accepting and open with self, others, and situations?
- How are you being curious, thoughtful, engaging, and empathic?
- How can you become increasingly more abundant and a better Learner?
- Who do you need to begin building trust from a Learner mindset perspective?
- As a Learner, how would you like to act and behave more effectively?
- What choices can you begin to make as a Learner that will benefit your role as a leader?

As a Learner-coach, you will begin to gain greater self-awareness in how you influence others more effectively. You will also begin to act in new and better ways that will better engage, motivate, and empower those around you.

Modeling the Abundance Mindset ——

Scarcity mentality measures out life by the ounce; it always
concludes that the needs outweigh the resources.
— Erin M. Straza, writer and speaker

I joined Covey Leadership Center (now FranklinCovey) as the 35th
employee, after returning from a spring and summer university study
abroad experience in London, England, in August 1987. Dr. Stephen R.
Covey was one of my early career teachers and mentors. A key insight
I learned from him was the value of thinking and acting in win/win
ways (for fans of his book *The 7 Habits of Highly Effective People,* this
is Habit #4, the principle of mutual benefit).

Dr. Covey taught that thinking win/win is the abundance mindset
in action. "Win/win sees life, and those we need to engage effectively
with as a cooperative, not a competitive arena. Most people tend to
think in terms of dichotomies: either or, good or bad, right or wrong,
strong or weak, hardball or softball, win or lose. But that kind of thinking is fundamentally flawed. . . . Win/win is based on the paradigm
that there is plenty for everybody to enjoy. The idea is that one person's success is not achieved at the expense or exclusion of the success
of others" (Covey 1989, p. 218).

For years, Dr. Covey was told that thinking win/win in a competitive business environment was naïve, unrealistic, and unattainable.
He did not back down. He understood that many leaders, managers,
and supervisors came to work each day with a scarcity mindset. This
mindset would focus on statements such as:

- "There is not enough . . ."
- "That will never work . . ."
- "There is no way to do that . . ."
- "I cannot share . . ."
- "I cannot not trust . . ."
- "We can't risk . . ."
- "They owe me . . ."
- "If they win . . ."
- "We're all in trouble . . ."
- "If they get credit . . ."

This language reveals a scarcity and Judger mindset. How do you reset a fixed position into a win/win position?

Some competition is good and even necessary, but when you need to partner, collaborate, work interdependently, and cooperate, then the only realistic option is a true win/win approach. Dr. Covey suggested beginning by recognizing abundant and trustworthy people around you. Learn from them, associate with them, and choose to model them (Covey 1989, p. 231).

For me, an example of abundance thinking and behaving is Stephen Covey's son, Stephen M.R. Covey. Early in my career, as I mentioned earlier, he was my boss at Covey Leadership Center. I've worked with Stephen M.R. for many years and continue to partner with him personally and professionally to this day. He models the win-win, abundance mentality in every possible way.

Before he meets personally with a client, Stephen wants to know more about them. He is deeply curious about their back story and their future. He wants to understand his client's needs and seeks to engage with them in a custom, flexible, and value-based way. He models what it means to be empathic, creative, adaptable, and flexible to meet clients' needs. He is a deal maker and a champion of making sure everyone benefits and wins in negotiations.

He practices an abundance mindset with his colleagues as well as his customers. When we meet together, he genuinely wants to know about my life and my career interests, and how I am feeling about my contribution at work. How am I progressing? How am I doing personally? He has no political or hidden agenda other than a sincere interest in helping everyone around him be successful. He is also very honest and transparent, and has a trustworthy agenda.

I wanted—and still want—to be more like Stephen M.R. Covey. An effective leader as coach will be like him—a model of the Learner and of the Abundance mindset.

Coaching as a Learner

Not to know is bad; not to wish to know is worse.
—Nigerian proverb

Before you can ever hope to coach or influence another person, you must build personal relationships and rapport. If you are a Learner, it doesn't take long. Of course, it takes time to build trust, but your genuine, sustained interest in others or with your clients will make the process easier. Over the years, I have done a lot of work and partnering in businesses in Asia and have found that deep, trusting relationships are critical to establishing credibility.

Here are a few powerful questions to get you started in the process of building stronger and more engaged relationships at work.

- "Tell me about your background. Where did you grow up? What are your favorite things to do in your free time?"
- "What are your personal interests? What do you like to do, and where do you excel and find your passion in life?"
- "If you had to return to a favorite vacation spot, where would you go?"
- "If you had unlimited time and resources, what would you choose to do?"
- "Name a time in your life when you were happy. When was it?"
- "What do you think your greatest achievement has been to date?"
- "What is your role here at work?"
- "How do you feel about your contribution here?"
- "What is your greatest contribution to your team?"
- "What are your natural gifts, strengths, and talents?"
- "What is the best part of your job?"
- "When do you feel that you are at your best?"
- "What part of your job do you wish you had more time for?"
- "What part of your job do you wish you could do less of?"
- "How do you think your job could be more fulfilling?"
- "How does this job fit in with your overall goals for your life?"
- "What would you like to be doing in your career within the next five years?"
- "What is the gap between where you are now versus where you want to be? How can you close that gap?"
- "How can you live a more engaged, connected, fulfilled, and balanced life?"
- "What stands in your way of achieving more balance in life?"
- "How will you know when you have achieved that balance?"
- "What are the most important relationships you want to invest in?"
- "How can I best help you to achieve your goals, dreams, and aspirations?"

Conducting Effective Conversations to Achieve Better Outcomes

Here's a case study to help you think through the process of holding effective conversations to achieve better outcomes.

Sarah is a business unit leader with a reputation for refusing to collaborate or to accept ideas from outside her own department. She doesn't play well in the organization, distrusts people, and communicates poorly. She's built a silo for herself within her organization.

Other units that want and need to work with her are frustrated. Imagine that you are Sarah's peer, a leader of another business unit. You want to improve relations by using some coaching skills. But where and how do you start?

Start with a respectful lead-in question. "Sarah, would you be willing to have a conversation with me on how our business units can get better together?" Stay away from accusing, judging, or anything that would get in the way of Sarah sharing her story or desiring to hold further discussions.

Ask what unmet needs and opportunities Sarah sees in the marketplace, with shared mission or purpose, customer needs, or better alignment across your business units. What are your shared objectives, needs, or opportunities going forward? Are there better ways to partner, to add value, and to improve your contributions together within the organization? How can you overcome your silos, conflicts, or differences and explore common interests and shared purposes?

Look for common purposes, shared mission, or aligned goals: What's in your collective pool of opportunities to get better in serving customer needs, modeling your values, and clarifying your shared objectives? Side-step functional silos, historical problems, or misaligned work areas at first, and look for the bigger picture and purposes where both departments can add better value, service, and support. You and Sarah can begin to identify and outline co-mission areas, shared customer needs, and market opportunities to partner in the future. Make sure you both are clear and transparent and understand what the bigger picture is and what the benefits might be for working in new and better ways.

Listen with empathic accuracy: Ask Sarah for her views on how the business units can begin working together to achieve the shared interests, objectives, and goals that will better satisfy the mission, customer, or marketplace needs. "What do you see?" "What do you think?" "How do you feel?" "What might be getting in the way?" If she expresses frustration, respond with empathy. "I am sorry to hear that; you must be feeling very frustrated." Capture and restate the key issues heard and then ask which issues are most important. Ask any clarifying questions, like "Can you say more about that? What have you observed? What have you learned? Can you tell me more about your concerns about quality, costs, pricing, service, or launching a product timely and successfully to market?"

Separate the person from the problem: this coaching conversation is not to fix, blame, or judge Sarah. It is to discuss how the key issues of quality, costs, pricing, services, or timely product launch impacts confidence and credibility. "How does this situation or issue impact your business unit? How might this situation impact your customers?"

Focus on Solutions to Problems and Challenges, Not Who's to Blame

When you're coaching a peer to build a relationship, you are not blaming anyone, you are simply examining facts, data, observable behaviors, events, issues, or areas of concern that are causing problems. The idea is that you can improve collaboration and seek to fix problems together. The focus should be on first making sure both groups identify what the problem is with complete honesty, transparency, and openness. Many times, people seek to solve the wrong problem or go after a problem the customer doesn't care about.

Go in with an abundant mindset of how to get better, how to do continuous improvement, and how to learn from customer and partner feedback. All the focus should be on the marketplace, the customers, co-mission opportunity, and shared objectives going forward. Key questions are: "What do you see as being best for the business and for the customer? What do you feel is the right thing for your business unit to do differently? What are your best choices and alternatives going forward to better serve both internal partners and external customers?"

When asking these questions, be silent. Let others share their intent and their understanding of the situation. Don't fill in the silence with your advice, stories, or input. Let them engage in discovering their part of the story.

Interpersonal Maturity and Effectiveness Requires Balancing Courage and Consideration

Balance both courage and consideration. Doing so is the essence of high maturity. Dr. Covey taught that a leader can be both courageous (honest and direct) and considerate (loyal and respectful) at the same time. Courage is a willingness and ability to speak your thoughts, feelings, issues, and challenges with complete transparency. Consideration is a willingness and ability to seek and listen to others' thoughts and feelings with affirmation, courtesy, and respect.

A leader as coach should be courageous, which focuses on honestly and directly confronting the brutal facts about goals, targets, measures, numbers, scoreboards, ethics, values, rules, policies, guidelines, and laws. At the same time, a leader as coach should be considerate and give feedback in a way that is helpful, safe, kind, and respectful. Keep in mind feelings, context, circumstances, capabilities, differences, history, expectations, and personality differences.

A leader as coach who is courageous but inconsiderate can be perceived as being "win/lose" a thinker. However, if a leader as coach only seeks to be considerate and not courageous, they will be perceived as being "lose/win." Neither of these approaches is sustainable for long-term success. The leader as coach should practice using a balance of both approaches in conversations (Covey 2006, pp. 230–232). To be successful, you must start first with kindness, respect, and considerate language and behaviors. Then seek to be courageous, honest, and transparent about the goals, measures, targets, laws, and objectives.

Clarify your intent. Be open and explicit in sharing your motives. "This is what I intend to do and why." Based on your observation and your personal experiences, you can say, "I see the problem as . . ." "From my perspective, this is what I've observed . . ." "Here is where I come from . . ." "My perspectives may be limited or short-sighted, but this is what I've seen . . . or this is what I intend to do." Always come first from a place of openness, consideration, and respect. When we begin with consideration, people open up because they feel safe and not judged. Ask your clients, customers, or partners how to move forward and get better together. "What are the shared objectives or the shared pool of opportunities for us to work better together? What are ways can our teams begin to work better together going forward?"

Validate, and gain mutual commitment and a path forward together. Close the conversation by expressing confidence in your successful future together. Show a genuine commitment to act and perform in new and better ways. "Based on our conversation today, I want to express how excited, how motivated, or how confident I am about our future opportunity to work together. I know we can accomplish great things. Let's recap what we are committing to do in the future. "What are your responsibilities going forward?" "What are my responsibilities going forward?" "Who else do we need to engage in this project to make it a success?" "How will we measure success?" "How can we track our progress?" "How will we resolve any future problems?" "How often should we meet to discuss our progress?" "With whom and where should we meet?" and "What are the best next steps going forward?"

Ensuring That "Your Success Is My Success"

Talent is God given; be humble. Fame is man-given; be grateful. Conceit is self-given; be careful.
—*John Wooden (1972)*

One leader who exemplified an abundance mindset was the late US college basketball Coach John Wooden. Wooden led the men's basketball teams at the University of California at Los Angeles to 10 NCAA championships, winning 88 consecutive victories and 38 consecutive tournaments. ESPN called him the greatest coach of all time. He was known for his high character and humility as a servant leader. The teams that John Wooden coached had unprecedented success on the basketball court, but more than what they achieved was how they achieved it.

His advice to other coaches was, "Remember, you didn't win the championships—the players did." Coach Wooden saw his role as a teacher and mentor. He treated everyone with respect. He set very high expectations and insisted on absolute integrity for himself and everyone around him.

He humbly deferred his personal and professional fame and success to his teams and players. He defined his success in terms of their success, not only in basketball but also in life. He spent hours drilling and practicing, but he never talked about winning. He focused on being prepared and maximizing everyone's potential.

You can be abundant only when you feel good about yourself. Only then do you want to help those around you feel good about themselves, too. This comes from inner security and confidence. When you see people acting in a controlling, abusive, arrogant, or demeaning manner toward others, their behavior is a symptom of their lack of self-esteem and inner security. They need to put someone else down to feel good about themselves.

By contrast, Coach Wooden always sought to build people up. All players knew that Coach Wooden cared deeply about them as persons above and beyond any of the Xs and Os or basketball drills.

"Outstanding leaders go out of the way to boost the self-esteem of their personnel," as Wal-Mart founder Sam Walton said. "If people have confidence and believe in themselves, it's amazing what they can accomplish."

Embracing the Abundance Mindset

Before you are a leader, success is all about growing yourself. When you become a leader, success is all about growing others.
—*Jack Welch, former CEO of General Electric*

A scarcity mindset is natural and tends to come from a selfish, fearful, ego-driven perspective, or a perceived notion of limited resources. Each circumstance of scarcity may come from various drivers. Picture the average day of a young toddler:

- "My toy, my ball, my bottle, my binky, my blanket, my turn, my mom . . ."

You can hear the tantrums around these phrases, right? We hear this stuff from kids, but unfortunately, we also hear it from adults. Some adults may say:

■ "My title, my position, my office, my power, my decision, my team, my recognition, my promotion, my bonus, my credit, my need to be famous and constantly recognized . . .

If scarcity can be a natural response from childhood, then how do we embrace an abundance mindset as we grow into higher levels of personal security, self-worth, and maturity?

Coach and author Naphtali Hoff suggested several ways to live your life and lead abundantly at work (Hoff 2017). One way is to write down the benefits of the abundant life. This can help you to become more self-aware of the benefits of being abundant and to rewire your thinking and make positive changes. Other methods may be to reward those around you who choose to act in abundant win-win ways. Find a way to bring generosity, civility, and mutual benefit into your work environment and into your home. Remember that what goes around, comes around. What you give to others you get back in return—eventually. "People appreciate generosity and often find ways to give back," Hoff says.

While I was preparing for a workshop on trust with the CEO and executive team of Zotec Corporation, the company's head of human resources came to me and said, "We have a leadership advisor who will be attending your trust and culture work session today. His name is Coach Lou Holtz, the head football coach at Notre Dame University from 1986 to 1996. He has been advising Zotec's leaders for years and would like to sit in and learn from you today."

I was surprised and taken back—you could even say "shocked"—because I seriously thought, "I would rather listen to Coach Holtz talk about leadership and trust throughout the day, rather than listen to myself." Coach Holtz was gracious, kind, witty, intelligent, and insightful. I would raise a topic and say, "Hey coach, can you share with us your perspective and experience on this topic? What have you done in this situation?" He would captivate the group with his vast experience and his simple, yet profound ideas—always sprinkled with a bit of humor. At the end of the day, I said to him, "I wish I could have you travel with me and work with my clients each week." He smiled and said, "Much of what you taught today is how I ran my team at Notre Dame."

Coach Holtz is a hero of mine. It was an honor to spend the day learning from him and his generosity, experience, abundance, kindness, and wit—I can honestly see why so many people played so hard for him and are still so loyal and connected to him to this day. He developed an abundant mindset on the football field with his players and prepared them to lead in business, in their families, and in their communities.

After our session, Coach Holtz sent me the following e-mail: "Dear Michael, just had to drop you a note to tell you how impressed I was with your presentation that you made for Zotec, and I am glad I had the opportunity of to be part of it. You obviously did a great deal of research and I appreciate your efforts. If I can help you in any way, give me a call. I just wanted to let you know—thanks for a job well done! Lou Holtz."

After 40 years of legendary coaching leadership, Lou Holtz thanks *me* for training *him*? What a model of generosity, humility, and abundance.

PRACTICE: YOUR COACHING PLAYBOOK

As you seek to coach other in more abundant ways, use the following abundance questions to help frame your ongoing coaching conversations:

1. "Who are great examples for you of people who operate in abundant, win-win ways?"
2. "What are the key benefits of living and leading others with abundance?"
3. "In what ways can you choose to be more abundant in your personal and work life?"
4. "How can you reward those around you who choose to act abundantly?"
5. "With whom do you need to practicing being more abundant?"
6. "In what ways can you be generous today? This week? This month? This year?"

References

Adams, Marilee. (2016). *Change Your Questions, Change Your Life.* Berrett-Koehler Publishers.

Covey, Stephen M.R. (2006). The 13 behaviors of trust action plan. In *The Speed of Trust.* Free Press.

Covey, Stephen R. (1989). *The 7 Habits of Highly Effective People*. Free Press.

Hoff, Naphtali. (2017). 7 strategies to lead with abundance. Tanveer Naseer Leadership. http://www.tanveernaseer.com/how-leaders-tap-power-of-abundance-naphtali-hoff.

Wooden, John. (1972). *They Call Me Coach*. Word Books.

5 Coaching with Authenticity

By now, you've probably realized that your success as a leader-coach depends on the kind of person you are. You're aware that successful coaching starts within you. You know that you need an abundance mindset. But you can't fake the personality and mindset of an effective coach. In this chapter, we'll talk about the importance of being *authentic*.

We have all been around leaders who are fake, inauthentic, and phony. When interacting with these types of leaders, you learn very quickly that they are self-centered, expedient, and narcissistic. For over three years, I had the opportunity to work closely with a man I believe exemplifies the authentic leader. His name is Brent Smith. When we first met, he looked at me and my colleague and said, "Michael and Barney, we are going to have a lot of fun, and we are going to do a lot of good—in that order."

And we did! When working with Brent, I felt engaged and empowered. I was never scared of making a mistake. He always had my back. I did not have to think about covering my tracks. Brent offered us a clear vision and sense of purpose and trusted us in our roles. I came to know that he would do anything for me and our team, and we would do anything for him. I used to say, "I would run through a brick wall for him."

Why was Brent such an influential leader? He was genuine, smart, hard-working, and humble. He served others and cared deeply about them. He was more than just a loyal leader—Brent was completely focused outward on what he could do for others and how to coach those around him. He made everyone on the team feel valued, needed, and respected. He treated others with kindness and honesty, never playing "gotcha!" games. His style was unassuming, and he preferred to look for and leverage the strengths of those around him, rather than focus on their weaknesses and mistakes. When I was with Brent, I actually felt smarter and better for being around him!

"We are building future leaders," he would remind us. "When our team members move on from here, they will have the confidence, skills, and resources they need to be successful throughout their lives."

In more than 30 years of coaching, I've constantly asked myself, what differentiates leader-coaches like Brent Smith? A key answer: they choose to be authentic. My four boys and my wife get a heavy dose of leadership talk from me—I'm always asking them, "What type of leader do you want to be? What leaders would you like to follow? Whom would you care not to follow?" Their answers are the same: you can always tell a fake leader from a genuine leader.

How can you tell?

A friend of mine loves to binge watch self-help improvement programs, particularly weight-loss shows. To justify the time spent, he tells me that he was considering writing a thesis about the kind of language people use in these programs.

He feels he can tell with some accuracy how successful the participants will be based solely on their opening monologue. Do they discuss the path ahead with hope, confidence, and excitement? Or do they look forward with pain and despair, dreading the huge gap between where they are and where they want to be?

In all honesty, most people are motivated by both gain and pain. Great coaches inspire with a vision of what is to be gained. They ignite our passion and inspire the best within us. When we try to explain why they are so effective, we focus on their ability to engage positively with our emotions—the heart and the spirit. Plus, brain science now tells us that a focus on the gain releases motivating and positive chemicals such as serotonin and dopamine. Authentic leaders help others focus on the right mindset, habits, disciplined actions, and exciting possibilities of a desired future state. They do not simply focus on new age jargon, quick-fix formulas, or cosmetic and superficial solutions.

By contrast, poor leaders seek to influence through fear, control, manipulation tactics, and anger. These toxic behaviors engage the amygdala: the primitive, reactive portion of the brain that spews protective and defensive chemicals into the body, such as cortisol.

Dr. Daniel Goleman, in *Working with Emotional Intelligence*, demonstrates that everything a business wants—profits, productivity, engagement, motivation, collaboration, innovation, and teamwork— go up when positive and healthy emotions prevail in an organization. Organizations are dependent on teams, not just individuals, for decision-making, problem-solving, and goal execution. When negative and diminishing emotions prevail, the net result is disengagement, lack of loyalty, poor execution, silos, distrust, and turnover (Goleman 1988).

What's even harder is dealing with fake emotions—the leader you can't read or connect with, and who pretends to be interested in you (but you can tell it's a ploy). There are leaders who want to be the hero, who want to be famous, who need your approval, and for whom phony emotiveness is a way to get what they selfishly want. They "fake it until they make it," which is at heart just lying to themselves and everyone else. These counterfeit motivations will always backfire and work against a leader. In the end, people will not be loyal or go the extra mile for them.

The problem is, emotions are contagious. Negativity and phoniness spread and undermine results. A leader's key to high performance, then, is to become a model of authenticity and good intent with and for those they serve. But, you may say, "I am authentically a cynic" or "I can't muster up positivity all the time." If cynicism is your deep-down truth, you probably will not make a good coach. And faking a positive mental attitude is still faking. Just be authentic—be true to yourself and others. Accept that failures happen. Recognize successes. Make sure people can trust you, because you can trust yourself. Authenticity starts with seeking to model good motives and intent.

Leading by Example

Children close their ears to advice, but open their eyes to example.
—ZsaZsa Bellagio, artist, designer, and photographer

When it comes to modeling influence, a great place to start is in your mindset, your language, and your conversations. Mahatma Gandhi said, "Become the change that you seek in the world." Recognize that your words matter, so mean what you say—and say what you mean. Begin by genuinely caring about people, and let people hear that you care about them. There is no replacement for sitting down and having a one-on-one conversation to understand them and connect with what is important to them. Talk about how you appreciate them. Express concern, listen and get to know them, and validate them. As a coach, you must have this emotional connection with people, or nothing you say or do will have lasting value.

Some leaders get lazy and apathetic about their roles as influencers. They abandon people or use people as things or simply as a means to get what they want. They disengage. Weeks and months go by with little contact except in routine meetings. Or, they do the opposite—they micromanage and paralyze independent action, holding people hostage in a victim cycle of blame and judgment. Or, they may proverbially disregard people and throw them under the bus without loyalty or support.

Recall what my friend Dr. Marilee Adams says about Learners and Judgers. Learners are emotionally intelligent leaders whose language and behavior offer a positive influence, while Judgers are emotionally unintelligent. Their language and actions create anxiety, helplessness, and resentment. Here are some examples of both Learner and Judger language (Adams 2015):

Judger language

- "I can't . . .
- "I won't . . ."
- "It's impossible . . ."
- "What's wrong with them . . ."
- "What's wrong with me . . ."
- "Why did they do that . . ."
- "It can't be done . . ."
- "It's not my responsibility . . ."
- "I have all the answers . . ."
- "What a bunch of idiots . . ."
- "The rules don't apply to me . . ."
- "I'm entitled, because . . ."
- "I don't care . . ."

- "I'm not the one to blame here . . ."
- "It's not my fault . . ."
- "Whose fault is it . . ."
- "It's their fault . . ."
- "I'm being told to . . ."
- "I guess I have to . . ."
- "I was not given a choice . . ."
- "There is nothing that can be done . . ."
- "They have no idea what they are doing . . ."
- "Those mistakes are bad . . ."
- "They always act like that . . ."
- "They just don't get it . . ."

Learner language

- "I will . . ."
- "I choose to . . ."
- "I know we can . . ."
- "I am responsible for doing this . . ."
- "What helpful feedback do they have for us . . ."
- "I am curious to know more . . ."
- "Let's brainstorm all our options and alternatives . . ."
- "What did we learn from this situation . . ."
- "How can we learn more about this . . ."
- "How can we get better and improve . . ."
- "What obstacles or barrier do we need to remove . . ."
- "What are our choices . . ."
- "What are the possibilities . . ."
- "What resources do we have available . . ."
- "What big opportunities do we see here . . ."
- "What is our responsibility . . ."
- "How can I help solve this problem . . ."
- "How do you think we can improve this situation . . ."
- "What are they thinking, feeling, or wanting from us . . ."
- "What are the best solutions for everyone involved . . ."
- "What seems to be the most practical thing to do . . ."
- "How can we help . . ."
- "We can do this . . ."
- "What will work best . . ."

- "I will commit to do this right now . . ."
- "This is what we will commit to doing right now . . ."

I was recently coaching Anthony, a smart and experienced leader in a global consumer products company. Anthony shared with me confidentially, "My boss said that I was not showing up very well in our recent leadership meetings. He said that I tended to overreact with him and my general managers."

I asked him, "What might be triggering your negative or reactive responses?"

He said, "I get very impatient and have outbursts and negative reactions when I'm under pressure and when I observe that people are not getting it." He continued, "I tend to be critical of my boss because of his lack of focus and clarity around our goals. I have responded impatiently with my direct reports when they make mistakes or do and say stupid things. I often ask myself, what is wrong with my team? Why don't they get it? Why are they not prepared?"

The good news: Anthony was completely aware of his diminishing and demeaning behaviors. The bad news: he didn't know what to do about it. "It is hard to change my behavior and my language. I don't like the way I respond and need to work on better ways to engage my boss and team. Furthermore, I don't like how my team gets defensive, shuts down, and disengages during some of our tense interactions." Anthony was in a bind.

Clearly, Anthony had a Judger mindset. After talking with many of his direct reports, I learned that my task as his coach was to help him become more self-aware of his bad behavior, understand his negative impacts on his team, and help him shift to a Learner mindset.

I asked him, "Can we role-play a few scenarios where you get triggered?" We practiced using Judger language and then Learner language. It began to dawn on him that the Learner responses would be more productive. He saw that curiosity and asking good, open-ended questions during tense, difficult situations would help to open people's hearts and minds and diffuse negative energy when the pressure in a conversation was highly emotional.

As we talked, it was as if a light came on in Anthony's head. He said, "I am 60 years old, and I cannot tell you how excited I am to learn this new and better way of responding when the emotions are high." He became extremely excited about coaching his team instead of ragging on them. He realized at his age, it is never too late to improve his Learner mindset and language.

To help Anthony, we created a new game so he could track his behaviors. Each day, he started with 10 pennies in his left pocket. The goal was to move the 10 pennies from his left pocket to his right pocket by the end of the day. Every time he was negatively triggered and wanted to respond in a judgmental or emotionally negative way, he would take a deep breath and practice his new Learner behaviors; for every positive interaction, he moved a penny into the right pocket. Though no one else knew about this little game, he was able to enjoy many private victories each day as he became more self-aware and chose new and better responses to difficult situations.

Changing behavior is hard, but people play differently in life and at work when they start keeping score. People also play better when they are treated better.

In time, Anthony became a great leader-coach. He was able to be authentically helpful instead of hurtful.

Becoming Emotionally Intelligent

Emotions are contagious. We've all known it experientially. You know after you have a cup of coffee or a drink with a friend, you feel good. When you have a rude clerk and negative interaction in a store, you walk away feeling bad.
    —Dr. Daniel Goleman, author, speaker, and psychologist

My client Alison helps manage corporate travel for an international company. Her team is small, around 19 people, but they can be tracking hundreds of travelers each day, ensuring that everything goes smoothly around the world.

When she steps into the office each morning, she checks in with a couple of co-workers to do what they call a "mood check." "Who has seen the boss? Was he smiling? Did he greet anyone on the way to his corner office? How is he today?"

"It's exhausting," Alison confided to me. "Every day is a different mood, and we have to adjust everything we do based on that."

Unsurprisingly, turnover in the office is very high, with workers being fired or deciding to leave on their own. "Only four people have been here for more than a year," Alison says.

When Alison reports to work on a good-mood day, she appreciates it the way we might enjoy a sunny day in January: we take it while we can. But these sunny days do not fool Alison. Unfortunately, she has learned that they do not last.

A good leader, a good coach, does not have a mindset as fickle as the weather. A good leader-coach chooses their own weather. They choose to be positive, optimistic, curious, and emotionally intelligent.

Dr. Daniel Goleman wrote, "When leaders habitually use displays of bad moods to motivate, more work may seem to get done—but it will not necessarily be better work. And relentlessly foul moods corrode the emotional climate, sabotaging the brain's ability to work at its best" (Goleman 2014).

Goleman continues, "The leader can drive an employee's emotions to a better or a worse state." Which state do you choose?

It depends on how emotionally intelligent you are.

Emotional intelligence is the ability to control one's own emotions and to handle interpersonal relationships "judiciously and empathetically," according to the dictionary. Simply put, emotionally intelligent people connect effectively and consistently with others.

Emotionally unintelligent leaders don't control their emotions well. They play victim, they fight, they abandon, they micromanage, they manipulate—they don't know any other way to get results. Unfortunately, their toxic emotions are contagious. Goleman compares them to viruses: "A steady dose of toxic energy from higher-ups will encourage valuable team members to update their resumes rather than their to-do lists" (Goleman 2015).

Such energy can also go from peer to peer. A study of 70 work teams across diverse industries found that people in meetings together ended up sharing moods, good and bad (Goleman 2015).

Emotionally intelligent leaders coach their teams toward awareness. For example, IDEO Corporation, known for innovating world-class products, intentionally banishes victimization, blaming, and shaming. IDEO's website (https://www.ideo.com/about) states that it is "a global design company committed to making a positive impact." IDEO believes failure is necessary for innovation. The company lives by these standards:

1. Be optimistic.
2. Collaborate.

3. Embrace ambiguity.
4. Learn from failure.
5. Make others successful.
6. Take ownership.
7. Talk less, do more.

As a leader-coach, you will want to model the kind of emotional intelligence that sets apart a company like IDEO.

A great place to start is with how you see others, what you allow to come out of your mouth, and the behaviors that follow. Great things and sustainable results will follow.

Seeing Yourself as a Servant, Not a Master

A leader is one who knows the way, goes the way, and shows the way.
—*John C. Maxwell,* New York Times *best-selling author*

It's tough to find models of authentic leadership. When we check the news about government, education, business, and international relations, we find mostly examples of how *not* to lead.

Robert Greenleaf, well-known researcher and teacher of leadership and author of the book *The Servant Leader*, was one of the first to research and define the concept of *servant leadership*. He states, "The big idea is that leadership must be about service. You cannot separate great leadership from service." He realized that people in the best organizations see themselves serving one another, easing their burdens, and enabling them to succeed (Greenleaf 1998, pp. 5–10).

According to Cheryl Bachelder, the former CEO of Kentucky Fried Chicken and AFC Enterprises, conventional leadership suffers from a "spotlight problem." In her book *Dare to Serve: How to Drive Superior Results by Serving Others*, Bachelder says most leaders are "drivers and high achievers, though perhaps a bit self-absorbed. We tolerate that, because they are going places that we want to go. If they are successful, we will be successful."

Bachelder contrasts conventional leaders with humble servant leaders who shun the spotlight and choose to listen to people more than they talk. "They involve the people in decisions. They make decisions that serve the people well; they give others credit" (Bachelder 2015).

We see the difference. We *feel* the difference. But nonetheless, Bachelder notes, we fear servant leaders. "We fear they will not get us to success. Could they deliver superior performance results? We doubt it." Why do we doubt it? She says it's because we've been told that nice people always finish last.

Bachelder pleads with us to reframe our perspectives. "Have you worked for a leader who loves fame, power, or the spotlight? Were *you* served well?" she asks. She encourages leaders to move out of the spotlight and get to work serving their people and their customers with their finest efforts.

Too many leaders see themselves as "in charge," when as far as their customers are concerned, they are "in service." Too many coaches see themselves as the star in the spotlight. As a coach and a leader, you have a choice to make every day: Do you want to serve, or do you want to be served? Do you want to talk at people, or do you want to connect with people? Do you want to be the person on the pedestal or the person who helps others to succeed? Great leader-coaches subordinate their own ego and interests and put the needs of others ahead of themselves.

Building Trust

> *The culture of any organization is simply the collective behavior of its leaders. If you want to change your culture, change the collective behavior of your leaders.*
> —Ram Charan, professor, business consultant, and author

Last summer I had the rare opportunity to flip through a few channels to see if there was anything worth watching on television. Eventually, my eye was caught by a show with a premise so over the top, I thought it could not be real.

Of course, it probably was as real as most "reality" television shows, but for a few moments I was hooked. An individual was looking for love on national television in a 60-minute show. While this person hid behind a darkened panel, potential companions were paraded across the stage. The individual had to filter through the potential companions knowing only a name, age, profession, and maybe one hobby. At the end of the episode, the individual emerged and offered a marriage proposal, complete with a diamond ring provided by the show.

Yet in the end it didn't seem that far-fetched. Maybe we know love when we see it. Trust is along the same lines: we know it when we *feel* it. Who knows whether our short-term judgment is good?

Authentic leaders should be consistent and the same person in every circumstance. They are credible and trustworthy. They are not laid back in the off hours and tyrants in the workplace. Trusted leaders are people of integrity and credibility, which means they consistently choose to live by their values and walk a moral path even when no one is watching.

In coaching, trust and credibility are essential. To be a trusted coach, you must continually practice the skills of a coach and keep up with new developments. Just as important, you must be an authentic model of integrity. It's about being both competent and caring. It's about defining the contribution you can make as a servant leader and then carrying it out. It's about helping your team members define and carry out *their* contributions.

Servant leaders contribute. Servant leaders know the job to be done for the people they serve. Servant leaders gain the trust of those people around them by consistently contributing value to their lives both professionally and personally. As a servant leader, here are a few questions to ask yourself and the people you coach:

- What is the greatest contribution that I can make in my role at work?
- How can living a life of contribution lead to fulfillment and happiness?
- What is the mission of our organization? What is our specific contribution to that mission?
- What impact does our contribution have?
- What are some specific things you can (and would) do to better contribute?
- How can I best help others make a meaningful and significant contribution in their work?

Creating a Safe Space for Coaching ━━━━

There is no innovation and creativity without failure, period.
—Dr. Brené Brown, New York Times *best-selling author, psychologist, counselor, and speaker*

Only when people know they can trust you will they feel safe opening up to you. Servant leaders exist to create comfort and happiness for those they serve. For coaching to be successful, there must be a safe environment. The timing, climate, and setting for your coaching are crucial to your dialogue. By asking the following questions, you can ensure that people will trust you and feel safe about opening up:

- Are you open to having a conversation?
- Would you like to have a conversation?
- Is this a good time to talk?
- I would really enjoy getting together soon and catching up. When would be a good time to connect?
- I would like to get your advice on a few things and also share some of my thinking.
- I would like to check in and make sure everything is going well for you.
- Would you be willing to have a conversation about how we could get better together?

As a coach, always get permission to proceed *before* you start coaching. This is a good way to declare good intent and show value and respect at the same time.

Recently, I gave a keynote presentation to a group called the Association for Contractors and Builders on improving the execution of safety standards in the workplace. Under federal law, your employer must provide a safe workplace free of known health and safety hazards and violations. As I spoke, I noticed a banner in the room with a picture of a mom, dad, and kids. The sign read, "Every family is entitled to have their loved ones come home from work every night safe and free from accidents, injury, or death." I was deeply touched with this all-important message about safety.

Like physical safety, everyone is entitled to psychological safety in the workplace. Coaches ensure that every interaction is open, respectful, inclusive, trusting, and safe. Confidentiality and no fear of retribution is also critical to safety.

In their book *Driving Fear Out of the Workplace,* Daniel K. Oestreich and Kathleen Ryan ask, "What does it mean to feel psychologically safe at work?" Their findings: when people know they can tell the truth without fear of repercussions, then indicators of quality, innovation, collaboration, and productivity all dramatically improve (Oestreich and Ryan 1991, pp. 65–67, 86–94).

So, how do you break a cycle of fear and mistrust and create a trusting and safe environment?

One way to create a safe environment is to allow people to make mistakes and learn from them. I have a close friend, Tanios Viviani, whom I have coached as he has led several multi-billion-dollar companies. Over the years, we have shared life's ups and downs and many successes along the way. I have found it refreshing to discuss lessons of life with Tanios. One intriguing topic we've talked about is failure. We've tossed around four key lessons about failure:

1. *Fail fast.* Overcome hubris, ego, and arrogance. Failing fast means you have open, two-way feedback loops that are transparent and offer fast, honest feedback so you can make a course correction.
2. *Fail cheaply.* We have all learned from very expensive mistakes when we go all in. Reduce the cost of failures by alpha and beta testing—piloting and testing the waters—before a big investment of time, money, and resources.
3. *Fail publicly.* Don't be embarrassed by failure. Everybody fails! If you fail publicly, you will gain respect rather than lose it, because you are demonstrating absolute honesty and commitment. Put failures out into the public domain so everyone can learn from them and get better.
4. *Fail forward.* There is no shame in failure. Adapt and keep moving forward! You cannot innovate and collaborate in an environment of fear. If a toddler falls, we don't yell at them. We know they're going to fall down a hundred times, but each time they fall, they arise a little stronger and a little wiser, and move forward. Learn and reflect on the past, but focus all your efforts on a successful future of continuous improvement.

Embracing Authenticity

So, what does it mean to be authentic? Simply stated, it is being real and being who you are. No false pretense, no act, no deception, and no arrogance or hubris. Be your real self, and hold to your values, principles, and integrity in all situations. NBA basketball coach Pat Riley would say to his team, "Be willing to take a punch in the mouth. Stand on your own two feet and keep them placed firmly on the ground. Never be intimidated by anyone. Always remember who you are and where you came from."

The question is, how do we get there? And how do we gain that high level of connection with the people we coach?

I suggest four things we've discussed in this chapter. An authentic leader as coach is:

- An example of integrity
- Emotionally intelligent
- A servant of others
- Trustworthy and safe to talk to

Authenticity requires you to be principled: to be honest, transparent, sensitive, humble, and kind. I believe that many people in leadership positions fight these things because they perceive that being authentic means giving up control. Vulnerability may be hard, but it is critical for any leader's or team's success.

The problem is, control is an illusion. The world shifts constantly, and just when you think you have control, you realize it was never yours to begin with.

You'll remember that early in my career, I worked for a man who could not and would not let go of his desire for control. He did not lead; he controlled others with his title, his ego, and little else. What were the consequences? A lot of internal backbiting and complete lack of respect for him. The team resented him, made jokes about him, and exhaled with relief when the board finally dismissed him.

A title or position is not power: Effectively influencing others is power. People do not control: true principles control. The authentic leader as coach is humble and genuine enough to understand this.

PRACTICE: YOUR COACHING PLAYBOOK

Think about those people—leaders at work, teachers, coaches, mentors, instructors, trainers, family members, friends—who made and continue to make a difference in your life. They believed in you. They trusted you. They brought out the very best in you.
Now it's your turn to do the same:

1. What is your vision? How and where can you best make a difference?
2. What is your unique contribution?
3. Whom are you going to help and inspire?
4. What lives are you going to seek to influence for good?
5. When do you plan to do this?
6. What actions will you take to make this a reality?
7. Who else needs to be involved?

References

Adams, Marilee. (2015). *Change Your Questions, Change Your Life.* Berrett-Koehler Publishers.

Bachelder, Cheryl. (2015). *Dare to Serve: How to Drive Superior Results by Serving Others.* Berrett-Koehler Publishers.

Goleman, Daniel. (1988). *Working with Emotion Intelligence.* Bantam.

Goleman, Daniel. (2014). Emotional intelligence. http://www.danielgoleman.info/daniel-goleman-be-mindful-of-the-emotions-you-leave-behind.

Goleman, Daniel. (2015). A relaxed mind is a productive mind. Mindful. https://www.mindful.org/a-relaxed-mind-is-a-productive-mind.

Greenleaf, Robert. (1998). *The Power of Servant Leadership.* Berrett-Koehler Publishers.

Oestreich, Daniel K., and Ryan, Kathleen. (1991). *Driving Fear Out of the Workplace.* Jossey-Bass.

Coaching the Individual and Teams

6 Knowing When to Coach

Coachable people seek out those who speak truth to them, even if it is a painful truth, because it protects them, and it makes them a better person and leader.
—Gary Rohrmayer, author and speaker

U p to this point, we've focused on you, the coach. We've helped you examine your own readiness to be a coach—the power of your example, your abundance mentality, and your personal authenticity. The next section of this book provides resources, examples, and specific tools for coaching specific individuals.

Before we dive in, however, there's one warning. Coaching is powerful. Coaching is transformational. And coaching can change people's lives. But it's not a silver bullet. It cannot solve issues that require education, training, or counseling. Also, you cannot coach people if they are not willing to be coached. You cannot force them to undergo coaching, so you should ask yourself if they are ready to be coached.

Ask:

- Does this situation require coaching?
- Is this person ready to have a coaching conversation?
- Is this person coachable right now?
- Is this person motivated to begin a coaching relationship?
- How can I best structure the coaching conversations?

Does This Situation Require Coaching?

Team members who lack the competency to do a job do not need coaching—they need training, skill building, work experience, or education. Coaches help people who are already competent to choose their own paths and make their own decisions. If, for example, a nurse isn't qualified to do a certain surgical procedure, she may need a course or training, not a coach. Once she's certified, you can coach her as her practices and skills improve, and she can leverage her new skills.

Often, there's a fine line between the need for training and the need for coaching. You might be coaching a person who is a poor communicator. You might be asking them questions that will surface that difficulty and then coaching them to decide how to deal with it. But you cannot teach them to be better communicators; your task is to guide them toward self-awareness and the desire to create an action plan that will help them allocate time and attention to communicate better with key stakeholders. That plan might include training courses in speaking, listening, or writing, but the coach is not the one to teach those courses.

Is This Person Ready to Have a Coaching Conversation?

Often, a person who would benefit from coaching isn't ready for it. They may not feel safe being coached by you. No one wants to be "fixed" or become a "project."

Remember, it is not your job to fix, judge, or change the participant. If you hand out orders about what to do and how to do it, whose fault is it if the advice doesn't work? Coaching is an ongoing dialogue with a team member where you do not counsel, advise, judge, or tell them what to do. Instead, you ask the right questions, in the right way, at the right time, in a safe environment. Through open-ended questions, you engage team members to discover their own answers for themselves.

Obviously, you don't need to take off the table all your wisdom, experience, and judgment. But you need to get team members to do the heavy thinking and lifting to solve their own problems. As a coach, you are a guide on the side to help co-create mutual understanding, thinking, creative problem-solving, and action planning. You can also offer tools, resources, and support to help them on their path to get better.

Is This Person Coachable Right Now?

A trusting relationship is probably the most important element in coaching. You'll go crazy trying to coach someone who doesn't fully trust you or feels unsafe. Dr. Terry Maltbia, our director from the Columbia University Coaching Certification Program, would invite us to ask these critical questions prior to coaching someone:

- Who is the customer or person you are coaching? Who will be paying you for coaching? What are their expectations or needs?
- Who are all the key stakeholders that need to be involved in the coaching process—talent management and development, finance, the business unit leader, the team members, the individual, etc.?
- What is the readiness of the participant? Are they willing, motivated, and ready for coaching? If not, don't waste your time, or theirs.

You can lead a person to coaching, but you can't make them coachable. Coaching can only take place when both parties are open, willing, and wanting to get better together. To determine if the person is coachable, ask these questions:

- Why are you considering coaching this person?
- What is your agenda? What are you trying to achieve with this person?
- Why do they want coaching?
- What is their agenda or need for coaching? What do they want to achieve?
- Is this person open to change and improvement?
- What is the current level of trust in your relationship?
- Do you have the time and resources to coach this person?
- Are there any expectations that you need to clarify prior to coaching?

- Is coaching clearly linked to a business strategy, talent management, performance management, a business challenge, career development, behavior change, work-life balance, or other opportunities?

These questions are crucial when deciding whether you are ready to coach a person. Try to determine in advance as much as you can about the person. Gather data from different sources in order to target areas for coaching. Surveys, interviews, and questionnaires such as 360-degree assessments can help gauge the person's needs, gaps, and level of desire to address those needs.

Personally, when I am hired as an external coach for a client or leadership team, I like to send a 10-page confidential Coaching Scope Document for the participant to fill out prior to our first intake scoping session. This document helps the coachee or client and me gain personal insights about what matters most to them both professionally and personally. Then I can customize my coaching to many of their needs, dreams, aspirations, and desired outcomes. But it's also important to know how things are going from the viewpoints of bosses, peers, direct reports, partners, and so forth. One-on-one personal interviews, 360-degree assessment, and surveys are ideal to gain data and needed context. Is this person delivering results? Is performance at a high level? Is there a work-life balance? Does this person want to change or improve certain behaviors? Here are some of the sample questions asked in my Coaching Scope Document:

- "What is happening in your world, right now?"
- "How open are you to change and improvement?"
- "How do you view your current level of performance?"
- "How do others view your current level of performance? How do you know?"
- "What seems to be working well for you right now?"
- "What is not working well, and what does that mean to you?"
- "What specific goals and objectives do you wish to achieve?"
- "What do you want to focus on in our coaching session?"
- "What aspects of your professional role do you want to improve?"
- "What aspects of your personal life do you want to improve?"
- "Listing your top stakeholders or key relationships, with whom do you need to improve trust and credibility?"
- "What aspects of your work-life balance would you like to improve?"

- "Are there any derailing or ineffective behaviors that you would like to improve?"
- "Is there any additional data, input, or feedback that would be helpful for me to review?"
- "Which targeted areas do you believe are the most important to focus on?"
- "How will you know if our coaching engagement has been successful?"
- "How will your success be measured from our coaching engagement?"
- "What ways do you prefer me to hold you accountable to your coaching game plan?"
- "How often would be reasonable to meet for accountability reviews? Weekly, bi-monthly, or monthly? In person, virtually, a combination of both?"

Is This Person Motivated to Begin a Coaching Relationship?

The way to get started is to quit talking and begin doing.
—Walt Disney, entrepreneur, animator, director, and
film producer

The Buddhists have a proverb that states, "To know and not to do, is really not to know." Confucius said virtually the same thing: "I hear and I forget. I see and I remember. I do and I understand." Moving from conceptually knowing to doing is the key. This is a tricky. Personally, I find that motivation is less about what people know or feel than about what they do and why they do it. Walking, talking, practicing, and performing with the person will be the key to getting and keeping them motivated. The more participants do, the more motivated they become. The key is to get them started. Once participants brainstorm action steps, prioritize them, and carry them out, they will move forward.

In graduate school at Columbia University, I was fortunate to have Dr. Victoria Marsick as a professor. She is one of the world's leading experts in adult learning, training, and development. Much of her research and client work has been in adult learning and action-learning.

She taught about the critical need for all people, teams, and organizations to invest much of their time in learning how to reflect on good questions and getting diverse perspectives with innovative and collaborative learning around brainstorming, curious exploration, and asking rigorous questions that test assumptions.

Coaching offers the same rigor as action-learning. The participant does the heavy lifting. The coach's job is to bring to the surface their barriers, their challenges, their motivations, their values, and what matters most to them, through rigorous testing, questioning, and brainstorming.

To help discover and stimulate motivation, ask these powerful coaching questions:

- "What are you most motivated to focus on? Why?"
- "Where do you see the biggest opportunities for your improvement? Why?"
- "What are the intended benefits of changing (topic/situation)?"
- "What are the costs for not changing (topic/situation)?"
- "What are your clear expectations for improvement going forward?"
- "On a scale from 1 (low) to 10 (high), how motivated are you to improve this situation?"
- "What are you motivated to do about the situation?"
- "Are there any barriers or obstacles that might get in your way?"
- "How will know you know you've achieved success?"
- "How would you measure and track success?"
- "What strengths, gifts, or talents can you leverage?"
- "What resources or support do you need, in order to act?"
- "How would you like things to be different going forward?"
- "What support do you need from me to accomplish this goal?"

How Can You Best Structure the Coaching Conversations?

We can't help everyone, but everyone can help someone.
—Ronald Reagan, former US president

When planning a coaching engagement, recall that every individual's time commitments and energy levels are different. Also, the resources available to them vary widely. Of course, these things are true of you, too. You have to gauge what you are able to contribute to the engagement as well.

Remember the administrative aspect of any coaching engagement and relationship, which needs to be clarified up front. Both parties will need to plan, schedule, and make the time to converse and check in. Effective scheduling and time for ongoing follow-up and accountability are critical. Determine the logistics with the participant's needs in mind. Ask these questions:

- Whom will you schedule coaching with?
- When will you coach?
- Where will you conduct each coaching session? Space? Location?
- How often will you meet for your ongoing coaching sessions? Time commitment? Dates?
- What barriers or time constraints might stop you or get in the way of your coaching sessions?
- How can you best support the person—through brief check-ins? In-depth conversations? Case studies? Field work? Tools and resources? Ongoing development?
- What specific topics will you plan to cover in your coaching sessions?
- What actions will you take to ensure consistency and success with each interaction?
- What are the best methods for follow-up? Frequency?
- What are your next steps?

PRACTICE: YOUR COACHING PLAYBOOK

Hold a practice coaching session in which you strive to follow the key principles in this chapter. Invite someone you trust to be coached, and explain to them the key elements outlined in this practice session. Remember to:

1. Care about the person you're coaching.
2. Ask questions that support their agenda, not yours.
3. Clearly identify the topic of the conversation.
4. Be courageous in the moment.
5. Ask coaching questions that were highlighted in this chapter.
6. Bring all conversations to focused actions.

7 Setting Priorities

*It is not enough to be busy . . . the question is: What are we
busy about?*
*—Henry David Thoreau, American author, essayist,
poet, and philosopher*

Thoroughly and physically beaten, a man collapsed near a major
thoroughfare. He struggled on the side of the road. He was not
alone, but that did not mean people rushed to his aid. In fact, people
passed this man without stopping to help—out of fear or disinterest,
we do not know.

This horrific event did not occur on the busy streets of New York
City or a hot, sunny sidewalk in Los Angeles. The story is found in the
Bible, and it is simply known as the story of the Good Samaritan.

At last, another traveler—a Samaritan—stopped and not only
helped the man but quite literally went "the extra mile" to ensure that
the man was able to recover, even though it came at considerable cost
to the Samaritan in terms of both time and money. The Samaritan had
no reason or obligation to help the victim but did so anyway.

In 1973, college students at Princeton Theological Seminary decided
to reenact this classic story. Forty students preparing for the ministry
were asked to participate in a general study. Their task was simple:
report to one building for an assignment and then go to another to
fulfill a task.

In the first building, they were given a questionnaire and instructed
to go to another building for their actual task. They were told, in vary-
ing degrees (slight, medium, and extreme), to hurry to their next location, where they were to give a talk about either their future career
or the parable of the Good Samaritan. On the way—directly on the

path to the second building—was staged another student, who was hunched over and clearly in need of help.

Did anyone stop to help? Some did.

The variable of what they were going to do next—either talk about their career vocation or talk about the story of the Good Samaritan—was found to have no direct correlation to the outcome. However, what the researchers called the "hurry" factor did. The greater the time constraint, the less likely participants were to stop. Only 10% of the "high hurries" stopped to help, while 63% of the "low hurries" did.

What's the takeaway? Perhaps it's this: if you're trying to make a difference in someone's life, the result depends on how you feel about the time involved. Do we get too caught up in the urgency of the moment and lose sight of what is truly most important?

We focus intensely on time and the impact of how much or how little we have. Consider how many times you check your watch, your phone, your calendar, or the clock on the wall. Jude Rake, author of *The Bridge to Growth*, observes that people drowning in urgent responsibilities tend to stay afloat by dealing with the task that is "loudest"—that is, the most urgent matter that the most people are screaming about.

What suffers in a world like that? Far more important but less urgent matters like vision, values, strategy, goals, talent development, coaching, and culture building. We'll take care of those very important, but less urgent, things "when time permits."

"Unfortunately, time rarely does permit," Rake says, "and leaders who travel down this well-worked path deliver sub-optimal results, while wondering why their workforce doesn't perform at a higher level" (Rake 2017).

Coaching another human being is one of those "most important" but "least urgent" tasks. If you're a leader, nothing is more important than helping your people succeed. But coaching requires building relationships. It requires trust. It requires frequent interaction.

It requires planning, time management, and allocating time on your calendar.

Coaching Must Be a Priority

Those who say "absence makes the heart grow fonder" know little about leadership. A leader who abandons people builds no relationships. If the coach is absent, the team languishes. This means you must make time for coaching as a key leadership priority—in fact, *the priority of coaching and connecting with your people is your key role as a leader.* Consider who you need to connect with and coach.

A comedian once said to his audience, "I'm sorry I'm late. I got here as soon as I wanted to." Whether you're the CEO or the brand-new hire, you have the same 24 hours in a day and 168 hours in a week to work with. It's the same for everyone. So, as a leader, what do you spend your time on? Or, more important, what do you *want* to spend your time on? The strength of your commitment to coaching says a lot about your leadership, and the time you give to it is the measure of that commitment.

What you spend your time on says a lot more about your values than any plaque on the wall or verbal declaration that proclaims, "We value our people and culture."

My colleague and co-author of the book *First Things First,* Roger Merrill, observes, "There is a constant struggle between two powerful forces: one is 'The Clock' which represents our time, goals, commitments, appointments, schedules, tasks, and activities. 'The Clock' deals with urgency, speed, and efficiency. The other is 'The Compass' which represents our mission, vision, values, key relationships, principles, conscience, purpose, and direction in life. 'The Compass' offers us direction and helps us clarify what we value, what we believe is most important, and where we are going" (Covey et al. 1994).

Execution of our Compass priorities is a daily and weekly challenge because the pressing demands of the Clock keep urgently pushing at us.

Business success depends on leaders who can successfully coach people to plan and create space for leveraging their most important values, priorities, relationships, time, and resources. Great execution is not simply accomplishing a goal. It is executing a goal in the midst of noise and hundreds of urgent tasks and priorities.

For a meaningful life, it's important to have big goals, to dream, and to dream big! I know this is hard to do because so many of us get caught up with day-to-day urgency and short-term priorities and never step back to give attention to the big picture.

But big changes only happen when you have a big "why" to shoot for. That big why has to be greater than your moods, your distractions, and even your urgencies. (Admit it: many things that seem urgent aren't really that important.) Unless you're ready to go all in, you might as well stop reading now and take a nap.

Eliminating the "White Noise" ━━━━━

Before everything else, getting ready is the secret of success.
—Henry Ford, inventor and founder of Ford Motor Company

Like bad jugglers, we try to balance meetings, conference calls, texts, and fires—no wonder we burn out under the myriad demands on our time, both personally and professionally. There are always more good things to do than time to do them, but we try anyway. Stephen Covey and Charles Hummel referred to this condition as "the tyranny of the urgent": the tension between what is most important and what is merely urgent.

In fact, most of what is merely urgent is not all that important. Think about it. It's "white noise," buzzing in our ears and distracting us from what truly matters. If you want to be an effective coach, you need to identify and eliminate the white noise as much as possible and guide your team to do the same.

Fortunately, coaching is a discipline that requires people to pause, reflect, and consider new and better options and solutions. In that space, you can create new possibilities, explore options, and do some innovative thinking. The following coaching questions will help you reduce and get away from the white noise and help plan what is most important:

- What vision or dreams do we have for a desired future state?
- What is our most important mission and purpose?
- What are the one to three most important goals to achieve?
- What is it about these goals that energizes us?
- What is distracting us from focusing on these goals?
- How can we eliminate those distractions?
- What few actions must we focus on to achieve those goals?
- How can we better schedule our time and focus on those few actions to drive our goals?
- How will we know when we've achieved these goals? What are the measures of success?
- What milestones will we achieve to ensure success?
- How will we know if we are winning or losing on our goals?
- How will we hold ourselves accountable each week on our path to success?

Setting Priorities and Leveraging Time ▬

How tragic it is to find that an entire lifetime is wasted in pursuit of distractions while purpose is neglected.
—Sundaty Adelaja, author, speaker, and pastor

An important part of your coaching agenda is to help others set priorities for action. Stephen Covey compared true priorities to big rocks and lesser priorities to gravel (Covey et al. 1994, pp. 75-89). Too often we smother ourselves with gravel while ignoring the big rocks. "What are our big rocks? What are our team members' big rocks? What are our organization's big rocks?" Knowing what's most important and what direction we are heading is the first thing that must be established.

It doesn't matter how quickly and efficiently we travel if we're heading in the wrong direction! Furthermore, if the direction is vague or undefined, people tend to wander around and get distracted by the white noise.

The coach's job is to guide people toward a clear purpose, vision, values, strategy, and goals. The key is not to prioritize what's on your schedule, but to plan and schedule based on your most important priorities.

By the way, don't forget to invest time in yourself. You are your own greatest asset. Schedule time for recreation, relaxation, relationships, rest, and personal renewal. Read a good book, enjoy a hobby, get some exercise, watch a movie, improve a relationship, and develop talents and skills. These things are big rocks that are essential to your well-being and become white noise only if they take too much of your time.

Planning and scheduling big-rock priorities is itself a big rock we must take care of before we jump into executing the year, quarter, month, week, or day. In this way, we can say no to the flood of urgent or unimportant gravel that will occupy all our time if we let it.

Following are important coaching questions about setting priorities (Allen 2001, pp. 18–19, 35–36, 138–140):

- Do we have honest self-awareness about those things that matter most in our lives?
- Do we have a clear shared mission, vision, and values that are more important than anything?

- Have we defined our clear roles, responsibilities, and relationships?
- Have we defined clear strategies and goals for achieving that mission?
- Have we scheduled the activities—the big rocks—that will enable us to achieve those goals?
- Are we being disciplined to the priorities we've established? Are we able to say no to the distractions (gravel) that slow down our progress or push our priorities to the side?
- Which of our less important tasks can we let go of or say no to?

The key is to have a well-defined mission, vision, values, strategy, and goals. Only then can you set intelligent priorities for how you use your time.

PRACTICE: PRIORITIES AND TIME—COACHING IN ACTION

Take time now to identify with your team your most important priorities, starting with your vision, mission, strategy, and key goals. Also, identify your common time wasters, distractions, and what to say no to. Then, schedule the most important activities or big rocks for the upcoming year, quarter, month, and week in alignment with your key roles, goals, and priorities.

PRACTICE: YOUR COACHING PLAYBOOK

Here is a list of questions you might ask while coaching people toward setting their most important priorities, vision, and clarity of purpose:

1. "How meaningful is your work?"
2. "What is your mission, vision, values, strategy, or goals?"
3. "What roles do you have in carrying out your most important goals?"
4. "Who are your most important relationships (customers, partners, stakeholders)?"
5. "How can you be more effective with your time and key priorities?"
6. "What do you want to start doing more of?"
7. "What should you continue doing that is working well?"

8. "What is distracting you from achieving your key goals more effectively?"
9. "What low-leverage, nonessential activities should you stop doing?"
10. "What do you want to stop or let go of?"
11. "What urgencies are you caught up in that are really not that important?"
12. "Where can you delegate nonessential or low-value-added activities?"
13. "How can you intentionally give more time to your key priorities?"
14. "What are you committing to do differently?"
15. "What will be your most effective next steps?"

References

Allen, David. (2001). *Getting Things Done: The Art of Stress-Free Productivity.* Penguin Books.

Covey, Stephen, Merrill, A. Roger, and Merrill, Rebecca R. (1994). *First Things First.* Simon & Schuster.

Rake, Jude. (2017). *The Bridge to Growth: How Servant Leaders Achieve Better Results and Why It Matters Now More Than Ever.* Skyhorse.

8 Asking the Right Questions

When you coach others, be as curious as a 10-year-old child.
—Dr. Terrence E. Maltbia, professor, Columbia University
Coaching Certification Program

I was raised in the era of physical libraries, card catalogues, and encyclopedias. If I had a question, I could look for an answer in an encyclopedia. If it wasn't there, I could go to the library and search through long rectangular drawers for the right card in the catalogue that would take me to a book with the answer.

After growing up using this formal, tedious process to access books and information, I love the convenience now of being able to ask Google or Siri my questions and get many answers immediately.

Ironically, even with so much information available, research shows that we stop asking questions as we get older. We even expect information to immediately surface at our fingertips. In a *Newsweek* article titled "The Creativity Crisis," Po Bronson and Ashley Merryman say, "Preschool children, on average, ask their parents about 100 questions a day. . . . By middle school they've pretty much stopped. . . . It's no coincidence that this same time is when student motivation and engagement plummets. They didn't stop asking questions because they lost interest: it's the other way around. They lost interest because they stopped asking questions" (Bronson and Merryman 2010).

Why do we stop asking questions? Maybe because we get more familiar with the world or think we have it all figured out. Maybe we hear that questions are annoying. At school, we cram and memorize and hate the kid who's always asking stupid questions when all we want to do is get out of there.

Maybe we stop getting rewarded for asking questions. Author Warren Berger asked Richard Saul Wurman, creator of the TED Talk

Conference, why people stop asking questions. "In school, we're rewarded for having the answer, not for asking a good question," Wurman pointed out (Berger 2011). Maybe that's why kids who start off asking endless "why" and "what if" questions gradually ask fewer and fewer of them as they progress through school.

Well, it's time to brush off your carpet square, open that fruit snack, and be a kid again. It's time to revel in the art of asking good questions. My wife Cynthia owns and directs a private school: Ivy Hall Academy in Provo, Utah. Her school's vision for each child is "To develop responsible and interdependent life-long learners who lead lives of meaningful contribution." The school is "inquiry based," meaning students are encouraged to focus on big, open-ended questions to research and respond to in their groups. In the process, they develop outstanding researching, critical thinking, creative, and collaborative skills.

The process is the same for leaders who become coaches: They make it their business to ask stimulating questions all day long, motivating people to research, think, collaborate, and create their own solutions.

Joshua, a leader I know, has gone all-in on coaching. He was surprised by the response of his team. "I have found that everyone wants an easy answer," he told me. "They want me to tell them what to do because they are frustrated, and they just want to move ahead. That's not how coaching works. We help people by asking questions and then step back and let them find their own answers. This is how you really learn. You recognize what you are capable of in your work and in your life. And you succeed!"

Asking Provocative Questions

> One of the coach's primary jobs is to be curious and ask provocative, open-ended and inviting questions that will invite the client to look in a direction or another, but with no preconceived conclusion.
> —Laura Whitworth, Karen and Henry Kimsey-House, and Phil Sandahl (Whitworth et al. 1998)

I've personally observed the transformations that come when a coach asks effective, powerful questions. I've thoroughly enjoyed helping countless clients discover for themselves what's most important to them, move away from unproductive mindsets, and create their own solutions to big problems. I always feel that I am walking on sacred ground when I engage in such transformational, inspiring work.

My job is to be genuinely curious and ask questions that provoke clients to examine their mindsets, missions, values, strategies, goals, customer needs, and leadership style—the many issues that affect business results. Mediocre bosses don't like questions. They need to have all the answers and are scared to let people know that they don't know it all (of course, some think they really do!). To such bosses, questions threaten their security and raise fears of losing control.

In contrast, the leader-coach sees questioning as an essential art and science. The science is the formulaic aspect: how to structure an open-ended question, for example. There are rules for that. The art is the fun part, the creative part, the dance in the moment with others, the excitement at arriving at solutions no one ever thought of.

But first, let's go over the rules for asking provocative, open-ended questions.

Rule 1: Care About the Person You're Coaching

Caring—about people, about things, about life—is an act of maturity.
—*Tracy McMillan, author, writer, and relationship expert*

The most important thing to keep in mind while planning coaching questions is to be genuinely curious about the answers. You must care. You must demonstrate your respect for the person you're coaching, be present, and focus on them. You can be listening; but if you really don't care to understand the person, or if you try to fake respect, they will tune in to this insincerity and question your influence.

Being authentically curious can take practice. You must keep trying to connect and show interest intentionally. You must accept the idea that others may be as smart or smarter than you, and at least temporarily suspend asserting your own opinions and viewpoints.

Here are some questions to ask yourself before the coaching conversation:

- What is my intent?
- Do I genuinely care about this person?
- Do I truly value others' ideas, input, and perspectives?

- Am I being curious, open-minded, and empathic with others?
- Am I being a team player and valuing the differences of all people?
- Have I checked my ego at the door?
- Have I created a space for safety and learning?
- Am I acting in the best interests of everyone involved?

Rule 2: Ask Questions That Support Their Agenda, Not Yours

> *Curiosity is, in great and generous minds, the first passion and the last.*
> —*Samuel Johnson, eighteenth century English critic, biographer, essayist, and poet*

Just because you're asking a question does not mean you're coaching. There's a big difference between questioning and interrogating. Executive coach Alain Cardon warns that Gestapo agents and Spanish inquisitors also "asked questions"—a lot of them. Respectful intent and genuine curiosity, therefore, are vital when asking questions.

Cardon reminds coaches that their team members are intelligent and well-informed, qualified in their own fields, and often the only people "capable of finding original and appropriate answers to achieve [their] personal or professional objectives" (Cardon 2008). The coach must shift from directing their own agenda to fully engaging and supporting their agenda. Coach and team member together discover and co-create that agenda, the coach by querying and the team member by doing the heavy thinking in order to answer.

Consider these contrasting pairs of questions. In each pair, there is a typical "interrogating" question coupled with a provocative question that demonstrates curiosity:

Typical

"Shouldn't you plan and live your life based on what your parents tell you to do?"

Provocative

"I wonder what your life would be like if you could design it any way you like?"

>>>

Typical

"Is that project going to be done on time?"

Provocative

"What stands in the way of meeting the project deadline?"

>>>

Typical

"Did you do a quality check on that process?"

Provocative

"What quality issues concern you the most about that process?"

Can you see the difference between the typical judgmental questions and the provocative, open-ended questions? Can you sense the difference in mindset between the two questioners?

The typical questions are diminishing and disempowering. You're treating your team member like a servant who is expected to jump at your commands. The provocative questions are empowering: You're treating team members like equals who can make their own professional judgments and decisions.

Avoid putting people on the defensive by asking questions that by implication judge or diminish them. Move towards more open, exploring, collaborative, and creative inquiry without judgment.

If your goal is to have an open conversation, use open-ended, non-directive queries: "Tell me about the situation." "Why do you think about this?" "What is your opinion about?" "When this situation arises, how do you feel about . . . ?" "Why is this such a big issue for you?"

Open questions tend to produce more information. Closed questions tend to produce short, limited responses. For instance, "Tell me more about how this all began" will produce more information than "Why have you been acting this way?"

If your questions are met with silence, *use* the silence. In his book *Find Your Why,* Simon Sinek observes that silence is an important tool for a leader: "If you ask a question and feel they are struggling to answer, let them struggle. . . . Resist the temptation to fill the silence with another question or a suggested answer. . . . Emotions are difficult to articulate, and it may take the person a little time to formulate the right words" (Sinek 2017, p. 52).

My general rule is this: after you ask a question, count to 15. Silence is uncomfortable, and people naturally want to fill it—just make sure it isn't you! If you don't get an answer after 15 seconds, then you rephrase the question if you want to.

Listen carefully to the individual's or team's responses. You've permitted them the space and luxury of thinking through your question. From there, you can guide their thinking: help them reframe their thinking or move toward solutions of their own.

Rule 3: Clearly Identify the Topic of the Conversation

> *The main thing is to keep the main thing the main thing.*
> —*General John Paxman, US Marine Corps*

Coaching is always about context. What is the situation? What is going on? What is the defined topic and scope of the coaching conversation? You may know why you want to have a coaching conversation with the employee, but does the employee share the same vision and commitment? To get on the same page, the following coaching questions are very helpful in clarifying the topic of conversation:

- "What's your understanding of the purpose of our coaching conversation?"
- "What topic or issue do we want to focus on today?"
- "Why are we here? What are the issues, challenges, or opportunities that bring us together?"
- "This is what I perceive as our purpose for coming together. . . . What do you think? How do you see it?"
- "What do you feel is the most important thing for us to discuss today?"

Rule 4: Be Courageous in the Moment

> *Do not fear failure but rather fear not trying.*
> —*Roy T. Bennett, political statesman and author*

Challenging a person's viewpoint, testing their assumptions, or encouraging different choices may help stretch them beyond their comfort zone. Your questions might disrupt how they see things or what they do or plan to do. Be courageous. Never be afraid to ask a tough question even if you don't know where it will lead.

Author Andrew Sobel writes that the simplest question—"Why?"—can be wonderful and needed (as long as it doesn't "come across as cynical, critical, or reproachful—especially when asked of a subordinate or a child"). Sobel says good questions are authentic, sincere, and non-manipulative (Sobel 2012). The most powerful coaching questions help:

- Dig under the surface to uncover root causes
- Clarify the issues and focus the conversation
- Create a common understanding of the situation
- Uncover dreams, ambitions, and aspirations
- Understand and connect with the most important priorities and needs
- Motivate people to see their own experiences and issues from a new perspective
- Test for alignment with values
- Reframe problems in more productive ways
- Create learning and innovation
- Inspire commitment
- Lead people to draw their own conclusions
- Validate and affirm your confidence in them

For over three years, I taught as a part of the leadership faculty with Dr. Stephen R. Covey, Dr. Ram Charan, and Dr. Mette Norgaard at FranklinCovey's Executive Leadership Summit in Deer Valley and Sundance, Utah. All three of my colleagues were master teachers, but Ram Charan, author of *What the CEO Wants You to Know*, stood out to me for his ability to ask very good, penetrating questions. He would ask questions after the questions, to dig deeper into what a participant was saying or experiencing.

It was magical how he could test, prod, question, facilitate, and pull out lessons from leaders' own experiences. He asked more curious questions than he gave answers. He certainly added in many of his own timely stories, as well; however, he pushed, pulled, challenged, tested, debated, and facilitated dialogue in a way that made people question their own assumptions and think deeply about their experiences and their answers. I have tried to model Ram's Socratic and insightful method of questioning. Following are some sample questions that can help a leader-coach facilitate dialogue and dig deeper, to ask more challenging and penetrating questions:

- "Why is this so challenging for you?"
- "Why would you want to focus on that?"
- "Why do you think that's the case?"
- "How does that inform your thinking?"
- "How would you like things to be different?"
- "What was most useful about this discussion?"
- "What stops you from doing that?"
- "What could you do to make that happen?"
- "What have you learned?"
- "Which do you see as being most important to focus on?"
- "How does that impact your team? Your organization? Your customer? Your position in the marketplace?"
- "When you say you are overcoming this issue, what makes it so difficult to change? Why?"
- "How will you apply that in your current role?"
- "Because you're finding it difficult to apply this in your leadership role, what specifically could you do differently to make a change?"
- "How could you apply that thinking with your team?"
- "What did you learn from this situation that will make a difference in your job?"
- "What are you committed to do?"
- "What actions will you take?"

Good questions can be shocking, but in a good way, like settling into a warm spa or Jacuzzi when it's snowing outside. We don't ask questions for their "shock value," but to create honest self-awareness and reflection. Provocative questions can help solicit insight and create new perspectives.

And there's an important benefit: as team members internalize the questions and own the answers, they learn how to coach and question themselves so when the next issue arises, they can be more self-aware and respectfully challenging with their team members.

Rule 5: Ask Clarifying Questions

It is not the answer that enlightens, but the question.
—*Eugene Ionesco, Romanian-French playwright*

Once you are comfortable asking your team open-ended questions, build on their responses. Asking clarifying questions invites the team members to tell you more; that way, you learn more.

Clarification means making sure you understand the answer. If you are unsure what someone means, just ask! "I am not sure if I clearly got your message. Please tell me more about . . ." You can also request specific examples: "When you say X, Y, or Z, what do you really mean by that?"

An important benefit of clarifying questions is enabling team members to think and express their thoughts more clearly, and perhaps to resolve their own issues.

Another benefit is building a stronger relationship. Your roles and responsibilities and your organizational level may be different, but coaching offers equal ground and mutual respect. The coach isn't answering, telling, or fixing. Instead, the coach and team member go on an expedition together to explore answers and co-create solutions.

As a coach, one of my biggest challenges was withholding my own knowledge and experience, at least for a time. I've been a management consultant for many years. As a consultant, you are paid to be the smartest person in the room, the one with all the answers: "Here's the problem," the consultant says, "and here's how to fix it." But coaching is not consulting, advising, or counseling. I had to get away from telling and advising. I had to move away from a position where I thought I knew the solutions, to a position of curiosity, questioning, and helping others co-create solutions, by asking good clarifying questions. Following are practical examples of key questions to help any leader or manager become a more curious, supportive coach:

- "I'm wondering about . . ."
- "Can you help me understand . . . ?"
- "Would you tell me more about . . . ?"
- "What have you observed about . . . ?"
- "Can you please explain more . . . ?"
- "What would happen if . . . ?"
- "How do you feel about . . . ?"
- "What do you think causes this . . . ?"
- "Why is this so . . . ?"

- "What do you see as the key issue/problem?"
- "What do you mean?"
- "Can you give an example?"
- "Tell me more about that."
- "Can you share the facts?"
- "What is the evidence?"
- "What is the impact?"
- "What do you think that means?"
- "What are the options here?"
- "How would you summarize your efforts?"
- "Can you tell me more about what aspects cause you the most frustration?"
- "What does success look like?"
- "What are the probabilities of success?"
- "What are the benefits?"
- "What are the costs?"
- "How do the costs compare to the benefits?"
- "What seems to get in the way?"
- "What are the biggest barriers?"
- "How will you get around those barriers?"
- "What actions will have the most impact?"
- "How will you start?"
- "Where do you go from here?"
- "When does this need to be done?"
- "What are your next steps?"
- "Who else needs to support this effort?"
- "How can I help?"

Teams need these powerful coaching questions. There may be vagueness, distractions, and barriers in their way. A leader-coach can help them get to a sharp focus on success by asking clarifying questions.

Rule 6: Perfect the Dismount

Remember watching gymnastics during the Olympic Games? Entire nations hold their breath during a routine, hoping their Olympian will deliver a perfect dismount from the balance beam. Failing to dismount perfectly can be devastating on the scoreboard.

While no gold-medal awards are on the line in coaching, it's still important to end each coaching session with a strong dismount—a strong conclusion. When it comes time to end the session, here are some ideas for closing remarks:

- *Express gratitude:* Thank the person you're coaching for being open and willing to participate.
- *Get better:* Ask for feedback on the coaching session. "What would you like to see more or less of?"
- *Align to purpose:* Help the person see the why, the bigger picture, organizational alignment connection, or stakeholder impact from your discussion.
- *Notice the details:* Discuss something you appreciate about the person.
- *Be affirming:* Affirm, show support, and express confidence in the person.
- *They do the heavy lifting:* Ask for the person's summary of the discussion.
- *Reinforce commitments:* Ask for a recap of any goals or commitments made in the coaching session.
- *Call to action:* Request that they summarize and recap their specific actions before the next session.

PRACTICE: YOUR COACHING PLAYBOOK

Hold a practice coaching session in which you strive to follow the key elements of asking the right questions, in the right way, at the right time. Invite someone you trust to be coached, and explain to them that it is a practice session. Remember to:

1. Express appreciation and respect to the person you're coaching.
2. Ask questions that support their agenda, not yours.
3. Clearly identify the topic of the conversation. Practice the 3Ds!
4. Be courageous and transparent about any key issues or opportunities of focus in the moment.
5. Ask good coaching questions to clearly summarize issues.
6. Help the participant narrow the focus on key actions and next steps.

References

Berger, Warren. (2011). Big innovations question the status quo. How do you ask the right question? *Fast Company.* https://www.fastcompany.com/1663429/big-innovations-question-the-status-quo-how-do-you-ask-the-right-questions.

Bronson, Po, and Merryman, Ashley. (2010). The creativity crisis. *Newsweek* (10 July). https://www.newsweek.com/creativity-crisis-74665.

Cardon, Alain. (2008). Powerful coaching questions. *Metasysteme Coaching.* https://www.metasysteme-coaching.eu/english/-powerful-coaching-questions.

Sinek, Simon. (2017). *Find Your Why: A Practical Guide for Discovering Purpose for You and Your Team.* Portfolio.

Sobel, Andrew. (2012). What is a good question? https://andrewsobel.com/articles/what-is-a-good-question.

Whitworth, Laura, Kinsey-House, Henry, and Sandahl, Phil. (1998). *Co-Active Coaching: New Skills for Coaching People Toward Success in Work and, Life.* Davies-Black.

9 GROWing by Setting SMART Goals

In the absence of clearly defined goals, we become strangely loyal to performing daily acts of trivia.
      —Jim Stuart, consultant practitioner and goal execution expert

Changing one's own behavior is hard. Changing someone else's behavior is even harder. I've asked audiences all over the world, "Have you ever had goals given to you that you could not influence at least 80%? Have you ever had goals that you could not measure objectively with good data every 30 days? Have you ever had too many goals? Have you ever been given unrealistic, unattainable or unmotivating goals?" Almost everyone laughs and says yes.

A few days before New Year's Eve, I asked my neighbor, Tim, "What are your New Year's resolutions?" An engineer, Tim is smart and organized and lives the structured life you'd expect of someone who loves detail and numbers. I thought if I could learn anything about goals and resolutions from anyone, it would be Tim.

"Michael," he said, "my resolution for this year is the same as last year's. It worked well for me last year, and I am expecting a second great year of success!"

"Really?" I asked. "What is it?"

"I have a goal that I know I can actually achieve and one that I'll feel good about. My goal is to eat more cake, especially the corner pieces where you find all the frosting."

I should mention—ironically—that Tim is very tall and one of the thinnest men I know. Clearly, he also knows something about cake and setting achievable goals that I do not fully understand. I think he simply has very good genes and a fast metabolism.

For most of us, a goal means going after a big opportunity or closing a gap. No gap, no goal. A good goal fills a significant gap in performance, a strategic opportunity to improve, or a stretch target to shoot for. Go from "X" to "Y": Reduce this body weight (X) to that body weight (Y). Increase this current level of profits (X) to a new level of profits (Y). Move from this measure of quality (X) to that measure of quality (Y).

Maybe because we usually fail at New Year's resolutions, we drag both feet when it comes to setting new significant goals. It's easier to coast, to get stuck, or to be indifferent to real, sustainable change. I once had a young family member who went through first grade refusing to learn to read. "She hopes it will just go away," her parents told me (ironically, she's now an elementary school teacher teaching other little kids how to read).

Like learning to read, some goals are just unavoidably important. There are performance expectations, quality standards to be met, and products to be launched. Besides, goals keep us motivated! It's easy to motivate people in the short term. A persuasive pep talk, an inspiring story, an immediate reward, an urgent threat—all these can motivate people to act. But once the urgency is gone, the short-term motivation goes with it. The only kind of commitment that lasts is internal commitment with clear, significant, objective, and achievable goals.

Following are a few rules to remember when coaching others to perform at higher levels.

Conducting the Goal-Setting Conversation

I don't focus on what I'm up against. I focus on my goals, and I try to ignore the rest.
—Venus Williams, American professional tennis player

Ultimately, focusing on goal planning and execution helps people grow, improve, and build discipline and confidence in their ability to accomplish important things in life and work. The American journalist Soledad O'Brien stated about goal achievement and transformation, "I've learned that fear limits you and your vision. It serves as blinders to what may be just a few steps down the road for you. The journey is valuable, but believing in your talents, your abilities, and your self-worth can empower you to walk down an even brighter path. Transforming fear into freedom—how great is that?" (O'Brien 2014).

Such vision and goal setting must meet certain goal planning principles and criteria (McChesney, Covey, and Huhing 2016):

- *Understanding the "why"* behind the goal is the first step. There must be a good motive for either pain or gain. Goals must have a strong benefit or business case that feels logical, rational, and motivating.
- Goals must be *practical but motivating.* If a goal is not realistic and winnable, there is no hope; but without a meaningful challenge or gap to close with the goal, there will be no motivation.
- Goals must be *measurable.* The goal must move us from X to Y with a clear gap, a clear measure, and a clear finish line or realistic target date for the goal to be achieved.
- Goals must be *influenceable.* The team must be able to influence the outcome at least 80%, or its achievement is out of their hands.
- Goals must be *collaborative.* There must be commitment to the goals by all parties involved. Goals must be legal, ethical, and environmentally and culturally sound.

Some of the best thinking on goals comes from Sir John Whitmore, world-renowned performance coach and international consultant, and creator of the GROW coaching model for achieving goals. I first encountered the GROW model while working at Pricewaterhouse Coopers in New York in the late 1990s. Since then, I've seen the model adopted worldwide because of its effectiveness in establishing clear goals and expectations for team members.

GROW is an acronym for Goals, Reality, Options, and Way Forward. Many coaches help people improve performance by defining their GROW process, as follows.

G = Goals

What are the team member's goals for improving performance? What are the goals for the coaching engagement? At this stage, you are defining in general terms what the team member wants to accomplish. At the end of this stage you should have one, two, or at most three narrowly defined goals. (Too many goals means none of them will be achieved with excellence.) Some key coaching questions to determine goals include:

- "What goals are you trying to achieve?"
- "What are the most important things you want to achieve?"
- "Why is that the most important? What makes you want to do this?"
- "What are the organization's most important goals?"
- "What are your boss's most important goals?"
- "Does your goal align up with the overall goals of your boss, business unit, and organization?"
- "If you could make only one goal for yourself or your team, what would it be?"
- "What would be the strategic value of this goal (i.e. to the organizational mission)?"
- "How would you rank this goal in importance in terms of other goals?"
- "What would this goal mean to other stakeholders (e.g. customers, other teams, shareholders, etc.)?"
- "Where have you seen this goal achieved before? How was it done?"
- "What are the benefits of achieving this goal? What is its economic value?"
- "What are the costs if you don't achieve this goal?"
- "What will ensure all team members will commit to this goal? How?"
- "Who needs to participate in executing this goal?"

R = Reality

What is the current reality? At this stage, you are taking stock of where you are now, what is achievable, and what current factors you are sure of or need to know more about. At the end of this stage, you should have goals properly defined in terms of "X to Y by when": i.e. the current state, the targeted state, and the intended deadline for completion. Ask these questions:

- "What is your situation in relation to this goal?"
- "What is the context?"
- "What are the issues and facts?"
- "Who is involved?"
- "How are you feeling about this situation?"

- "What is the current state (as measured by cost/benefit, customer retention, profits, etc.)?"
- "Which areas are most important to you?"
- "What is the ultimate measure of success on your goal (in terms of cost, benefit, quality measure, profit number, customer retention, etc.)?"
- "How realistic is this goal?"
- "What has been done or tried before?"
- "When do you expect to start/finish?"
- "Who else needs to be involved to achieve this goal?"

O = Options

What actions could reasonably be taken to achieve this goal? You are not looking for the right answer or perfect solution; rather, you are brainstorming as many alternatives as possible to get the creative juices flowing. At the end of this phase, you should have a short list of prioritized action steps and personal commitment for achieving the goal. Ask these questions:

- "What are your alternatives for action? What are your creative possibilities? What innovative solutions can you come up with?"
- "What have others done to achieve similar goals?"
- "What additional options could help you to achieve this goal? What else?"
- "What resources do you have available? What resources do you need?"
- "If resources of time, money, or people were not limited, what else would you need to be successful?"
- "What actions can you take that would have the most impact on this goal? How do you know?"

W = Way Forward

What are the action steps the person will take? What commitments need to be made? At this stage, you are agreeing on concrete decisions, expectations, and focused actions going forward. Ask these questions:

- "What two or three key actions are you going to take?"
- "How will you measure your success along the way? How will you know if you are succeeding or falling behind?"

- "What is the immediate next step?"
- "Who needs to do what and when?"
- "How will you do it?"
- "What could go wrong? What would you do about that?"
- "How likely and committed are you to do it?"
- "When will you do this?"
- "Who else will you need to support you in achieving this goal?"
- "What mentors are available to you to achieve your goal?"
- "What internal sponsorship, political support, or resources do you need to achieve this goal?"
- "How often will you meet to discuss performance and achievement on this goal?"
- "When, with who, and where will you meet for ongoing accountability?"
- "How can the organization best support you?"
- "How can I help you keep on track?"

Making Sure Goals Are SMART

Freedom means the opportunity to be what we never thought we would be.
—*Daniel J. Boorstin, Pulitzer Prize–winning author, historian, and educator*

I travel weekly to help companies and leadership teams worldwide design, set, and execute crucial goals. I've seen that a few narrowly focused and measurable goals affect focus, clarity, engagement, and accountability. When it comes to setting important goals, you must make sure they are SMART (Wilson 2007, pp. 42–47).

SMART goals are:

- Specific
- Measurable
- Attainable
- Realistic
- Time-bound

Introduced in 1981, SMART goals were developed by George Doran, Arthur Miller, and James Cunningham (Doran 1981). The goals your team sets should meet the SMART test, or they will likely fail. If your team can answer the earlier coaching questions, the goals will likely meet that test easily.

I once worked with a team of engineers responsible for managing impeccable research, writing readable and relevant reports, and providing technical reviews of all product development. To improve their performance, they recognized that they needed a better goal-setting process.

I encouraged them to define and establish a SMART goal for the upcoming quarter. Some understood goal setting right away. Kennedy, a very bright engineer, set a SMART goal that sounded something like this: "I will increase my peer review reports from 5 to 7 by end of quarter this March." SMART goals communicate the gap or performance result in a very clear, concise, and measurable statement, and this goal checked all the SMART boxes.

After Kennedy, I met with George, who had been marked down in his annual performance review for not taking advantage of the training opportunities available throughout the year. So George wrote a SMART goal: "I will attend two corporate training courses that have direct job skills/competency development related to my current role by the end of the quarter. I will receive boss sign-off when completed." This goal also checked all the boxes; but then George realized that with all his other work, his boss probably wouldn't let him meet the goal.

I asked, "Then why set that goal?"

George just shrugged.

"Would this SMART goal have significant business impact to help you grow in your current position?"

"Yes, of course it would. It's essential."

Working with George, we got his boss to agree on what was realistic, and he was able to set and achieve his goal.

For over two decades, I have had the privilege of coaching thousands of leaders and teams as they designed and executed goals. Following are some excellent goal statement examples, arranged by different organizational functions, that will help guide you to effectively coach others with SMART goal-planning rules and conversations:

Sales

- Achieve $15 million EBITDA in new sales growth by December 31.
- Increase net new sales revenue (above plan) from $250 million to $275 million by year end.

- Grow total top-line sales in the commercial product category by $4 million by Q4.

Marketing

- Increase database leads for sales by 30% by year end.
- Increase client marketing referrals from 0 to 12 per month (sustaining > 12 min. per month) by year end.

Customer service

- Increase customer Net Promoter Score (NPS) from 68% to 75% by Q4.
- Achieve 90%+ customer ratings in (customer supply scorecard) by Q4.
- Reduce customer response time from 48 hours to less than 8 hours for 90% of all customers by year end.
- Reduce network operations center tier one customer call wait time from 10 minutes to less than 4 minutes by Q3.

Operations

- Deliver operational cost savings of > $2 million over last year by Q4.
- Increase ship to request from 48 hours to 12 hours by end of fiscal year.
- Reduce quality omission error rates by 30% by Q4.
- Achieve productivity costs targets at 5% year over year by December 31.
- Achieve 95% production uptime (people and equipment) by year end.
- Achieve inventory turns > 12 by end of fiscal year.
- Achieve 0 safety recordable instances by December 31.

Information technology

- Reduce total duration of IT outages from 30% to 10% by Q3.
- Maintain stable IT platform with zero downtime by December 31.
- Reduce IT backlogs by 15% by December 31.
- Launch new sales software app project to 100% sales team users by Q3.
- Complete launch of new direct to retail product platform to 95% of users by Q4.

Project management

- Increase IT design applications with formal order requests from O to 25 by year end.
- Complete 2 Six Sigma projects achieving productivity target at 80% by Q3.
- Launch engineer project design to support new product sales from 10 to 38 by fiscal year end.
- Identify/execute two key projects for each of our top 10 customers by fiscal year end.
- Achieve 100% launch readiness as measured by green on 5Ps scorecard by Q4.

Finance/Accounting

- Reduce billing time from 2 days to 24 hours by Q2.
- Maintain budget accuracy by (+/- Y%) by fiscal year end.
- Reduce financial analysis/quotation times from 14 days to 48 hours by Q3.

Human resources

- Increase the level of talent retention (non-forced turnover) from 82% to 90% by fiscal year end.
- Fill 90% of all key positions reporting to the regional directors by December 31.
- Increase employee compliance in attending new hire onboarding orientation from 80% to > 95% within the first 30 days of hire by December 31.
- Successfully design/launch new sales manager skills training with 90% mid-level management adoption by end Q3.

As a coach, you need to ask yourself if your team members or client is ready for the rigorous goal-setting process I've described here. The quality of the relationship, the political situation at work, the goal-setting culture of the organization—these are all issues that typically arise when it's time to start setting goals (Oliver et al. 1997). Ask yourself these questions:

- Do I have a good relationship with this person?
- Is this person coachable, motivated, and capable of setting and achieving goals?

- Do these goals align with their performance management evaluation of success?
- Are those goals tied to an organizational plan with specific targets and measures that they are responsible for?
- Are they motivated, rewarded, and aligned to achieve this goal?
- Is there a clear line of sight between organizational, divisional, and team goals?
- Is there a clear business case for the goal? Can they describe it?
- Will the goal help them develop their own career success?

Following Up on Goals

Many of life's failures are people who did not realize how close they were to success when they gave up.
—*Thomas Edison, American inventor and businessman*

The key to achieving performance goals is to hold ongoing coaching conversations that focus on accountability for the goals. According to Olivero, Bane, and Kopelman's coaching research, "Follow-up coaching increases productivity more that 300% over training alone" (Olivero et al. 1997). Follow-up is critical to ensure that all members are clear on strategic objectives—aligned, focused, and moving forward to greater levels of success.

A former colleague of mine, Bill Bennett, used to say, "It is not the hard work that causes people to be tired, it is the fog or lack of clarity." Coaches can help teams clarify purpose, direction, and goals to get people out of the fog and focused in a motivated, passionate, and excited way. Still, it's easy for the team to get derailed or side-tracked. That's why coaches must hold people accountable frequently and regularly—preferably in weekly reviews where all parties account for their individual commitments and progress toward the goal. Team members run into roadblocks of all kinds: politics, resource issues, changing priorities, distractions. The coach's weekly review helps overcome these barriers and ensure that the goal is met.

Here are key questions to help team members stay on track in achieving important goals and objectives:

- "Are you winning or losing this week?"
- "What progress have you made in achieving your goal?"

- "How do you feel about your progress? What are your successes so far?"
- "Are you on track to accomplish the goal? If not, what are you doing to get back on 'track'?"
- "How do the boss and other key stakeholders perceive your progress?"
- "What lessons have you learned about what works? What doesn't work?"
- "Is the goal still realistic and achievable?"
- "What barriers are in your way?"
- "Who could remove these barriers for you?"
- "What is your plan at this point?"
- "What new opportunities do you see for moving forward?"
- "What resources are needed at this point?"
- "What issues need resolving?"
- "When would you like to meet about these issues?"
- "What are the realistic next steps going forward?"
- "How can I help?"

PRACTICE: YOUR COACHING PLAYBOOK

Think of a time when you achieved a goal that you set for yourself, your team, or your organization. Think of a time when you failed to reach a goal. What made the difference between your success and your failure?

Have there been times where you've set lofty and inspiring goals, and then lost commitment or focus on the goals? What happened? How can you avoid those problems in the future?

How can you help hold others accountable and committed to achieving their most important goals and objectives?

Can you improve performance and accountability by holding regular follow-up check-ins and ongoing performance conversations?

What are your most important goals for the immediate future? Are they SMART goals?

As you begin to design and align your goal-planning process, here's a way to write your SMART goals to ensure that they align across your organizational structure to the business unit or division level, the team level, and ultimately the individual level. Make sure your individual and team goals are aligned, up to the higher-level goals at the division and organization levels:

1. Organizational goals (strategic level):

   _____
   _____

2. Business unit/division/department goals (operational level):

   _____
   _____

3. Team goals (tactical level):

   _____
   _____

4. Individual goals (personal level):

   _____
   _____

References

Doran, George. (1981). There's a S.M.A.R.T. way to write management's goals and objectives. *Management Review* 70 (11).

McChesney, Chris, Covey, Sean, and Huhing, Jim. (2016). *The 4 Disciplines of Execution: Achieving Your Wildly Important Goals*. Free Press. pp. 127–132.

O'Brien, Soledad. (2014). Prime time with Soledad O'Brien. *Essence*. https://www.essence.com/news/prime-time-soledad-obrien.

Olivero, Gerald, Bane, K. Denise, and Kopelman, Richard E. (1997). Executive coaching as a transfer of training tool: Effects on productivity in a public agency. *Public Personnel Management* 26 (4), 461–469.

Wilson, Carol. (2007). *Best Practice in Performance Coaching: A Handbook for Leaders, Coaches, HR Professionals and Organizations*. Kogan Page.

10 Listening with Empathy

To be with another empathically means that for the time being, you lay aside your own views and values to enter another's world without prejudice. In a sense you lay aside yourself; this can only be done by people that are secure in themselves.
> —Carl Rogers, American author and twentieth-century humanist psychologist

When was the last time you spoke with someone who was a truly lousy listener? How did you know they were not listening? Was it the fact that they checked their phone or watch or email every few seconds? That they did not make eye contact? That they did not ask any follow-up questions? Did they try to interrupt you? Were they just waiting for their turn to talk?

In contrast, think about some of your most powerful exchanges when you interacted with a great listener. How did you know they were really listening? Did they appear zoned in to what you were saying, and only what you were saying? Were they present, available emotionally, and focused on the moment at hand? Did they make and keep eye contact? Did they ask timely follow-up and clarifying questions? Did you feel that they were not simply waiting their turn in the conversation, but were fully engaged nonverbally and verbally in what you were saying?

The times you feel listened to become priceless memories. You connect on a deeper level with those who listen, and you arrive at authentic understanding.

Evaluate Your Listening Skills ━━━━━━━

Many leaders are not very good at listening. Great listening skills are the pathway to gaining more connected relationships, influencing others, and effectively diagnosing problems and issues. Much of work is emotional, psychological, and cultural. Effective listening allows us to check our title, position, ego, wisdom, and competence at the door long enough to show respect and real understanding of what is happening with others. Not only do great listening skills help to build better relationships, solve problems, understand issues, and resolve conflict; but they also help to improve quality, speed, commitment, satisfaction, and engagement.

Here are some self-assessment questions to consider as you evaluate your own listening skills in the role of becoming a great leader-coach:

- On a scale from 1–10, how good a listener am I? (1 = poor listener, 10 = very good listener.)
- How well do I listen and show respect while communicating with others?
- Am I fully present and engaged in coaching conversations?
- Do I really want to set aside my agenda and listen with empathic accuracy to the other person's agenda?
- Do I create a safe environment for listening, confidentiality, comfort, and dialogue without distractions?
- Do I interrupt others while they are speaking?
- Do I schedule adequate time for the coaching conversation?
- How well do I understand the other's position, perspectives, and point of view?
- Am I okay with silence?
- Do I pretend to listen, or listen selectively?
- Do I listen in a way that leads to creative dialogue, innovation, and improved performance?
- Do I ask clarifying questions?
- Do people feel understood, valued, and respected during our dialogue and conversation?

Listening Empathically ━━━━━━━━━

Most people do not listen with the intent to understand; they listen with the intent to reply.
—Dr. Stephen R. Covey, professor, author,
speaker, and businessman

Great coaches take time to listen. Nothing makes a team member feel more supported and respected than an open-door policy where they can maintain a positive connection, offer input, and receive ongoing support and encouragement. Listening to your team members will do more good than almost anything else you do.

Why do people love good listeners? Because a good listener always lets people hear their favorite speaker—themselves! As a coach, listen more and talk less. Great listening begins and ends with making the other person feel respected and important. Talk-show host Larry King once said, "I remind myself every morning: Nothing I say this day will teach me anything. So, if I'm going to learn, I must do it by listening."

Listening is a lost art. As a father and as a global consultant, teacher, and coach, I have witnessed that many of our employees and our children spend so much time seeking digital connection with others, and even the masses online, that many have a difficult time engaging in real-time, face-to-face, old-fashioned conversation. In a world where we're increasingly connected online or with cellular devices, it's a sad dilemma to consider that more access to efficient digital connections with people can lead to a lessening in the art of connection, conversation, and deep listening skills.

Coaching allows leaders the opportunity to dust off that lost art. It's absolutely required. To be a great coach, you must listen with empathy and truly care about understanding another human being.

To listen well when practicing empathy, we must give up interrupting, advising, judging, interpreting, or evaluating. Good listening requires us to be completely present in the moment. It requires us to get lost in another person's world in terms of context (the overall setting), content (what is going on from their perspective), and feeling (how they are emotionally reacting and responding). We can't pretend we are listening while we are formulating our next brilliant comment. We can't successfully fake interest for very long.

Practical Applications in Developing Empathic Listening Skills

> *How does a leader make people feel important? First, by listening to them. Let them know you respect their thinking and let them voice their opinions. As a bonus, you might learn something!*
> —*Mary Kay Ash, business leader, entrepreneur, pioneer in direct marketing and consumer products*

Holding a black belt in any martial art requires mastery at the highest level of proficiency. Empathic listening is like the black belt of listening. Empathy is a skill that requires self-confidence, self-mastery, and self-control. By being a faithful translator, you engage in listening with your eyes, ears, and heart to understand the feelings of another person from their personal, intimate perspective.

Marshall Goldsmith wrote, "The thing about listening that escapes most people is that they think of it as a passive activity. You don't have to do anything. You sit there like a lump and hear someone out. Not true. Good listeners regard what they do as a highly active and connected process—with every muscle engaged, especially the brain and the heart. Basically, there are three things that all good listeners do: they think before they speak; they listen with respect; and they're always gauging their response by asking themselves, 'Is it worth it?'" (Goldsmith 2014, p. 47).

Imagine that a co-worker, Erik, calls you one evening. He wants to talk to you about a business situation that arose that day. If possible, he wants to meet first thing in the morning.

What are some practical steps to developing space, time, and effective listening skills when you meet with a co-worker like Erik?

- Ensure that you have cleared your calendar and that you have ample time to listen.

- Ensure that your meeting space is free of any physical, psychological, or social distractions—the room temperature is comfortable, and your cell phone and other electronic devices are turned off or silenced.
- Allow for time and space to not feel rushed. Do not look at your watch, phone, or laptop, or in any way signal that you are in a hurry and need the conversation to be done.
- Use body language to signal to the person that what they say is important and valued.
- Your first goal is to empathize with whatever they have to say.
- Intent is huge and cannot be faked. When it comes to empathic listening, intent counts more than technique. You are both equals in the conversation. If someone can see and feel that you are sincerely trying to understand their point of view, it won't matter if you don't get the technique exactly right. The important thing is to give them a safe place to share and connect.
- Use "I" messages when restating what you are hearing. "I" messages are nonjudgmental and safe. Here are some examples:
  - "I definitely hear the concern. You're not feeling that . . ."
  - "I appreciate your honesty. I'm hearing that you're frustrated with . . ."
  - "That is a very good question, just tough to answer. I am sensing that you're concerned about . . ."
  - "I definitely want to share my perspective and feelings on that. Let me make sure I understand first. You seem bothered by . . ."
  - "Well, let's talk about that. It sounds like you are struggling with . . ."
  - "If we can't find some good answers to that, I wouldn't want either of us to proceed. You're feeling strongly about . . ."

Once you have acknowledged the person's concern, you need to clarify understanding. That means asking good clarifying questions about their message, objectives, meaning, position, needs, and issues. By clarifying, you can restate and recap the other person's feelings, motives, and emotions accurately. By restating and clarifying, you aren't agreeing or disagreeing with their point of view; you're simply asking questions to gain accurate understanding. Clarifying questions not only help you understand, but also allows the speaker to move out of the emotional brain and into the thinking or conceptual brain by giving them space to verbalize their situation, concerns, issues, and feelings. Following are examples of clarifying questions to practice in your coaching conversations:

- "When you say . . . , what do you mean? Can you tell me more about that?"
- "Help me understand what you mean by . . ."
- "I'm interested in your perspective on . . . Can you tell me more about it?"
- "Can you give me some examples of . . . so I can understand better?"
- "Tell me more about . . ."

As a coach, after you have listened and asked clarifying questions, you are ready to identify the real problem and possible solution.

- Identify the problem:
    - What issues seem to be the most important to the person you're coaching?
    - What is the evidence of these issues?
    - What are the impacts of these issues?
- Clarify the solution:
    - "To make sure I am on point, what might be the best solution to this problem?"
    - "If we solved this problem right now, what do you think the impact would be?"
    - "What do you believe would be the best next steps going forward?"

Avoiding Pitfalls

We have two ears and one mouth, so we should listen more than we talk.
—*Zeno of Citium, founder of the Stoic school of philosophy and virtuous teachings in Athens, Greece, about 300 BCE*

Why is it so hard for many leaders to listen effectively? There are many reasons, but here are a few typical pitfalls:

- *Asserting control:* A conversation is always easier if you're in charge. You get to pick the topics and direct the conversation because you are much more interested in what you have to say than anything anyone else has to say. Giving advice can also be a form of control. We put ourselves in the driver's seat and jump in with our agenda, our solutions, or our need to be validated.
- *Being the smartest one in the room:* If you have a large ego, you want to be the hero of the situation. Everyone needs to know how smart you are and how brilliantly you solve problems. You don't need to understand other people's viewpoints, because their viewpoints don't matter.
- *Hurrying along:* You're busy! You have only so much time and a lot of competing priorities. It's hard to turn off that list and focus on the needs of others. You might be suffering from the common management syndrome called "chasing squirrels," or Attention Deficit Disorder (ADD). Everything is shiny, and you're too busy to stop and really hear people out.

Ineffective leaders view communication as an opportunity to promote their own personal agendas. Great leaders understand that the deepest need of the human heart is to be understood. Everyone wants to feel valued and heard, so effective leaders work at understanding and focusing on what matters most to the people they lead. They are then in a better situation to engage and release the talent, strengths, and passions of their team toward the organization's highest priorities.

Responding Empathically ━━━━━━━━

Unexpressed feelings never die; they are buried alive and come forth in uglier ways.
—*Dr. Stephen R. Covey, professor, author, speaker, and businessman*

Hand in hand with empathic listening is empathic responding. This means communicating back to a person that we hear, validate, and understand their feelings.

Suppose your close friend comes to you with the bad news that he has just been fired from his job. How should you respond? In Dr. Covey's 7 Habits book, he shows how to effectively connect with others by practicing empathy. He cites four typical responses, including advising, probing, interpreting, or evaluating what you've heard:

- *Advise:* "Well, you'd better update your resume. I would go to their competitor and get a better job and more money."
- *Probe:* "When? Who fired you? Why? What were they thinking? Where are you going to go next?"
- *Interpret:* "You didn't really like that job anyway. It would have taken you 10 years just to get a promotion at that lousy company."
- *Evaluate:* "That's terrible. They shouldn't have done that. I knew your boss was an idiot!"

None of these responses are very helpful when seeking mutual understanding. Empathic responses are quite different.

You start by allowing your friend to talk as much as they want. Before they can move forward, they need ample opportunity to express their feelings, which are probably confused, angry, or fearful. You can help by saying, "Tell me more about what happened." Or, "What was happening that may have influenced their decision?" Or, "In addition to what you've already told me, is there anything else that you believe influenced their decision?"

You can respond with affirmation and empathy: "This must be very frustrating and upsetting for you. I sense your frustration and your disappointment."

Help your friend find their own way forward by listening with sincere respect and kindness: "I am so sorry to hear that . . ." "What are your thoughts and feelings going forward?"

As an empathic listener, you have no agenda (Covey 1989). You are not jumping in and adding to or controlling the conversation. The speaker drives the agenda. Be curious, respectful, and kind. Your intent is only to clarify what happened and to offer compassion and support in a difficult situation. Many times, just being with a person and listening can add tremendous value.

PRACTICE: YOUR COACHING PLAYBOOK

In the Broadway musical *Hamilton*, Alexander Hamilton talks with Aaron Burr, who advises him, "talk less, smile more." Here's a coaching challenge: During the next week, pick one conversation where you talk less and listen more. In fact, make a concerted effort to talk less than the person you are talking to. Instead of talking, pause and reflect on what is being said, and listen. Instead of inserting or commenting, just listen. Instead of inserting ideas, overpowering, and dominating, simply listen. At the end of the week, take a moment to note: When were you successful in practicing empathy and when could you get better?

1. How did the other person respond to me when they noticed they had my complete attention?
2. How did I feel during the conversation? Was it hard to remain silent? Did it feel awkward?
3. Did I learn anything that I might otherwise have missed by talking?
4. What were the benefits of practicing empathy?
5. What barriers or challenge get in the way of me becoming a better listener?
6. What was the hardest part?
7. What was the easiest part?
8. Did others give any positive feedback—either verbal or nonverbal—due to practice with empathic communication?

References

Covey, Stephen R. (1989). *The 7 Habits of Highly Effective People*. Free Press.
Goldsmith, Marshall. (2014). *What Got You Here Won't Get You There*. MJF.

11

Coaching and Feedback

Sometimes you can't see yourself clearly until you see yourself through the eyes of others.
—Ellen DeGeneres, American comedian, television host, actress, gender equality activist, writer, and producer

Amy, the front-desk receptionist, believed that she was the face of the corporation to customers. When people came in, they saw and interacted with her first. She wanted to ensure that every interaction was a positive one. She smiled a lot, laughed a lot, and tried to help everyone who asked her for assistance.

Until the day came when she received the feedback that she was trying too hard to please everyone. Her mindset and feeling about her role shifted. What she once considered to be a positive thing—in fact, her very job—became a source of doubt and discouragement. Negative feedback robbed her of some of her confidence. She still tried to be helpful, but she was not as happy about it.

What is the purpose of feedback? To help people engage fully in their work by leveraging their strengths, skills, competency, motivation, and experience. After all, their success is your success! It is estimated that 70% of a customer's experience with a company's brand is through their interaction with front-line employees. We should seek to treat our employees as we do our finest customers.

The Balancing Act of Giving Feedback

Most of us have received job performance feedback throughout our career. Many leaders are equipped with great coaching skills and know how to give feedback to help people improve. Others use feedback as a hammer. Still others aren't quite sure how to give feedback.

Harsh feedback can demotivate and derail performance. Charles Schwab, former CEO and a great personal wealth manager and financial investor, says, "I have yet to find the man or woman, however exalted in their station in life, who did not do better work and put forth greater effort under the spirit of approval and support than under a spirit of criticism" (Schwab 2004).

Dr. Don Clifton, former head of the American Psychological Association and father of strength-based feedback and developmental psychology, gathered 50 years of Gallup research from 20,000 leadership interviews and 10,000 follower interviews to find out what effective leaders do well. Clifton discovered that the most effective leaders regularly and frequently seek and offer feedback in order to maximize the strengths of their people.

People get energized if they can approach the feedback process openly and positively.

But a lot of damage can be done, all in the name of feedback—which is perhaps why we dread giving it almost as much as we dread receiving it. If feedback is used as a punitive, punishing, "knife in the back" approach, engagement and performance will decrease rather than increase. Some people hind behind anonymous feedback surveys: like trolls on the Internet, they take aggressive, abusive shots at their colleagues, who are generally seeking to improve. There is instructive, helpful feedback; and there are very negative, abusive forms of feedback. Feedback should never be used in a punitive, manipulative, or abusive way.

Feedback has a purpose: most people think they know what they're good at, and they are usually wrong. They have not stopped to see where their natural gifts and talents lie. Feedback has the potential to fill in the blind spots and provide clarity on strengths, as well as the ability to recognize areas of improvement and opportunities.

Marshall Goldsmith has argued that feedback is necessary because some people are "incredibly delusional." He observes that 95% of workers believe that they are performing in the top half of their group. It is, Goldsmith writes, "statistically ridiculous" but "psychologically real." At the same time, "giving people negative feedback means 'proving' they are wrong. *Proving* to successful people that they are wrong works just about as well as *making* or *forcing* them to change. Not gonna happen. . . . But successful people's identities are often so closely connected to what they do it's naïve to assume they will not take it personally when receiving negative feedback about the most important activity in their lives" (Goldsmith 2014).

Coaches should balance both positive and corrective feedback. Too much negative feedback can feel abusive, demotivating, and demoralizing. On the other hand, all positive reinforcement without correction can feel insincere and hollow. A rule of thumb is to offer two to three times more positive praise, affirmation, and support than correction.

Often, formal style-and-strengths instruments along with 360-degree surveys can be useful in giving feedback because they add credibility to your view of the person.

The Practical Application of Feedback and Coaching

If you feel uncomfortable giving feedback, practice the following steps to help with improving development and action planning:

1. Explain that you're giving feedback to help everyone understand how they can better contribute to the team's goals or improvement in a particular area. Align feedback and link it with the culture, values, talent development, goals, behaviors, and performance standards of the company.
2. Describe with specifics what you or others have observed. Keep the feedback to the objective data or observation. Be respectful and helpful, never hurtful or demeaning in any way. Do not attack the person or get personal with any comments.
3. Explain the impacts of any desired behavior change. Lay out your clear expectations. Link to company values, goals, performance standards, or new and better behaviors expected at work.
4. Give team members a chance to respond and share their observations and reactions openly. Don't focus on the past; rather, focus

on the future and what they can do to effectively improve. Create a safe environment for feedback so people will not be resistant or defensive.

5. Brainstorm how things can be different. Don't focus on the problem but the possibilities, opportunities, and solutions. Target the future desired state, set goals, prioritize areas of focus, and collaborate on a commitment or a plan. Close the feedback session with affirmation, expressing encouragement and confidence. End on a positive note by offering your support.

All feedback and coaching should lead to a clear, accountable action plan. Marcus Buckingham, discussing how to improve human performance, says, "Leaders must develop a systematic process to find out and clearly identify what their strengths are and how to capitalize on them" (Buckingham 2001). Focusing on the positive and helping people play to their strengths, as opposed to just focusing on gaps or weaknesses, will go a long way toward empowering, energizing, and motivating them to improve their performance.

Following are some useful planning tools for better engaging and empowering people to effectively plan and use their feedback and coaching in a positive direction.

PRACTICE: MY "CURRENT STATE" SELF: WHO AM I NOW?

What are the issues, challenges, or opportunities? Where am I right now? What do I enjoy? What am I good at? Strengths? Targeted areas to improve? How do others see me? Any gaps?

_____

_____

What are my strengths—i.e. the things about me that move me toward my "desired state" self?

_____

_____

What are my currently observed and targeted areas to improve? Any key gap areas? The things that I want to/others want me to develop? How can I create more alignment between my "current state" self and my "desired state" self?

_____

_____

**PRACTICE: MY "DESIRED STATE" SELF: WHO DO I
REALLY DESIRE TO BE IN MY FUTURE STATE?**

What do I really want out of life? What kind of person do I really
want to be? What am I aiming for as a person? What is my purpose
or contribution?

_____

_____

What insights emerge as you compare what you captured related
to your "current state" self and your "desired state" self? Any key
actions? To complete by when?

_____

_____

Giving Feedback as a Coach

> *A leader is someone who can effectively get things done with
> and through people.*
> —*Warren Buffett, CEO of Berkshire Hathaway, business
> investor, speaker, and philanthropist*

Who has had the most positive influence in your life? Who is a person
who supported and encouraged you? Who is a person who criticized and
demeaned you? What was the big difference in their influence on you?

What does that mean in a business culture or environment? If you
tell a person four good things about them and one negative thing—
guess which type of feedback will stick? The one negative thing.
Remember the importance of three or four positive areas of feedback
to one instructional area for improvement. For example:

1. "McKay, you are very dependable. You show up on time, ready
   to work every day."

2. "McKay, your work is impeccable. Your sources are professional and dependable, and your research on your reports is flawless."
3. "McKay, people really like working with you. You have a great attitude, and you make collaboration easy and rewarding."
4. "McKay, you are really going above and beyond your job description. You're very talented, and you're expanding your work role in ways we did not even consider possible."
5. "McKay, your final work product is always outstanding, but you always seem to push right up to the very last minute of your deadline. You seem to procrastinate a lot. Is there any way you could stop procrastinating and produce the reports faster and on time?"

What do you think McKay will remember from the review? If he's like most of us, he'll remember most vividly that his boss told him he procrastinates and is too slow. To ensure that feedback is positive, remember to give the positives and strengths first, with abundance and generosity.

I talked with one leader after he concluded his quarterly performance reviews with his direct reports. One of his employees was known as the office top performer. Her overall evaluation rating was superior, but he noted on her review that she did not participate in enough training sessions throughout the year. She argued with her supervisor for three hours, even though her overall rating was superior.

If someone is on the wrong path and has serious derailing behaviors, it's vital to show them what the behaviors are, the evidence of what has been observed, the negative impacts, and how they can improve, in a helpful, supportive way. When people give feedback in a spirit of anger, hatred, guilt, or shame, many times the feedback will not be fully received. Blame, shame, and judgment are ineffective and overpower all other effective feedback processes. Feedback should be honest and transparent but should also be helpful around fact-based observations and support. Feedback should always create hope and a pathway to potential and improvement. Feedback is about helping people get better, not bitter. Never use feedback as a weapon, as a tool of manipulation, or to cause despair.

Let's look at some bad and good ways to give feedback.

1. Be specific when referring to observable behavior, and look for ways to get better:

- Bad—"Luke, you are lazy, you don't work hard, and you have a poor attitude at work."
- Good—"Luke, I've observed that you have been 15 minutes late for work three times this week. Can you explain·why you were late and how you would like to change this?"

2. Focus on observable behaviors that the person or the team member can do something about:
   - Bad—"Jacob, why are you so introverted and shy? You don't seem to like talking to other people in the finance department."
   - Good—"Jacob, we would appreciate your keeping your team well informed. How could we stay in closer communication about all our budgets?"

3. Don't be negative toward the person. Define the impact of the behavior on the team and the business, and focus on how to resolve the issue:
   - Bad—"Sabrina, why can't you ever get your reports to me on time?"
   - Good—"Sabrina, when your reports don't get to me on time, I can't get my reports to my boss and other leaders on time. This slows down their decision-making process, and they can't allocate resources back to us when we need them. Can we work together on ways to get the reporting done on time?"

4. Avoid putting negative labels on people. Focus on observable behaviors and exploring how to get better:
   - Bad—"Zach, you've been really inconsiderate to our team members from customer service. You cut them off, you don't listen to them, and your tone is rude."
   - Good—"Zach, I know how important it is for you to be a good team player. I recognize you're under a lot of pressure in sales. I received feedback from customer service that we need to improve our communication with them. Do you have any ideas on how we could do that?"

5. Give feedback in a calm, unemotional tone, and use good body language that shows respect and support. Focus on involving

the other person in the solution to the problem, without causing defensiveness through judgment and shame:

- Bad—"Steve, you blew it again! You obviously don't know how to run that machine, and you're constantly messing up our production line."
- Good—"Steve, I think there are some ways you can improve your quality and production runs with our machines. Were you aware of the quality and production issues? What are some recommendations that you have that could improve in these two areas?"

All feedback should be targeted at the development of the people we coach. If we focused solely on feedback without an eye on developing people, we might get short-term results but still have unskilled people. Always keep in mind your development goals for a person who's getting feedback from you.

Giving Strengths-Based Feedback

The best coaches offer feedback that builds on the strengths of the people they coach. In addition to strengths, it is about clarifying the person's purpose, meaning, and significant contribution. You should add to your coaching agenda questions that will help identify those strengths and motivating purposes:

- "What are your top two or three natural gifts, strengths, and talents?"
- "What have you always loved doing?"
- "What gets you motivated and excited to get up each morning?"
- "You feel smart, talented, and at your best when?"
- "When do you find yourself most engaged and enthusiastic about work?"
- "What would you like to do more of in your work?"
- "If money was not needed, what would you spend your life doing?"
- "What strengths do you want to more fully develop or leverage in your work?"
- "When working in teams, what do you enjoy doing the most?"

- "Where do you feel the greatest sense of purpose and contribution at work?"
- "What is going well in your work role?"
- "When do you lose your passion and become de-energized?"
- "You feel drained or de-motivated when?"
- "What would you like to do less of in your work?"
- "What type of work or role would make you disengage?"
- "When working in teams, what is your least favorite type of work to do?"
- "What would you like to shift, change, or improve about your work role?"

The following feedback worksheet can help you to identify an individual's strengths and aligned purposes, with practical plans for developing them:

PRACTICE: DEVELOPING LEADERS COACHING FEEDBACK WORKSHEET

Strength-based successes	Areas for development
Based on the review of your feedback report, data, or coaching, identify and list your leadership strengths in the left-hand column. Be sure to focus on those strengths that you are aware of and any that you tend to minimize or don't see, yet others recognize as strengths. Capture ways to leverage your key strengths in the right-hand column.	Based on the review of your feedback report, data, or coaching, identify your top developmental areas in the left-hand column. Again, target those key areas where you noticed the biggest gaps and opportunities for improvement. Capture any action ideas in the right-hand column.

Your strengths	Ways to leverage your key strengths	Developmental opportunities	Action ideas to improve
1.		1.	
2.		2.	
3.		3.	
4.		4.	
5.		5.	

Using tools like this coaching worksheet, you can review the following key questions to help in your planning and follow up in your ongoing coaching conversations:

1. Brainstorm actions in each priority area (strengths and improvement areas):
   - "How can you play to your strengths most effectively?"
   - "How will you address opportunities to improve your weaknesses/limitations?"
   - "How will you align your actions to advance the strategic priorities and goals of your team, business, and organization?"

2. Create leadership development/job performance action plans (job performance focus):
   - "List the concrete description of key job performance actions/behaviors/competencies."
   - "List the expected timing and measures of success in your current job."
   - "What quick wins can you expect to achieve in your job performance in the next 30, 60, and 90 days?"
   - "What longer-term wins can you expect to achieve in your job performance?"

3. Develop long-term career path goals (career focus):
   - "What are your career expectations and aspirations in the future?"
   - "Where do you want to be professionally in the next one to five years?"
   - "Who is your career mentor? Who is a part of your career network to support you?"
   - "What are your most important career goals in the future?"
   - "What skills, people, or resources do you need to develop to achieve these goals?"

4. Define stakeholder support, resources, and an accountability system:
   - "Which stakeholders do you need to enroll in your success (e.g. boss, peers, your manager, team members, other departments, family members, others)?"

- "What sustaining processes or support systems do you need for your success (e.g. external or internal coaching, additional training, information access, professional experiences, professional networks, mentoring/exposure, rewards/recognition, budget or time approval, etc.)?"
- "What barriers, obstacles, or path needs to be cleared or overcome in order for you to achieve success in your career path?"
- "What will you do to ensure that you have all the support and resources necessary to be successful in your career?"

Giving Feedback with Humility

Never look down on anybody unless you're helping them up.
—Jesse Jackson, American civil rights activist, Baptist
minister, and politician

The best leaders coach others from a position of humility. Remember that some feedback may cause anger, stress, discomfort, or withdrawal, and lead to further disengagement. In one of my earlier books, *Unlocking Potential: 7 Coaching Skills That Transform Individuals, Teams, & Organizations,* I observed, "It is critical to challenge paradigms in a safe environment because many false, limiting, or incomplete paradigms can stop us from achieving our full potential. Feedback helps to educate and shift paradigms that limit one's progress. Feedback is a gift to help increase self-awareness and lead to transformational change" (Simpson 2014, pp. 49–53).

As a leader, you must demonstrate to others that you are open to their input. Listen to them and understand their viewpoints, no matter how they differ from yours. Never let them doubt that you respect their views and that you believe in them. Show appreciation and gratitude for everyone's efforts and contributions. All of that takes humility.

In my experience coaching executives from some of the top organizations in the world, I have found that humility is the key to growth. The ability to accept and act on feedback is a hallmark of great leadership. Not everyone wants to change and improve. People see in themselves only what they are prepared to see. As a coach, you set the tone by the way you receive feedback from others: If you accept feedback with humility, others will more willingly accept feedback from you.

In his book *Good to Great*, Jim Collins uncovered through extensive research that the highest-performing leaders in great organizations are humble. They are generally quiet, reserved, shy, and motivated to act on good information rather than overwhelm everyone with their charisma and ego. In fact, Collins feels that humility is the number-one characteristic of great leaders, or what he terms a *level-five*, highest-level leader. Their humility surfaces primarily in their ability to leverage feedback—to listen to the customers, the marketplace, competitors, and employees—and adapt to the necessary changes based on input and ongoing feedback (Collins 2001).

I wasn't surprised by this research because we have all seen that the downfall of most civilizations, countries, companies, and individuals begins when they become self-centered, internally focused, arrogant, myopic, and isolated from honest, candid feedback.

Dr. Clayton Christensen, renowned Harvard Business School professor, once asked his MBA students to describe one person they knew who was very humble. It turned out that the humblest person they knew was also the person they admired the most. For the students, humility was not a self-depreciating behavior; rather, it was a sign of a healthy self-esteem accompanied by an openness to feedback.

I remember early in my career, Dr. Stephen Covey would often say that humility is the mother of all principles, and obedience to principles is the father. We need to be open and humble to market, customer, and employee feedback. Then, we need to obediently align to those principles of continuous improvement, innovation, and getting better.

I have been assigned to coach leaders all along the humility spectrum. For example, Austin was a very energetic, innovative, and experienced executive. After many years, he had worked his way up in the business to the proverbial corner office. Unfortunately, now that Austin had finally achieved everything he wanted in terms of professional success, he treated everyone around him as if they were idiots. He had to be the smartest person in the room. He was the source of all knowledge in his department, and if anyone spoke up independently, Austin quickly neutered their voice.

The consequences in Austin's department were dramatic and noticeable. His employees were disengaged. They went silent, which was fine with him.

I was brought in as a coach for Austin. I asked him, "Austin, do you realize how you are showing up in the office with your team?" Austin thought he was dynamic, engaging, and fun. He did have a very charming side, which his employees saw to an extent. I asked them, "What do you love about Austin?" They conceded he was bright and charismatic and possessed a lot of competence in his role—but he had a temper, he had his own agenda, and they couldn't trust him. He thought he was a smooth operator, but others disliked him intensely and saw him as an obstacle to the success of the team.

I asked him, "Are there any derailing behaviors you have that you would like to change?" He couldn't think of any. "What do you want to do about this?" I asked, confronting him with survey responses from his employees. He quickly turned into a victim. "What can I do?" he asked. "I'm doing the best I can with the staff I have; they're all idiots, and I can't help it if I get easily frustrated with stupid people!"

The ego is a hustler; it wants to protect itself against honest feedback. It needs to be the smartest one in the room. It needs to be in control, it can be very hard on other people, and it seeks to promote itself nonstop. Ego can even hide under the mask of false humility. Austin's ego was calling in reinforcements; he was not open to feedback, input, and change.

"But Austin," I said, "what will the cost be if you do not change?" Unfortunately, Austin soon afterward learned the cost: he was terminated from his position. Despite his solid financial results, he lost his influence because his values were contrary to the culture of the company, and he was unwilling to change. His demise was not about *what* [goals, financial results, measures, and targets] he produced; it was *how* [language, communication, behaviors, and values] he produced it. The how was not sustainable and was inconsistent with his ability to build a high-trust culture.

In contrast with my work with Austin, I had a far more satisfying experience conducting a leadership work session and coaching assignment with a billion-dollar global company in Dallas, Texas. I was working with the CEO, Duncan (who has become a very good friend), as well as with his executive team from Europe, Asia, Latin America, Canada, and the United States.

During a leadership team offsite retreat, we reviewed for each leader the aggregate data from their 360-degree leader profiles, which contained candid, direct feedback from their boss, peers, direct reports, and others.

I was amazed at how open, humble, and genuine the CEO was during this session. At one point he shared openly with the team key data from his own feedback report. He was very vulnerable intellectually and emotionally. He shared items he needed to work on: communicating at all levels within the company, holding others accountable, and focusing more on customer needs. He showed no defensiveness: "This feedback is true," he said, "and I need to do a better job in each of these three areas."

As I talked with members of Duncan's team the next day, they said, "It is so refreshing to see our CEO share his shortcomings. We already know his strengths and weaknesses, but with this objective data, I see him even more clearly as an amazing leader. He is humble and open. His shortcomings don't make him look weak at all. Rather, his genuine and sincere desire to improve gives all of us on the leadership team the courage to be open and vulnerable, and to improve as well."

Great leaders like Duncan are willing to confront the brutal facts in their business environment, assess their own performance, face their leadership shortcomings honestly, and make the necessary personal and organizational changes to lead in a turbid global environment.

Gaining Awareness Through Feedback

The capacity for faith and hope is the most significant fact of life. It gives human beings a sense of destination and the energy to get started.
—Norman Cousins, political journalist, author, professor, and world peace advocate

Sir John Whitworth believes that raising awareness is the most important work a coach can do. Both a telescope and a magnifying glass provide great clarity and insights into the galaxies above or the unseen microscopic world. The same is true with effective coaching.

The coach holds up a mirror to a person's mindset, thoughts, feelings, motivations, behaviors, and choices.

Our family loves going to Hawaii. When I go scuba diving or snorkeling with my family in Kauai, my diving mask helps me to see clearly the beautiful coral reefs, brilliantly colored fish, turtles, monk seals, and dolphins that would be just a blur without it. Like my diving mask, good feedback helps to clarify the key issues, possibilities, and opportunities around me.

One president of a large global technology company that I was coaching said he was struggling but couldn't pin down exactly why. Despite being at the pinnacle of his career and known as a high performer, he felt burned out and stressed, and told me, "The harder I work, the more disengaged I feel. I am losing my edge, my balance, and my ability to inspire success in my team."

Gradually, as we gathered and analyzed feedback, he became more self-aware. He began to see that he was too caught up in daily, urgent firefighting. He had lost sight of strategic priorities and became a micromanager around the tactical aspect of his job. He realized that his executive team was disengaged because he was trying to do all the work himself. And when he did delegate, they were never fully empowered to make decisions and take action. At last he concluded that he needed to lead more strategically, empower his team, give them more authority to act independently of him, and balance his personal and work lives.

Feedback helped this leader fully reengage in improving his company, delegating more to his team, and reconnecting with his family. He focused on setting clear targets, goals, and objectives that he and his team felt were more motivating and realistic. He found his excitement again, but self-awareness had to come first.

The following open-ended questions can guide a leader-coach in gathering and analyzing feedback.

Gathering feedback

- "Who are your key stakeholders—customers, peers, co-workers, team members—who could give you candid feedback?"
- "What information from them would be helpful to you? What data points, critical instances, or evidence would you like to gather?"

- "What issues do you anticipate hearing about in feedback from these people?"
- "What people are most affected by a certain significant issue? What are the impacts on them? What could they tell you about the issue?"
- "Describe how improving (the situation or issue) would provide greater benefits to you, your job, career, family."
- "Describe the effects if the issue remains unchanged."
- "Would you be willing to continue in the current state if nothing changes?"

Analyzing feedback

- "How do you feel about this feedback?"
- "What do you think is the impact of the issues shared in this feedback?"
- "Based on the issues shared, what would you like to be different?"
- "How do you see yourself influencing this situation in a more positive way?"
- "What possible strategies could you employ to remedy this situation?"
- "What would you say are your strengths to help improve this situation?"
- "What would others say are your strengths to help improve this situation?"
- "What are you most motivated to work on?"
- "What actions will you take to improve upon this issue or opportunity?"
- "What specific actions are you personally committed to?"
- "When and with whom will you begin? What are your next action steps?"

Separating the Person from the Problem

There is nothing permanent except change. It is in changing that we find our purpose.
—Heraclitus of Ephesus, late sixth century
BCE Greek philosopher

Ken Blanchard often says, "Feedback is the breakfast of champions." Effectively handled, feedback can be a great tool for continuous improvement. Being honest with feedback and discussing real issues can help increase trust and overcome fear. So, how do you provide effective feedback in a safe, productive, and instructive manner?

When people feel threatened by feedback—if they are harshly judged, criticized, or blamed, or receive negative feedback that they don't agree with—they get defensive or even resentful. To survive, they may create the illusion of having addressed the situation. They avoid the issues raised by the feedback, and they blame, avoid, or make attributions toward others in their unwillingness to face reality.

Good coaches can minimize these reactions by separating as far as possible the person from the problem or issue. This is partly a balancing act: emphasizing the strengths of the person while also approaching weaknesses with a mindset of continuous improvement. Consider these guidelines when offering effective feedback:

- Open respectfully, making specific, concrete, future-oriented statements.
- Give feedback that is descriptive, not judgmental. Use factual data, direct observations, and concrete examples rather than subjective impressions or gut feelings. Maintain objectivity, avoiding labels, stereotyping, and any negative bias.
- Use "I" messages to describe how you see the situation rather than "you" messages that create defensiveness. For example, "This is how I am seeing or am observing this situation." "This is what I hear you saying." "Let me see if I accurately hear your perspective." "This is how I am experiencing this situation." "This is how it is showing up for me." "I may not be seeing the entire picture here, but this is what I've seen and observed."
- Listen carefully and empathically to responses, and take time to understand the historical or situational context. Feedback can be hard on the emotions: let the person process the feedback by talking through it. Check for accuracy of understanding using clarifying questions.
- Focus on the person's strengths, possibilities, and opportunities. Identify their current state, and set goals toward a desired future state. Don't hold people hostage to the past.
- Talk about behaviors that can realistically be improved.
- Be willing to let go of your own agenda and focus on theirs.

PRACTICE: YOUR COACHING PLAYBOOK

Experiment with discussing feedback. Choose someone you trust to practice with. Here are some sample coaching questions you can use in end-of-year reviews, debriefing 360-degree feedback, planning conversations, and other ongoing conversations involving feedback:

1. "What was your initial reaction to your feedback?"
2. "What were your greatest strengths in your feedback?"
3. "What surprised you most?"
4. "What areas would you like to target for improvement?"
5. "What themes or issues emerged for you to pay close attention to?"
6. "Where are you most motivated to get better?"
7. "What short-term actions will you take based on your feedback?"
8. "What was your biggest success this past year?"
9. "What was the best decision you made this year?"
10. "What was the biggest risk you took?"
11. "What surprised you the most?"
12. "What do you want to keep working on?"
13. "What do you never want to do again?"
14. "What mistake did you learn the most from?"
15. "What is your biggest takeaway lesson from this last year?"
16. "Did you improve any relationships this year?"
17. "Did you eliminate any distractions this year?"
18. "What is the best compliment you received this year?"
19. "What compliment did you not receive about something that should have been validated?"
20. "Reflecting over the past year, are there any other key issues, items, areas, or relationships that you would like to discuss?"

References

Buckingham, Marcus. (2001). *Now, Discover Your Strengths*. Gallup Press.

Collins, Jim. (2001). *Good to Great: Why Some Companies Make the Leap and Others Don't*. HarperBusiness.

Goldsmith, Marshall. (2014). *What Got You Here Won't Get You There*. MJF.

Schwab, Charles. (2004). *Charles Schwab's New Guide to Financial Independence: Simple Solutions for Busy People*. Crown Business.

Simpson, Michael K. (2014). *Unlocking Potential: 7 Coaching Skills That Transform Individuals, Teams, & Organizations*. Grand Harbor Press.

12 Coaching for Engagement

To trust life, you must trust others; and to trust others, you must trust yourself.
—*Bhagavad Gita, Sanskrit Hindi scripture*

Winning lottery tickets. Pots of gold at the end of rainbows. Total employee engagement. These are things that we seek after but that most of the time seem out of reach. Companies that fail to encourage ongoing growth and development for their employees will lose their best people.

Many people feel frustrated, discouraged, unappreciated, and undervalued at work—with little or no sense that their voice is being heard or their contribution being recognized. They may say:

- "I'm not making a difference."
- "I'm in a dead-end job and have no passion or purpose for my work."
- "I'm afraid. I am fearful I might lose my job."
- "I'm stressed out, burned out, and exhausted; I have no time for recharging my batteries."
- "I'm micromanaged and suffocating at work."
- "I'm feel beat up to hit the numbers. The pressure to produce is unrelenting."
- "With a spouse who doesn't understand, and kids who don't show appreciation, home is no better than work."
- "I can't change my current situation. I don't even know where to begin."

Have you ever heard comments like these? Perhaps you've said such things yourself.

These are the voices of people at work—millions of executives, leaders, managers, supervisors, workers, professionals, teachers, and families all over the world. There is a lot of pain in people's lives. Many feel lost, overwhelmed, and full of resentment, and don't know how to "ignite the fire within."

Can you relate?

Of course, many people *are* fully engaged, contributing, passionate, fulfilled, and energized in their work and in their lives. But the happy, connected, and engaged are far too few. During many of my work sessions worldwide, I've enjoyed asking the following question: "How many agree that the majority of the workforce in your organization possesses much more talent, capability, creativity, and initiative than their current job requires or allows them to contribute?" Most people raise their hands.

Globally, there is a war for great talent. Employees face a new and increasing expectation to produce more in their jobs for less money. In the past, companies could offer employment for life; today, they can only offer employability. In this highly competitive, dynamic world, organizations need higher levels of trust and empowerment and the full engagement of their people. The irony is that many employees are not allowed to use a significant portion of their talents, innovation, drive, and intelligence. Because people are not fully engaged, there is a clear waste of underutilized talent, energy, and capability.

The High Cost of Disengagement

A Harris Interactive research group surveyed 23,000 US people employed full time in several different industries and across many different functional work areas. Consider a few of the most stunning findings from this research:

- Only 37% of respondents said they have a clear understanding of what their organization's goals are and what they are trying to achieve and why.
- Only 1 in 5 employees were enthusiastic about their team's and organization's goals.

- Only 1 in 5 employees said they have a clear "line of sight" between their work roles and their team's and organization's goals.
- Only 50% of the employees were satisfied with the work they accomplished at the end of each week.
- Only 15% felt they worked in a high-trust environment.

The data is sobering. The results are the same for employees in organizations all around the world. Despite all our gains in education, engineering, technology, product innovation, and global business, most employees are not fully engaged and thriving in the organizations they work for. They are neither fulfilled nor excited. Many are frustrated and disengaged. They are not clear about where the organization is headed or what its highest priorities are. Many don't feel valued or respected.

Can you begin to estimate the personal and organizational cost of failing to fully engage the passion, talent, and intelligence of your workforce? The cost of disengagement and lack of productivity is staggering. It is a far greater cost to business than taxes, interest charges, and labor costs put together!

In fact, Gallup Research stunned the business world by announcing that employee disengagement cost companies in the United States $450 billion annually. Only 30% of US employees are engaged at work, and only 13% are engaged at work worldwide. Gallup defined engaged employees "as those who are involved in, enthusiastic about, and committed to their work and workplace" (Gallup 2014). Sadly, in many organizations today, if a better-paying job or a more fulfilling and engaging culture was offered to people, most of the talent would leave.

The Benefits of Engagement

What makes an employee engaged? The greatest variable appears to be the employee's immediate boss or manager. Gallup estimated that managers accounted for at least 70% of the variance in employee engagement scores across business units (Beck and Harter 2015).

The Gallup research also shows that when a manager gets people in their work roles focused on applying their natural gifts, strengths, and talent, they score 75% or higher on job satisfaction and engagement.

Gallup found that people in organizations with a culture of engagement are 480% more committed to corporate success, 250% more likely to recommend improvements, and 370% more likely to recommend their company as an employer of choice.

These are all great things, but I'd like to assert one more. Employees who are engaged stay and effectively produce results, which impacts the bottom line of any organization. Those who are not effectively engaged and are not aligned to leverage their natural gifts, talents, and strengths will simply choose to go elsewhere.

Great leaders acquire the right talent, retain and develop them, and develop and coach their strengths and skills to achieve great performance. A leader can have the best talent in the world, but if those individuals are not aligned in the right roles, respected, trusted, valued, and developed—they will not be fully engaged, motivated, and productive.

There's usually little focus on talent development and retention. We do not take the time to consider, "What is happening with our culture?" "How engaged is my team?" "What is my bench strength, and what does my future talent pipeline look like?" "What are my opportunities and plans to help our people become more engaged?" "How can I invest in the development of a strength-based team and talent-based organization?" "How can I create a system to help our people develop their career paths?" As a leader-coach, your role is not only to recruit, align, develop, and retain your talent; your role is also to seek ways to empower, entrust, and engage your team members so they can perform to their best abilities.

Be Sure You Coach the Right People

In high-performance teams, the role of the team leader is less important and more difficult to identify because all members lead the team at different times."
—*Douglas Smith and Jon Katzenbach (1999)*

In his book *Good to Great*, Jim Collins advises, "You first have to get the right people on the bus (and the wrong people off the bus) and then figure out how to expand the seats on the bus and where to drive the bus" (Collins 2001, pp. 41–42). Do you have the right people in the right seats on the bus around you? If not, what needs to change?

Vincent S. Flowers and Charles L. Hughes published an article in the *Harvard Business Review* entitled "Why Employees Stay." They found that an employee will generally stay with an employer unless something happens to cause them to leave. It's the principle of inertia. You don't move unless acted upon by a force (Flowers and Hughes 1973).

What makes people stay engaged? Gallup research says, "It's great managers." Flowers and Hughes argued that there are a couple of additional issues: (1) job satisfaction and (2) company culture and environment and the degree of compatibility the employee feels with the organization. Those are "right" reasons to stay. Of course, there are "wrong" reasons to stay, such as a difficult job market.

The authors found that companies can strengthen the right reasons to stay by providing "conditions compatible with the employee's values" about working and living, e.g. work-life balance, flexible work schedules, expanding the employee's work role and responsibilities, and providing more autonomy, challenging and exciting projects, rewards and recognition, to name a few.

Additional studies have found that while compensation may be a leading cause for joining an organization, it stops being a reason to stay. Great coaching and ongoing development can strengthen "the right reasons" to stay.

People who play to their strengths in a good culture are more engaged, motivated, productive, and passionate in their work. Leaders should seek to create conditions where people feel safe, valued, and a part of something greater than themselves. They need to feel connected to a clear purpose and contribution in the work and understand why it is important.

The leader-coach should identify, select, recruit, and develop a talent pipeline. If you do not have a two-year, ready-now succession pool to take your place, you are putting your organization and team at risk. Another key to fully engage your team members is to use the right mix of training, development, and mentoring with formal and informal coaching. Our job as coaches is to help people feel smart, confident, and talented. Helping people find their passion and purpose and fulfill their potential at work is what can really help drive motivation and excitement each day.

Coaching to Keep People Engaged ──────

A leader is one who is more interested in the success of their people than the success of themselves.
　　—*Catherine Pulsifer, Canadian motivational author*

Now that you have "the right people on the bus," your next task is to coach them and keep them engaged and productive. This ongoing process of coaching and engagement will never end. It is an effort of all great leaders and managers.

As the third generation in an established and successful family business, Mario's success was nearly guaranteed. The business was thriving and growing at an unprecedented rate. But while the business was progressing, Mario felt unfulfilled with the direction of his own career. On one side was great success; on the other side was dissatisfaction.

"Everyone has their hurdles, but I'm sitting here, facing mine, not knowing what direction to go and how to get to the other side of the hurdle," Mario shared with me. "I'm helping my family members run our family business, but I'm stuck trying to find my own way, my own voice, and fearful that some of my family members will try to edge me out to make room for their own kids' legacy and to eventually take over. I'm frustrated, and my emotions are building up to the point where I'm angry and have a lot of resentments."

In coaching Mario, I started with his emotional triggers and his current dissatisfaction about his role and perceived contribution within the company. We had to unpack and uncover a lot of raw feelings, resentments, and areas where he was stuck.

"Mario, how do you feel about this company? Do you love it or resent it? Is it more than just a family obligation?"

He told me that he loved being a part of his family's company. He saw it as a ship. He loved his crew. He loved being a captain and driving it forward. The company was a positive place for him. Over the years he had carried out many interesting roles, responsibilities, and projects, and had learned every area of the business. He had developed great pride while building upon the legacy of his father and grandfather.

"But now I feel stuck, and I don't know what to do. I would like to build my own legacy and not simply fulfill the legacy of my father and grandfather," he admitted.

Mario was stuck intellectually and emotionally. He carried his frustration home in the evenings, which was taking a toll on his family. He was going through the motions for a paycheck but was not fulfilled in his current role.

Mario said, "I am fighting with more people now because I do not feel appreciation and respect. While I love the company, the daily work is a grind and I am stuck in a rut."

Through many coaching conversations over months, I worked with Mario to get him to slow down and assess where he was currently. We began by discussing what went on in the past, where he was now, and how his key relationships were going. This context offered great perspective into what was working and what was not.

Then, we discussed what a new or different desired state might look like. We assessed his strengths, where he had the most passion, and what new areas could possibly be profitable. We discussed and brainstormed myriad career options that might be more satisfying than his current path, where could he do more of the things he loves and find meaning again in his work.

At some point, many people find themselves unsatisfied, and their inner fire dims or goes out. Like Mario, they feel trapped, isolated, unfulfilled, and alone. They may have a high title, power, privilege, opportunity, and lots of resources at their disposal. Though Mario had a strong sense of mission and commitment to his family's legacy, he felt overlooked, undervalued, and unappreciated. This led to friction with family members and several internal leaders.

To re-engage Mario, we needed to help him reframe his limiting Judger mindset. As we explored the triggers of his negative feelings, we switched focus from what was not working to areas in his career where he had once felt passion, excitement, and drive, doing what he loved and was good at. We focused on those things he could control.

Using this information, we set some short-term goals and action steps so he could begin to define a new life for himself based on where he had real drive, passion, excitement, and strengths. It was as if a light bulb had come on in the room. As we brainstormed and explored, I could see on Mario's face that excitement and hope were returning. Relying on the framework of the whole-person, we addressed five key areas: physical, financial, relationship/emotional, career path, and spiritual/contribution areas of development. In each area, we planned around needs and key roles, and built a 30-day, 60-day, and 90-day plan to achieve success.

Mario realized anew that he was in a position of great authority and influence with his family business. He awoke to the insight that he could contribute much to the community, to the livelihood of others, to their customers, and to his family. We explored innovative and new career opportunities in what we termed "Blue Ocean Strategies": areas where he could make a huge contribution that was possibly profitable, was mission driven, and might leverage existing businesses and brands where others were not currently working.

We had met in Mario's office every month for a year for our ongoing executive coaching engagement. We took approximately six months off, and then Mario called and asked if we could re-engage for another six months. As I began meeting with Mario again, I asked: "How are you doing? What is different since we last met? What is better in your life and career? What area do you still need to work on? How do you see me best helping to support you?" He had made several significant career changes, and I was proud to see he had pursued some of the new business opportunities that we had discussed and that were most exciting and profitable to him.

Coaching had helped him reframe a potentially difficult career transition: moving from a disengaged, disrespected, and unfulfilled role to now sailing his own ship, building his own brand, playing to his strengths, and charting his own course toward a rich, fulfilling career and life. He said, "Thank you for our previous coaching engagement. I wish I would have made my career transition sooner. I am more happy and excited about my future than I ever have been before."

This story helps us to understand the need for coaches to better engage and align employees to achieve greater goals within a business or organizational context, within a marketplace or with customer needs, or with job performance and career development. Following is a series of practical coaching questions that can help engage, motivate, and inspire greatness with team members or employees:

- "How are you doing in your current role?"
- "What are you working on now? What are you learning? Where do you find the most joy in your role at work?"
- "What needs or opportunities do you see within your career or within the company?"
- "What are the biggest obstacles and challenges?"
- "If you could change one or two things, what would they be?"
- "What are the biggest opportunities that you see for growth, development, and improvement?"

- "What would you like to do that would add the most value to your team or your organization?"
- "What seems to be working well? What are you really good at? Your unique strengths?"
- "What have you always loved doing? What are you most passionate about doing?"
- "What would you like to be different in the future?"
- "What opportunities do you see for growth and development?"
- "How would you like to improve your knowledge, skills, experience, or competencies?"
- "In what ways would you like to feel more valued, trusted, respected, and supported?"
- "How can we help support you to improve in your job?"
- "How can we help support a better work-life balance?"
- "Physical: Anything from a health, wellness, or fitness perspective?"
- "Financial: Anything from a financial or recognition perspective?"
- "Social/Emotional: Anything from a work environment, safety, culture, values, or trust perspective?"
- "Professional: Anything to support your job performance, training and professional development, or career advancement? What job-related opportunities are you most passionate about?"
- "Spiritual: Anything to support your connection to mission, purpose, contribution, or making a difference at work or in life? What would make work more meaningful to you? How can you best make a difference?"
- "How will you best measure your success going forward?"
- "How can I best help and support you?"

Assessing and Coaching Skill and Will ──

> *Success consists of a series of little daily victories.*
> —*Laddie F. Hutar, Middle Eastern American, Muslim,*
> *author, and entrepreneur*

One way to look at and address employee performance is by assessing and coaching both *skill* and *will*. To keep people engaged, you need to know where they stand in terms of their skills and their will as it relates to doing the job. If their skills are not performing at base-level performance or if they are falling behind, they can disengage or lose confidence; likewise, if their will is lacking—their passion, drive, motivation, intensity, and excitement—their productivity and performance can lapse over time.

This was the case with Mario. We needed to determine where his skills would be best applied in his role and responsibility. We also needed to find opportunities that would energize him and help him find passion and greater motivation with his will.

Introduced by Max Landsberg in his book *The Tao of Coaching*, the Skill-Will Matrix is a tool to help you identify ways to motivate people and keep them fully engaged. The matrix allows you to gauge the current situation of a particular individual and guide them to finding new skills and new excitement in their work.

The Skill-Will Matrix assesses employees against two sections (Figure 12.1): the Skill section is the individual's capabilities based on their experience, training, competence, skills, and knowledge. The Will section is the individual's attitude, motivation, desire, drive, determination, and passion. People with high skill and high will are essential to any high-performance organizational culture.

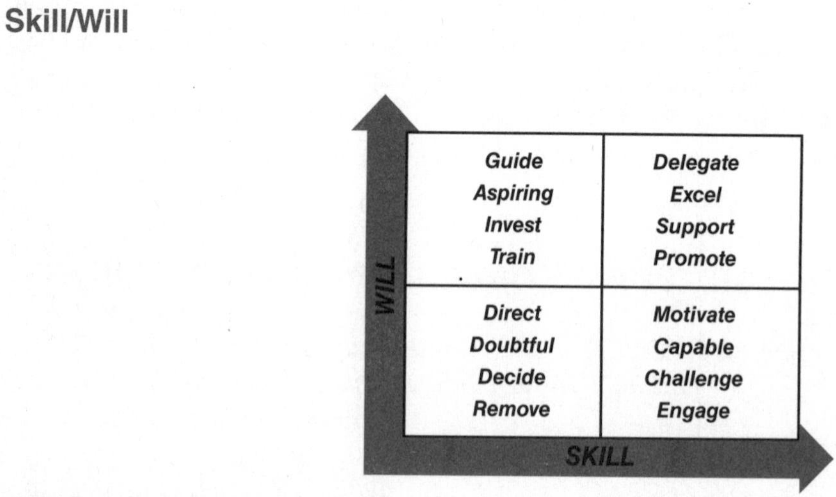

Skill/Will

Figure 12.1 The Skill-Will Matrix
Source: Adapted from (Landsberg 1997).

Low Skill/High Will (Aspiring)

How to best engage those aspiring:
- Invest time early on, with full coaching, training, explaining, and answering of questions.
- Create a risk-free environment to allow early mistakes and learning.
- Relax control as progress is shown.

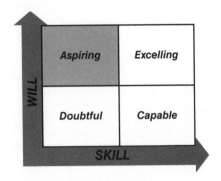

Figure 12.2 Low skill/high will (aspiring)

There are four quadrants in the Skill-Will Matrix:

- *Quadrant 1—Aspiring* (Figure 12.2): This is an aspiring person who has the desire to complete a task but lacks the necessary skills. Typically, this is an enthusiastic new hire. With employees in this quadrant, leaders should coach intensely with training, mentoring, explaining, and answering questions. The leader should create a risk-free environment to allow early mistakes and ongoing learning.
- *Quadrant 2—Excelling* (Figure 12.3): This is an excelling person who has both high skill and high will to perform the task or role at work. This is often an experienced person looking for more

High Skill/High Will (Excelling)

How to best engage those excelling:
- Promote freedom to do the job; set objectives, not methods.
- Praise, don't ignore.
- Encourage them to take responsibility and involve them in decision-making.
- Take appropriate risks, including more stretching tasks.
- Don't over-manage.

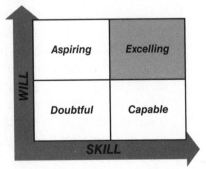

Figure 12.3 High skill/high will (excelling)

High Skill/Low Will (Capable)

How to best engage those capable:
- Identify reasons for the low will (e.g. task/management, style/personal factors).
- Identify and connect with their key motivating factors.
- Work on their confidence by developing a vision of how good they could be at completing the task.
- Monitor with feedback and praise.

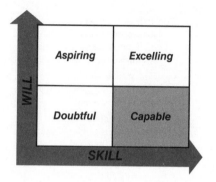

Figure 12.4 High skill/low will (capable)

opportunities to grow and develop. Coach this person to promote freedom and flexibility to do their job and set goals and objectives, not methods. Give them more autonomy, freedom, empowerment, and flexibility in their role. The employee should be praised, not ignored, and encouraged to take on more responsibilities and participate in greater levels of ownership, autonomy, and authority with decision-making and by expanding their role. The employee should be given the freedom to take on appropriate risks, supported and entrusted, but not over-managed.

- *Quadrant 3—Capable* (Figure 12.4): This is a capable person who has high skill but lacks the will and motivation to complete the job or task. They have hit a wall and need a new why, a purpose, or a challenge or support from others to overcome barriers with execution to get things done. The leader should find ways to connect with the person's motivations and leverage their strengths. Sometimes these employees may talk a good game and be highly analytical or very experienced, but they do not execute well or walk the talk. Coach them with regular feedback and praise. Surround them with people, resources, and things that can help them execute and make up for their limitations with will, motivation, drive, or execution capability.

- *Quadrant 4—Doubtful* (Figure 12.5): This person has neither the skill nor the will to complete the job or task to be effective in their role. They may also be a beginner who is risk-averse and afraid to fail. The leader should assess and coach first, to build the will by identifying motivations, values, and a vision for the

Low Skill/Low Will (Doubtful)

How to best engage those doubtful:
- First, build the will. Provide a clear briefing, identify motivations, and develop a vision of future performance.
- Then build the skill. Structure tasks for quick wins; coach and train.
- Finally, sustain the will. Provide frequent feedback; praise and nurture.
- Throughout, supervise closely with tight control and clear rules and deadlines.

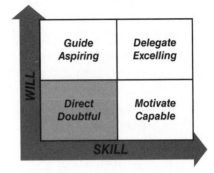

AU: these words don't appear in previous figs?

Figure 12.5 Low skill/low will (doubtful)

future. Build skills by structuring job tasks that ensure quick wins and ongoing mentoring. Finally, sustain the will and motivation by providing frequent feedback with rewards, recognition, and praise, and tasks that build confidence. If you don't see results in time, transition the person out. Don't waste too much time here. Protecting your nonperformers will backfire, as other workers will resent them for their nonperformance and you for keeping them on. They can also destroy the future success of your culture if not held accountable, offered corrective feedback, or transitioned out for nonperformance.

People can and do move from one quadrant to another, depending on their experience and knowledge and stage of life cycle in their career. An unwise change in role can even cause a Quadrant 2 (high skill and will) to become a Quadrant 4 (high skill and low will)! Dr. Stephen R. Covey's wisdom is appropriate here. You continually need to coach, engage, connect, and seek to inspire others. Dr. Covey has stated, "Leadership is communicating to people their worth and potential so clearly that they are inspired to see it in it themselves" (Covey 2007).

Following are a series of practical "Skill-Will" coaching questions to help engage and motivate your employees and keep your employees in Quadrant 2 (high skill, high will). These should be ongoing, frequent conversations to engage your people to higher levels of engagement and performance. Take time to identify those people in your areas of direct influence and begin asking yourself these questions:

- Is there worth and potential with this person?
- Are they in the right seat on the bus?
- As a coach, how can you develop high levels of skill and will in your team members?
- Do you have the right mindset to coach someone based on where they fall on the Skill-Will Matrix?
- Do you believe everyone is a leader and has high potential for great performance?
- Do you believe some people just need a little help, resources, encouragement, and support along the way?
- Do you see the value of assessing, training, developing, mentoring, and coaching this person?
- How can you assume the best in others and help bring about that best performance?

Here are some questions to help you connect with your employees and help them clarify and unleash their strengths and talents:

- "How would you describe the gap between your current skills, capabilities, or situation and where you would like to be in the future?"
- "What areas of your future job performance or career development would you like to focus on?"
- "What excites you about your future opportunities?"
- "Where would you like to start?"
- "What strengths would you like to build upon?"
- "What are you passionate about? What fuels your motivation, drive, and passion?"
- "What have you always loved doing? What are you really good at?"
- "Where do you excel? What are your greatest strengths and talents?"
- "What you would like to overcome?"
- "What you would like to achieve?"
- "What is there about your job that you would like to improve?"
- "What skills would you like to develop?"
- "What additional capabilities do you desire to improve?"

- "Is there a mindset that is impeding your growth?"
- "Do you have work-life balance? Are you in balance or is there a risk of burnout?"

Coaching through Potential Burnout ━━━

Dear Stress, I would like a divorce. Please understand it is not you, it is me.
—Thomas E. Rojo Aubrey (2019)

This last area—burnout—is paradoxical because it can affect team members who are intensely and maybe even excessively engaged. They are often your most valuable people; because they are so valuable, they are often overburdened and risk breaking down.

For example, a great executive that I coached was worried about losing one of his best managers. Her name was McKenna. She was a very hard worker and was good at execution. Her work ethic was impeccable. She always came in early and left late. She connected well with people and was very empathic to those around her. She was on top in her production with nearly 100% of the assignments that she was given. An ideal employee, right? But this executive wasn't worried about squeezing more productivity out of McKenna. He was a talent leader. He had enough vision to know there would be trouble ahead if she stayed on this path of aggressively doing too much.

"In our organization, being the first in and the last out is not a merit badge for success. Staying in the fast lane with a focus on completing all the urgency tasks coming at you will lead to burnout," McKenna's boss says. "We value people. We value seeking balance in their lives and their families. We want to model the right culture of work-life balance from the top. It is critical for our people to look after their physical health, to manage the emotional costs of work on their personal life, to effectively manage time with personal and family relationships off the job, and then find a way to scale things back to achieve that balance."

With McKenna, his coaching agenda was all about helping her find work-career-life balance. This is coaching at its best. Nothing was "wrong." Nothing was "broken." But the risk of future problems was real. We've all seen it. The company keeps pushing for more and more and more. If left unchecked, work can become 24 hours a day, 7 days a week, 365 days a year.

McKenna's boss checked in with her frequently. They brainstormed creative ideas for achieving a better mix of work, career, and personal life. McKenna liked putting out fires, being in all the meetings, and making most, if not all, of the day-to-day business decisions. She needed to better engage her team members and better clarify roles, delegate and entrust her direct reports to make decisions, and work on getting out of their way—particularly on the more operational and tactical sides of the business.

She realized that most days, she left the office late in the evening, and that wasn't working for her. She decided to begin clearing emails between 2:00 and 4:00 p.m. every day, instead of starting around 6:00 p.m.; the new timing would help her be home with her husband and children for dinner.

For a long time, she had felt that her workday never ended. "It never feels complete, and I'm tempted to take it home with me and stay connected online all night." An external coach was able to help her to establish a consistent ritual: she now took 15–20 minutes each day before leaving the office to plan the next day. This seemingly small ritual made a big impact. McKenna was gaining self-discipline as she became better organized. Coaching helped her plan, prepare, prioritize, delegate, entrust others, clarify roles, and stay at a more strategic level, while pushing the more operational and tactical tasks to her team members. McKenna now had the tools not only to elevate her own work and life, but also to enable those around her to learn and develop.

We live in an urgent whirlwind environment with constant 24 × 7 access from emails, texts, calls, meetings, and social media posts from smartphones that push constant reminders and urgent requests with an endless onslaught of data and information. Work is demanding and can feel relentless. It's becoming increasingly difficult to find work-life balance among our various roles and responsibilities. It is hard to switch on and off among the workplace, home, family, friends, communities, and those with whom we have daily interactions. Burnout can lead to anxiety, depression, insomnia, strained or ruined relationships, health issues, disconnection, fatigue, and resentment.

We all have different capacities to respond to emotional stress, negative triggers, and physical strains. Burnout should be a wake-up call for all employers to help treat chronic stress that has not been successfully managed as a performance, work health, and safety issue. Following are some practical coaching questions to help assess and reflect on the stresses in life, burnout, fatigue, and life management skills with those we lead and manage:

- "Do you currently feel you have work-life balance?"
- "Do you feel burned out and stressed at work or in your personal life?"
- "On a scale from 1–10, where are you currently now in terms of your stress and burnout?"
- "What are your biggest triggers and areas of imbalance in your work or your life?"
- "Which areas are influencing your stress, burnout, anxiety, and lack of balance?"
- "In recent weeks and months, have you become angry or resentful about your work or about colleagues, clients, family, or other colleagues?"
- "Has anyone close to you asked you to scale back and cut down on your current workload?"
- "Do you feel guilty that you are not spending enough time with your friends, family, or even yourself? In which areas? Tell me more about your situation?"
- "Do you find yourself becoming increasingly emotional or depressed, e.g. getting angry, shouting, being negative, being pessimistic, or feeling anxiety for no obvious reason? Tell me more about why this is happening."
- "What are your values toward improving your work-life balance and reducing your stress?"
- "What could lead to a more positive condition to reduce stress and find more balance in work and life?"
- "Which areas do you believe would be the best to improve?"
- "How would you like things to be different in your work and life?"
- "Can you envision a time in your life when you had more time and space for balance, physical and emotional renewal, and inner peace?"
- "How do you see yourself getting more balance, rest, renewal, or relations in your work and personal life?"
- "How can I help remove any obstacles or barriers to help you reduce burnout, stress, and find more balance?"

PRACTICE: YOUR COACHING PLAYBOOK

1. Do you have the right people on the bus? If not, who needs to be eased out of position or placed into another position? How and where will you find the right people?
2. Who appears to be disengaging? Do you know why? What is your plan for re-engaging this person?
3. Experiment with putting your team members into the Skill-Will Matrix. Who has high skill and high will? Who has high skill and low will? And so on. What will you do about the results?

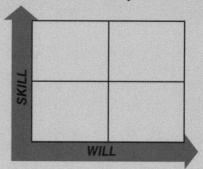

References

Aubrey, Thomas E. Rojo. (2019). *Unlocking the Code to Human Resiliency: Building Professional Resiliency Against Burnout, Traumatic Stress and Compassion Fatigue*. XanEdu Publishing.

Beck, Randall and Harter, Jim. (2015). Managers account for 70% of variance in employee engagement. Gallup. https://news.gallup.com/businessjournal/182792/managers-account-variance-employee-engagement.aspx.

Collins, Jim. (2001). *Good to Great: Why Some Companies Make the Leap and Others Don't*. HarperBusiness.

Covey, Stephen R. (2007). *The Leader Formula: The 4 Things That Make a Good Leader*. Lead News.

Flowers, Vincent S., and Hughes, Charles L. (1973). Why employees stay. *Harvard Business Review*.

Gallup. (2014). State of the American workplace: Employee engagement insights for U.S. business leaders.

Landsberg, Max. (1997). *The Tao of Coaching*. Knowledge Exchange.

Smith, Douglas, and Katzenbach, John. (1999). *The Wisdom of Teams: Creating the High-Performance Organization*. HarperBusiness.

13 Coaching for Contribution

Your time is limited, so don't waste it living someone else's life.
—*Steve Jobs, inventor, businessman, co-founder Apple, Inc.*

Much of the confusion, pain, lack of focus, burnout, and disengagement today comes because people have little sense of direction, purpose, or contribution. Many people feel that what they do doesn't matter much. They feel isolated and disconnected, and wander hopelessly without direction. In the mundane tasks of the day to day, they feel themselves sinking into irrelevance, being silenced or directionless. At the end of the day, week, month, and year, many feel they have made no significant contribution to discuss or point to as a means of making a difference.

Why do so many people lead mundane or aimless lives? Why are so many people unfulfilled in life and in work? Henry David Thoreau said it this way: "Most men [and women] lead lives of quiet desperation." So, how do people find their unique purpose? How can we help ourselves and others find purpose, passion, and contribution by effective coaching?

When a person discovers work that taps into their talent and fuels their passion—that rises out of a need they feel drawn to by their values and conscience to achieve their highest and best use of their talents, intelligence, capabilities, and strengths—some call it finding their calling in life, their soul's focus and meaning, or their unique contribution to the world.

The late founder of Apple Corporation, Steve Jobs, made famous this idea of passion and purpose when he challenged others by stating, "We're all just renting time here on planet earth. We're here to put a dent in the universe! Otherwise, why else even be here?" (Snell 2011).

Apple Corporation was his passion. Not just the company that he founded and then rescued, but what Apple represented. Apple was a vehicle that took the highest technology applications to the human race to make life and work better. People were and are passionate about Apple's products. Apple's brand becomes an extension of their brand.

Think of how many amazing creations have come from a Steve Jobs–managed company. The Apple II, the world's first mass-produced personal computer. The Macintosh, the basis for almost every personal computer interface on the planet today. Pixar, one of the most successful and innovative movie studios of all time. The iPod and iTunes, which transformed the music industry and changed how we access and listen to music. The iPhone, which upended the stagnant cellphone industry and created the concept of a modern smartphone. And the iPad, which defined a new, smaller computing category that paid off the original Mac's promise of being a "computer for the rest of us."

If you want peace, if you want purpose, if you want wholeness, discover the great contribution only you can make. As a coach, one of your highest callings is to help others discover that purpose, passion, and contribution for themselves. Your colleagues and team members may never find their purpose as Steve Jobs did, but they can find how they truly want to make a dent in the world and live an inspired, fulfilled life of meaning and purpose in their own way.

"Your time is limited, so don't waste it living someone else's life. Don't be trapped by dogma—which is living with the results of other people's thinking. Don't let the noise of others' opinions drown out your own inner voice. And most important, have the courage to follow your heart and intuition" (Jobs 2005).

Coaching to Help Define Contribution ───

At the highest level, the work of a leader is to lead conversations about what is essential and what is not.
—*Ronald Heifetz, founder, the Center for Public Leadership, Kennedy School of Government, Harvard*

In 2017, I co-authored a leadership and coaching book entitled *Talent Unleashed: 3 Leadership Conversations to Ignite the Unlimited Potential in People.* I spent over three years writing and researching this book with my FranklinCovey colleagues Roger Merrill, Shawn Moon, and Todd Davis. We also received tremendous leadership insights from Dr. Stephen R. Covey and the brilliant writing of Dr. Breck England and Rebecca Merrill. My professional colleagues and I were all on a professional journey to find the components of a meaningful work-life contribution and offer coaching questions to help every manager and leader become a great coach. We agreed that professional contribution depends on four key discoveries:

1. Finding a targeted need or a big opportunity in society, the marketplace, with customers, or at work
2. Uncovering our unique gifts, strengths, and talents
3. Engaging our passion and joy in our work and life
4. Aligning what we choose to do to be in full alignment with our values and conscience

Sometimes, the catalyst for defining your contribution comes as a response to an external problem, challenge, or need in the community or society at large, in the marketplace, or in your organization or team. Other times, the catalyst may come from your values or conscience, a calling to serve others. Or, you may start contributing as you fulfill a deep passion or personal interest.

But at the intersection of all four discoveries comes your unique purpose and contribution in life. Let's look at each element in sequence.

Finding a Need or Opportunity

We never know which lives we influence, or when, or why.
—Stephen King, American novelist of suspense and science fiction stories and movies

As important as it is to identify our strengths, talents, and passion, most people will never rise above work as a hobby unless they meet a need in society or in the marketplace. We must align our passion and values to what people truly want and need from us. I love the statement "No organization inherently has a right to exist." No company exists without customers willing to pay money for a product or service; once you lose sight of your market, you will lose your value. And those needs change, meaning we must continually learn, improve, and adapt as we seek to add value. Similarly, in government, education, or nonprofits, the organization exists to add value to a societal need, community values, or a particular mission-driven need.

Your contribution must drive one great overarching purpose: to serve a series of identified human needs. It's not only a societal or marketplace imperative. We grow personally when we are giving of ourselves to others. Viewed this way, leadership really is a creative, innovative, and enabling art more than a science.

According to some of the great psychologists—Abraham Maslow, Clayton Alderfer, and Frederick Herzberg—each of us has five basic areas of need: financial, physical, emotional, mental, and spiritual. As a coach, you guide your team through these five areas as they formulate the contributions they want to make. Help them to examine their skills, capabilities, talents, and desires to improve in each of the five areas.

As your team members develop their own definition of what they can contribute, the following coaching questions might be helpful:

- "What unmet needs or opportunities do you see among society at large and your external customers, suppliers, distributors, investors, business partners, team members, and other key stakeholders?"
- "What unmet needs or opportunities do you see among our internal customers?"
- "What financial problems are they facing? How could we help?"
- "What physical, mental, or spiritual challenges are ahead of them? How could we help?"
- "What are the biggest gaps or opportunities that need to be satisfied?"
- "What does anyone need from *us*?"
- "What is the great value only we can provide our customers?"
- "What could we contribute to help them grow and achieve their purpose?"
- "Where are their opportunities for growth and success?"

Uncovering Your Talents

The purpose of life is a life of purpose.
—*Robert Byrne, author*

Where do you find your natural strengths, gifts, and talent? Often people are skilled at things they enjoy doing. You may be very good at putting your thoughts onto paper, or you might be skilled at web design or the most capable person on your team to manage the budget or the project. Sometimes we are skilled at things we love; other times we are skilled at things we are not passionate or excited about. Some of the following coaching questions may be helpful in assessing gifts and talents:

- "What are your talents, abilities, and strengths?"
- "What have you always been able to do easily? Where do you most naturally succeed?"
- "What do you love to do? What do you do better than anyone else on your team?"
- "What tasks do other people rely on you to do? What are you naturally good at?"
- "What needs do people turn to you to fulfill?"
- "Have you ever been assigned a task at work that you did very well, even though you may not have enjoyed it particularly?"
- "Have you discovered that you do certain tasks quickly and effectively, when you didn't expect to?"

Engaging Your Passion

*The meaning of life is to find your gift. The purpose of life is
to give it away.*
—*Pablo Picasso, artist*

Our passions are a great source of energy and satisfaction in life and are uniquely part of our DNA. Differing from person to person, passions involve tremendous emotional drive, determination, and energy. Our passions are those values, beliefs, and things that we care deeply about. They are the things that intrigue us, that motivate us, and that are housed where our most creative energies and interests lie.

Our passions can often frustrate us, because they are so consuming and absorbing; but if we can connect them to market and customer needs, we are in good shape for making a contribution. Here are a few key coaching questions that can be useful for engaging others' passions:

- "What have you always loved doing?"
- "What drives and motivates you?"
- "Do you have an interest, passion, or hobby that you love?"
- "What are you most passionate about?"
- "Do you feel deeply drawn to a cause or a belief system that seems to bring out the best in you and others around you?"
- "Is there something you enjoy doing so much that you would go without pay just to be able to do it?"

Aligning to Your Values, Conscience, and Beliefs

Life is not about having and getting, but being and becoming.
—Matthew Arnold, English poet and cultural critic

Finally, to find our contribution, we must connect to the inner voice that Steve Jobs was talking about: the voice of contribution that speaks to us based on our deeply held values, beliefs, and desires. We listen to that inner voice to tell us if we are truly contributing and adding value to our customers, organization, and team, and to the lives of people. The following coaching questions will help with aligning values, beliefs, and conscience:

- "What values, beliefs, or principles are most important to you?"
- "What fuels your purpose and meaning in life?"
- "What aspect of work and life bring you the most passion and joy?"
- "Which of your work-life elements offer you the most satisfaction, joy, and fulfillment?"
- "What part of your life or work do you feel best about?"
- "Is this job the right thing for you to be doing?"
- "Will your work serve others and the greater good of society?"
- "Are you serving a moral imperative—an ethical basis for your work?"
- "Do you feel uncomfortable about some of the things you are asked to do?"

- "When do you feel most disconnected, unfulfilled, and hopeless in your job?"
- "Are there any potential legal or ethical conflicts with your work? Why?"

Talent, passion, and need are not enough. We want to align these factors with our internal moral compass and inner beliefs and ask, "Do I feel good inside about what I'm doing? Does this work align with my values and my conscience?"

Call to Action: Coaching for Contribution ▬

Having a specific meaning and purpose in your life helps to encourage you towards living a fulfilling and inspired life.
—*Vic Johnson, Major League Baseball player*

Every person can choose a path to fulfillment and greatness. We find greatness in making the contribution only we can make. For each one of us, this quest or path can be a bit different. There is no "one size fits all"; it is more like, "one size fits one." We must constantly question the needs of others, the talents unique to us, our innate passions, and the voice of conscience. Listen to your inner voice: it will tell you who you are, what you should do in life, and how to make a difference.

One of my clients, Robert, had a "crisis of finding his unique and important contribution." He was feeling deep frustration in his role and turned to coaching to help him regain his sense of purpose.

Robert's father had founded a business when his two sons were both very young. Robert remembers being frequently told, "Robert, one day you'll run this business with your brother." Sure enough, the business grew stronger and more profitable every year until his father was ready to retire and hand over the reins to his two sons.

But things turned sour. Robert was the "little brother," and his older brother never let him forget it. Robert had been in the shadow of his brother his entire life.

In our coaching conversations, we spent a lot of time working through Robert's mindset—helping to shift from a resentful, Judger mindset to a Learner mindset. Maybe his brother was a "complete idiot." Maybe his brother was selfish and controlling. Maybe his brother had to constantly prove that he was the smartest man in the room. Maybe his brother never listened and never recognized Robert's contributions. But Robert still had a choice of how to respond.

We worked to reframe his negative inner story and his perspective on himself, his brother, and his key stakeholders. Here are a few of the key coaching questions we explored in our coaching conversations:

- "What is your current situation?"
- "What's the story about your father, your brother, and your family business?"
- "What is working well? What is not working well?"
- "What areas of your career would you like to focus on?"
- "What barriers are getting in the way of your career goals?"
- "What triggering events or people are influencing your negative feelings?"
- "What false or limiting beliefs are keeping you from moving forward?"
- "What choices could you make to best move forward in your life and your career?"
- "What if you choose forgiveness?"
- "What might be the benefits to you and others of letting go and moving forward?"
- "What are the costs to you and others if you don't move forward?"
- "What are you good at?"
- "What have you always loved doing?"
- "How can you focus on leveraging your natural gifts and strengths?"
- "What are your passions and strengths?"
- "What needs to change currently so you can leverage your passions and strengths?"
- "How would you like your current situation to be different?"
- "What is your inner voice telling you about what you should do differently?"
- "What would your ideal future look like?"
- "Where do you see opportunities for growth, development, and making a difference?"
- "How do you see your future contribution being successful and more fulfilling?"
- "What are your best next steps?"

- "Who would be possible partners? How could their strengths be added to your strengths?"
- "Where would you like to begin planning your new game plan going forward?"
- "How can I best help support you with your new game plan?"
- "What are some possible quick wins or successes in the next 30 days, 60 days, and 90 days?"

It turned out that Robert was good at numbers: he was very creative and innovative, and he had many big opportunities and potential partners to help leverage his skills, experience, and passions.

"Michael, I do not have to be held hostage in this position in my career," he told me. "I can choose differently! I feel liberated, as if I am being let out of prison. I am excited about planning my future and transitioning from those areas of my work that drain me and cause doubts, and where I am simply not happy. There has been a dark cloud over my head for some time, and I am now starting to see rays of light and hope."

Before coaching, Robert was focused on past injustices, feeling disrespected, and the perception that he was not adding value in his role. Strong comparisons were made by his brother and by others on their senior staff. With coaching, he recognized that he could choose his response, stop competing and comparing his success against his brother, and live for his own dreams. "I have a great brand, a great education, tremendous resources and work experience. I have a great opportunity to chart my own course and leave a great legacy. I have a whole future of opportunities that lie ahead that I can see and that I am passionate about."

At the end of our coaching engagement, he said, "Michael, thanks for the coaching on helping me brainstorm and explore a successful transition from my past successes [and failures] to my future success. It has been life changing, and I am on a very good path now. I can say that my business partners and I care as much about each other's success as we do our own. Life is about working with and surrounding yourself with good people that you trust, and help you make a significant contribution that is profitable, while you do work that you love."

Many people lack passion, purpose, and clarity with their direction in life. Coaching for contribution can offer a dramatic impact on individual and team performance, engagement, and overall contribution. By using the coaching questions in this section, any leader-coach will be able to help people clarify desired state outcomes with their vision and goals, the intended results they want, changes in attitudes, mindset, underlying values, and motivations to better execute their unique gifts, strengths, talents, and aspirations for making a significant dent in the world.

Finding Satisfaction in Your Contribution ▪

> *The one thing that you have that nobody else has is you. Your voice, your mind, your story, your vision. So, write and draw and build and play and dance and live as only you can.*
> —*Neil Gaiman, English author of novels, theater, and films*

Few things are more powerful than discovering the contribution you can make in life—except, perhaps, inspiring another person to discover theirs. Think about those people who have contributed so much to your life and career. How do you feel about those people? What did they do to have such a profound influence on you?

They believed and saw something in you. They trusted you. They challenged and helped you become the best that you could be. They encouraged your growth. When you failed, they helped you learn and grow, and inspired you to get better. They offered feedback, course correction, affirmation, and accountability. They were loyal and had your back. By the fact that you worked with them, you were better and felt inspired to make your greatest contribution.

Surely there is no greater role for a leader than to help others realize and maximize their own potential, and then to help them achieve it. We really have no idea what a given person may be capable of. Discovering the unlimited potential of people can be one of the great experiences in life.

Becoming a Change Agent ▬▬▬▬▬▬

> *Some men [and women] see things as they are, and ask why. I dream of things that never were, and ask why not.*
> —*Robert F. Kennedy, US Senator, US Attorney General, politician, lawyer, and activist*

You will find yourself coaching people who are in less-than-ideal circumstances; in fact, there's a lot of toxicity and despair out there. Real leaders want to make a significant dent in the universe and make their world dramatically better. But change is hard, and many circumstances can be very difficult.

Still, as a coach, you can become a mighty agent for change. To decide to be a change agent is a huge, self-empowering choice. In your role as a coach, many times formal leaders many not empower you to make real change. Further frustration may happen as the organizational structure or culture may not inherently empower you to be a change agent. In addition, your job description, the title on your business card, or your lack of authority may not empower you. Many times you may not be rewarded or recognized for making or sustaining change. Many people and political obstacles may also stand in your way. Having said this, every leader-coach must view themselves as real change agents. As a coach, much of the time you will need to empower yourself, authorize yourself, and motivate yourself to impact others—or no change will happen at all. It's your proactive choice to embrace the role of coach, change agent—or not. Despite all of the insurmountable obstacles, you can be a great force for good, for positive change, and for making a significant difference.

You might have known some highly effective change agents. They lead themselves and their teams in a way that positively affects the entire organization. Who have you encountered that changed a bad situation into a great success on their own initiative? Did they have great obstacles and barriers to overcome? What did they do to bring about such a transition? How did they operate from a place of courage, purpose, and passion? What resources, drive, and initiative were required in their quest for change? Are you that person? What is your choice?

Your freedom to be a change agent means you don't have to put up with the mess or discomfort any longer. As a coach and change agent, you have two rational choices in any toxic and difficult situation: you can allow the past to hold your future hostage. Or, you can learn from the past, reframe your mindset, and begin to re-create and reset a new, brilliant, and creative future. Coaches as change agents clearly identify and understand the vision, future state, and targeted areas for change. They sidestep negative influences, they develop an optimistic and positive mindset, and they focus on building strong relationships, networks, and partnerships with others around the desired future state for change. They help themselves and others get clear on organizational and team strategies, goals, and objectives, while they help identify others wins and opportunities for their growth, development, and success. They help co-create new and better habits and action plans for success. They are empathic and affirming, and value others' opinions and feedback; and they overcome fears, apathy, failure, and resistance to change. Coaches as change agents help map out and define realistic actions and plans for success. They hold people accountable and are impeccably honest and supportive while change initiatives are successfully implemented.

Coaching can offer life-changing tools to help people on their road to happiness, fulfillment, and great success. Understanding a person's life history, context, experience, and roadmap will go a long way to influence their personal mindset, strengths, behaviors, limitations, incongruencies, and frustrations, and much of the pain and shame they may experience on life's journey. Coaching must offer a safe and confidential place to be curious, explore truth, challenge assumptions, be empathic, focus on the client's agenda, explore choices and options, and help to reframe the right mindset or story if a false story has held them hostage or unable to overcome life's challenges.

Let me share the coaching context and how it can lead to understanding your life journey and how to find passion, purpose, and meaning despite setbacks and challenges. One of my good friends and former work colleagues, Sam Bracken, grew up in an unthinkable family environment as a young boy in Las Vegas, Nevada: poverty, drugs, gambling, and fighting; emotional, physical, and sexual abuse; and lack of parental support. Eventually, Sam had to transition to foster care as a teenager.

Given his many early setbacks, Sam's mindset could have been "poor me, life is terribly unfair, and nobody loves or cares about me" (these things were essentially true for Sam!). He could have sunk into self-victimization and easily ended up on the streets or in prison like other family members or similar teens in his situation.

But something deep inside Sam said, "Not me. I'm not like them, and I will not be like them." Instead of blaming, moaning, complaining, and becoming resentful and bitter, Sam got better! Blessed with a big athletic body and a big heart, he followed his passions, running track and playing football. Although every voice in his life told him that he was stupid, worthless, and a failure, he discovered the truth: he was not worthless, not a failure, and not stupid.

With counseling, a supportive foster family, and many people who noticed and cared about him, Sam was able to reframe his inner negative dialogue. He began to have daily inner conversations that became positive, affirming, and full of hope. He realized he was smart, he could be a good student, and his hard work ethic could pay off in the classroom and on the football field. He also found peace in attending a local church and claimed further light and hope in who he was and what his destination could be through his faith. He connected with God and found happiness in worship, which helped him overcome the negative life challenges that young people should never have to face in their lives.

Ultimately, the "dirty little kid" (as Sam calls himself) played Division-I football on an athletic scholarship at Georgia Tech University, and was a four-year starter, a team captain, and all ACC newcomer of the year. He received two academic All-American honors his junior and senior years. He graduated from Georgia Tech with honors, served a full-time, two-year mission for his church in Toronto, Canada, and received his MBA from Brigham Young University. Sam has been happily married to his sweetheart, Kim, for over 30 years, and they have four beautiful children.

In telling his inspiring story, my friend Sam says, "My proactive change all started first with gaining a bold vision for my life. I had to reframe my negative experiences and see a new and better future of who I was and who I wanted to become. Don't ever be happy with where you are. Don't look back on negative life experiences with anger, regret, or resentment. I realized, life is hard, life is full of setbacks and opposition. I had to look forward and find my passion and purpose in life. I realized that I could choose a different path in life than the one I was heading down. People along the way helped me develop a vision of who I could be and who I wanted to be. They helped me realize that I could make choices in life to achieve a unique contribution despite my awful past. Once you've made substantial progress along your path, reflecting upon how far you've come and what you've accomplished with the help of so many, life can be humbling and gratifying—it is a sweet life" (Bracken 2012, pp. 1–31).

There is a lot to unpack with the life story of Sam. We are all products of our life's story with all its twists, turns, ups, and downs. Life can be hard and full of challenges. A great coach can help to assess history, story, beliefs, views, and choice. There are tremendous breakthroughs in coaching when the coach helps the client or performer assess where they are now and any gaps or areas in which they need to get better; needed changes or negative impacts; and the ability to overcome false inner dialogue, poor behaviors, or areas where they may have failure or need improvement. Coaches can help people shift their mindset, attitude, old habits, and ineffective behaviors to a more effective, functional, and desired state of success.

Take a moment to coach yourself. Take time to reflect and think about a challenging situation at work or home that is very frustrating or negative, where you feel powerless, have lost faith or perspective, or are unable to control the outcome. In what ways could you become a change agent and move out of the victim role into that of a responsible leader? What mindset needs to change? What are your responsible choices? What is your bold, courageous vision of your desired future state? What will you do differently to change this situation? What resources and people can you leverage to help support you along the way?

PRACTICE: YOUR COACHING PLAYBOOK

The following activity cannot be done in a few minutes or in a day. Sustainable change is often a process of self-discovery and illumination that will sometimes come quickly but may require long contemplation and planning, and change in behaviors and actions over time.

Consider two or three of the primary roles in your life where you would like to make change or a significant contribution, and ask yourself the following:

1. What changes do I need to make that would be beneficial to me and others?
2. What unmet needs or big opportunities do I see for change?
3. Why is change so important to me and others?
4. What is my bold vision for change?
5. What are the benefits of making these changes?
6. What are the costs of not changing?
7. What have I always loved doing? How can doing those things contribute to the world or those around me?

8. Where could I be an agent for change or make a significant difference?
9. What would make my life more meaningful, joyful, and fully engaged?
10. What inner need must I satisfy in order to feel like I'm making a contribution?
11. Does the need or the opportunity for change tap into my passion and excitement?
12. What values, beliefs, or principles are most important to me to advance or pursue?
13. Do my values and conscience inspire me to take action and become involved?
14. Do I possess the right skills, talent, and resources to make the contribution I want to make?
15. What does my desired future success or contribution look like?

References

Bracken, Sam. (2012). *My Orange Duffel Bag: A Journey to Radical Change.* Crown Archetype.

Jobs, Steve. (2005). *Commencement address*, Stanford University.

Snell, Jason. (2011). Steve Jobs: Making a dent in the universe. Macworld. https://www.macworld.com/article/1162827/steve-jobs-making-a-dent-in-the-universe.html.

14 Coaching the Whole-Person

Determine what motivates you and you can find your path to love, happiness and influence and that which you seek to make your life complete.
—Louis Howard, professor of mathematics at MIT

Life can be difficult and stressful. No one is entitled to anything, and no one owes you anything. Life can also be full of false expectations, unrealistic demands, ups and downs, detours, setbacks, empty experiences, thrills, meaningful moments, and real connections with people in a number of diverse ways. Our human experience is full of change, challenge, adaptation, and a precious life that can be fulfilling, adventurous, and joyful. The nature of the work-life balance can be difficult and feel unrealistic and unobtainable. How do we balance living, working, health, and relationships? How do we find meaning and purpose? How do we succeed and find joy and real happiness? How do we fulfill our unique gifts, strengths, and contribution? How do we find a high quality of life? These are all important questions to consider in our life's journey. As George Bernard Shaw stated, "Life isn't about finding yourself, life is about creating yourself." So how do we create the life that we want? How do we engage our whole-person?

When we seek to improve and sustain our happiness, performance, and success in life, it begins by overcoming the mindset that we are one-dimensional beings. We need to love what we do and overcome the focus on our work dimension. Professional success is very important. However, many believe that happiness, security, and success in life are found by building financial wealth. Others focus on personal health, diet, nutrition, and exercise, believing that a focus on physical wellness will lead to overcoming stress and anxiety. Some believe that working on cognitive thinking skills, academic success, and intellectual development leads to ultimate self-actualization and fulfillment. Many feel that happiness is found by having strong, connected, and loving relationships with family, friends, or work colleagues. Others find high levels of satisfaction and enlightenment based on spiritual connections, inner peace, and service. Still others focus on work with public service, advancing social justice, a political platform, or offering community service that work to solve larger social or global community needs.

Each of these dimensions is essential. To improve higher levels of performance, fulfillment, and happiness, we need to examine and be thoughtful about how we plan and integrate all areas of our body, finances, heart, mind, and spirit. At times, life can feel one-dimensional, unfulfilling, or lacking in any real purpose. The pressure to perform in our academic or work area can be unrelenting. Life can feel like one pounding wave after another is hitting us and knocking us off our feet. Many feel stuck in a rut, overworked, underpaid, or as though they are running fast on life's treadmill and cannot get off. Many of life's events can negatively or adversely impact our personal health, worth, value, or satisfaction.

A coach with a whole-person mindset can truly help people self-assess where they are now and gain insights into each dimension of their lives. Coaches can help people examine what matters most to them. Each person has diverse needs, aspirations, passions, expectations, and desires. The key is to remember that each person is a whole-person, and their interests, dreams, pursuits, and needs are as diverse as there are stars in the universe. Coaches can help people examine their financial wealth and security goals; their physical health, wellness, and nutrition goals; their key loving relationships and social connection goals; their academic, professional, and career development goals; and their spiritual wellness, inner peace, and aspirations regarding their purpose in life. Again, all too often people are blinded by short-term career success, money, or professional aspirations at the expense of burning out or destroying key relationships. A coach can offer great insights, creativity, and innovation in helping people explore areas of meaningful service, social or political causes, religious connection, online networks, and innovative projects that positively impact the larger community.

Whole-person coaching is a simple yet transformational way to enable vast connections across a wide range of needs and determine what fulfillment and happiness means to each person, in a wholistic and meaningful way.

Embracing the Whole-Person ━━━━

Life isn't about finding yourself; it's about creating yourself.
So live the life you imagined.
—Henry David Thoreau, American essayist,
poet, journalist, and philosopher

If you look at life holistically, you can divide it into five key areas. Work on improving yourself in each of these areas, and you'll enjoy a more abundant, integrated, purposeful, and fulfilling life. If you seek to improve your whole-person mindset, you'll want to consider investing time in clarifying and defining your whole-person needs and statements. Consider the following whole-person aspirational statement examples:

1. *What is your financial needs statement?* "I will choose to invest time and resources in life by hard work, savings, wealth creation, innovation, financial leverage, and investment into business ideas and entrepreneurship areas where I have a passion and purpose. I will improve my money-making model, time, and resources to solve big problems, to satisfy a big market need, to increase my future business and revenue-generating opportunities, to improve cash flow, to expand my financial resources, and to better manage and control expenses. I will seek to become a better entrepreneur, to invest time and money in startup business ideas, and to get rid of 100% of credit card debt and high-interest payments. I will effectively manage time, capital, and all my assets and resources. I will partner, expand my professional network, and learn from other entrepreneurs, business partners, and investors in future business and financial growth opportunities."

2. *What is your physical wellness needs statement?* "I will proactively invest my time and energy in taking better care of my body and my overall health and wellness with constant exercise and enjoyable sporting activities. I will eat with more discipline, portion control, and better nutrition. I will make time for rest, relaxation, sleep, and renewal. I will invest time each week in sports, hobbies, and personal interests that help me improve my health, wellness, and energy."

3. *What is your emotional relationship needs statement?* "I will choose to invest time in responsible relationships and positive connections with family, friendships, and business colleagues. I enjoy building positive, healthy, loving, and mutually beneficial relationships. I will expand my social networks and connections. I have clear boundaries and choose who I will spend time with and who I will not spend time with. I am lovingly and genuinely interested in others, as I seek to listen better and be more empathic, more optimistic, and positive with others. I will be present and available to those I love by helping them be seen, heard, affirmed, and valued. My time with others with be based on uplifting activities, fun, humor, and enjoyable activities. I encourage my success and others' successes abundantly."

4. *What is your intellectual, academic, or professional career needs statement?* "I have a wide range of creative, curious, and innovative intellectual interests. I will invest my talent, skills, mind, and resources in reading, education, professional development, career development, and skill building, becoming a thought leader in my profession. I will sacrifice time and be resilient to invest in professional education courses with a minimum of one professional development experience per year. I will join two or three professional networks. I will take on two or three board or advisory positions with businesses in areas where I have friendship, financial, or career interests. I will proactively invest time in ongoing career training, mentoring, and certificate programs."

5. *What is your spiritual, purpose, or contribution needs statement?* "The glory of God is intelligence, light, and truth. The more intelligent I become, the more my faith will grow, develop, and expand. I choose to invest time growing spiritually by clarifying my values and purpose, improving my motives and behaviors, and seeking inner peace, happiness, and spiritual connection. I will grow my faith through prayer, meditation, personal study, community worship, and meaningful service to others. With my family and friends, I will invest time enjoying culture, art, music, nature, and inspiring music, and make a contribution to society. I will do simple acts of kindness and engage others with service, compassion, love, and forgiveness."

Practice clarifying your whole-person needs statement here. Take 10–15 minutes to write down your whole-person hopes, dreams, principles, and desired future state aspirations.

1. **Financial needs statement**

   _____

   _____

   _____

2. **Physical wellness needs statement**

   _____

   _____

   _____

3. **Social relationship needs statement**

   _____

   _____

   _____

4. **Intellectual, academic, or professional career needs statement**

   _____

   _____

   _____

5. **Spiritual, purpose, or contribution needs statement**

   _____

   _____

   _____

Here is a comprehensive list of coaching questions that can help lead to whole-person engagement:

- "Have you developed a whole-person game plan?"
- "When looking at the whole-person development, on a scale from 1–5 (1 = low effectiveness, 5 = high effectiveness), how is your work-life balance?"

- "In which dimensions of the whole-person are you most satisfied and fulfilled?"
- "Which dimensions of the whole-person are neglected or unfulfilled?"
- "What would you like to achieve this year?"
- "Where are your biggest barriers or challenges in gaining whole-person balance?"
- "What dreams, aspirations, or goals really excite you in the upcoming year?"
- "What changes will have the biggest impact on your whole-person life style?"
- "How are you currently doing in each dimension of the whole-person?"
- "Where are your strengths? Where might you find the most happiness, joy, and fulfillment?"
- "In which areas do you need to improve? Where can you get better?"
- "Which areas do you believe you can work on to gain better work-life balance?"
- "Where and how do you spend most of your time during the week?"
- "How about your time on the weekend?"
- "Where are you most productive with your time? Where are you least productive? What are your biggest time wasters in your week?"
- "Where can you spend time more effectively on those areas that matter most?"
- "What are the benefits of making time to focus on these important areas?"
- What could be the negative costs if you don't spend time and effort in these important areas?"
- "What will you commit to do to get better?"
- "What important things do you want to improve upon first?"
- "How will you measure success in each area?"
- "When will you commit to block time for yourself? How much time each week/day?"
- "When will you commit to block time for others? How much time each week/day?"

- "On a yearly basis, I will improve my effectiveness [in topic area] by . . ."
- "On a quarterly basis, I will improve my effectiveness [in topic area] by . . ."
- "On a monthly basis, I will improve my effectiveness [in topic area] by . . ."
- "On a weekly basis, I will improve my effectiveness [in topic area] by . . ."
- "On a daily basis, I will improve my effectiveness [in topic area] by . . ."

While I was attending Columbia University's Executive Coaching Certification Program in 2008, each coaching cohort group was filmed as we practiced improving our coaching skills with others. Filming and reflection were very important aspects for continuous improvement for each coaching cohort, so we could learn from each other's successes and mistakes and seek to get better. In one supervisory coaching session, our cohort leader, Ann Powers, helped me gain greater insights into the importance of whole-person needs, challenges, and self-awareness. She used some very powerful and transparent questions to assess and help expose various areas of my life, where I was not balanced and not paying enough time and attention to critical aspects of my own whole-person development.

As she asked questions about my intense work-travel schedule and imbalance in life, Ann began to assess and examine the health and relationship aspect of my work-life balance. I was feeling a lot of guilt, stress, and imbalance because I was traveling and away from home approximately 150–160 days per year. Virtually every week for the past 25 years, I was away somewhere in the world working with my coaching and consulting clients. I was dancing and ducking many of the real issues where I felt guilt. Ann saw right through my façade and began to ask me questions that caused me look deeper and more honestly and vulnerably at what I was saying and how I was acting. My deepest values were to be a good husband and father and that I valued my health and wellness. Her pointed coaching questions helped to expose that my values and beliefs were very inconsistent with what I was doing. This exposed gap was very uncomfortable.

During our public coaching session, I was being filmed for everyone to examine this gap. I visibly became emotional and felt really bad about the inconsistencies between the truth and what I believed. With great empathy, Ann helped unpack my inconsistent values, my espoused beliefs, and my guilt with increased self-awareness. We began to explore new and better choices about how I spent my time with my wife and children and how I could get better with the limited time I was home on the weekends. She then asked me to make a few public commitments about how I wanted to behave differently—all on film! Then we discussed how she could help hold me accountable in changing my mindset and behaviors so I would live in a way more consistent with my values, my beliefs, and what was most important to me in my life.

My personal experience with Ann Powers as a coach was life trans-formational and life changing. She helped me uncover my guilt, pain, and imbalanced needs. She coached me without shame, blame, or judgment. She used honest labels to help me honestly look at the truth and gap areas for improvement. She then helped me recommit to liv-ing a life according to my values, beliefs, truth, and actions that would better serve my health and wellness, my family, and my connection with my most important relationship going forward.

One thing she said that stuck with me was, "Michael, when you are home on the weekends with your family, you need to be more present and available. When you are home, can you see how you're wasting time doing many non-valued-added activities that you can delegate, or outsource, or simply choose not to do? Focus your time better by connecting with your family emotionally, spending time together for lunches and dinners, watching your children's sporting events, attend your worship service together, and eliminating urgent activities and distracting events that don't add lasting value. Also, given your demanding work and travel schedule, can you see how you need to make time to invest in your own health and wellness? Otherwise, you will be stressed and burned out, and this imbalance will impact your overall energy and effectiveness."

Ann found that I was driving myself to pack too much into my weekends. Golfing with family and friends, doing community ser-vice projects, and coaching sports teams are all good—but not at the expense of relationships and connecting with the people who matter most. I was trying to overcompensate for being gone so much. Say-ing no to extended family, friends, and community service was very hard—I value these people and community connections tremendously. However, they should not be at the expense of the things that matter most, given my limited time with my family.

It's still hard to stay balanced. But now, when I am home, I have learned to be better about saying no to a lot of "good things," "good relationships," and "worthwhile urgent activities." With limited time, I am learning to dedicate blocks of time for myself and exercise or renewal, my most important relationships with my family and friends, and other key community interests.

There will always be more worthwhile, urgent, and good demands on your time than you have time and capacity to execute. The key to whole-person balance and discipline among the five dimensions is to review each area every week. Do not neglect one of them at the expense of the others. Don't get caught up in the good things in just one or two dimensions. As Jim Collins says, "The enemy of the great is the good." Keep a holistic, balanced view across every dimension.

This "aha" moment from my Columbia Coaching cohort practicum helped me realize I needed to better plan, prioritize, and fully commit to my mission and vision statements. Then, I needed to responsibly commit to improving my own wellness and energy levels while finding better ways to connect with my wife, four boys, and others who mattered most. The German writer and statesman Johann Wolfgang von Goethe said it best: "Things that matter most, must never be at the mercy of things that matter least." As I reflect on my coaching experience with Ann Powers and on Goethe's quote, I am coming to understand that choices in life are not always between good and bad or right and wrong; many times responsible choices are between good, better, and best.

We all make decisions and place goals, values, needs, and importance on where we choose to spend our time and where we choose not to spend our time. Defining why and where is critical to self-awareness about where we allocate our time, effort, and resources. Losing my father at age 19 brought a more intense focus on why I desired to be more "present and available" as an active part of my wife's and boys' lives. I sincerely desire to connect and engage with them, to teach and affirm them, and to raise these great boys to be responsible men who lead lives of integrity and make meaningful contributions to society and their future families.

Coaching the Whole-Person

A long, healthy, and happy life is the result of making contributions, of having meaningful projects that are personally exciting and contribute to and bless the lives of others.
—Hans Selye, Hungarian Canadian scientific
pioneer on stress

As my experience with my supervisory coach Ann Powers shows, you are never just coaching an employee, a team member, or a performer; you are coaching a whole-person who has key stakeholders and people who matter most to them. When you choose to coach the whole-person, you choose to address and engage people in all five areas of their life: financial, physical, emotional, intellectual, and spiritual. In this way, you are better able to engage and unleash their full creative potential. You understand more of what is important to them personally, and how to align their priorities with their team, organizational, and key stakeholder priorities. The whole-person is about finding an individual's innovation, passion, excitement, aspirations, future development, and motivation.

In practice, what are you asking about when you coach the whole-person? You're thinking holistically, so your questions are also holistic at the personal, team, or organizational levels of development. Consider asking coaching questions that cover the following whole-person topic areas:

1. **Financial area**
   Personal:
   - Self-reliance
   - Income
   - Budgeting
   - Spending habits
   - Investments/business acumen
   - Savings
   - Debt reduction
   - Financial planning/tax strategies
   - Entrepreneurship
   Team/Organizational:
   - Total rewards package
   - Fair-equal compensation
   - Rewards and recognition

- Paid time off (PTO)
- Bonus incentives/401K/stock options
- Benefits/healthcare/medical/dental
- Insurance/disability/workers compensation
- Investments/retirement/savings/pension
- College tuition reimbursement
- Professional and career development
- Professional associations/networking/mentoring

2. Physical/Health/Wellness areas

Personal:

- Work-life balance
- Health and wellness
- Exercise and recreation
- Nutrition/diet/eating habits
- Nutritional supplements
- Sleep/rest/renewal
- Meditation/yoga
- Stress reduction

Team/Organizational:

- Safe work conditions
- Work-life balance
- Culture of engagement and trust
- Virtual work/flex schedules/tele-work
- Family leave/childcare/sabbatical time off

3. Emotional/Relationship areas

Personal:

- Partner/spouse/significant other
- Family members and relationships
- Friends/colleagues/partnerships
- Community/social networks

Team/Organizational:

- Company culture
- Business unit/teams/projects
- Professional networks/associations
- Board of directors
- Advisory groups
- Community service
- Unions/memberships/advocacy groups

4. Intellectual/Professional areas

Personal:

- Academic/educational training
- Study abroad/travel/hobbies

- Internship/trade-skill experience
- Professional work experience
- Professional networking/associations/clubs

Team/Organizational:

- Professional work experiences
- Professional training/job competencies
- Financial, technical, and job skills training
- Management and leadership development
- Networking/associations/certifications
- Mentoring/coaching/career development

5. **Spiritual/Purpose/Contribution areas**

   Personal:

   - Journaling/reading/prayer/meditation
   - Board of directors/advisory boards
   - Advocacy and service groups
   - Volunteerism/community/civic service
   - Faith-based/religious organizations

   Team/Organizational:

   - Corporate social responsibility
   - Charitable/nonprofit agencies
   - Educational/vocational/community and global outreach
   - Children/disadvantaged/minority and elderly support groups
   - Legal/social justice/political and environmental advocacy groups
   - International service organizations

Maybe you're not used to asking questions about many of these holistic topic areas. Some of them are quite personal. But these questions get at the many of the issues, needs, and things that matter to people. Coaches can provide a safe and innovative setting to help people explore and find their voice, passion, and interests in those areas they care most about.

People are being asked to work longer hours, do more with less, and work in more complex, diverse, and competitive global environments. When coaches focus on the whole-person, they are more likely to care about and build up that person in every way possible.

As Henry David Thoreau said, many people "lead lives of quiet desperation." They wonder if anyone cares about the stresses they face on so many fronts. Health problems, financial issues, family concerns, alienation—all these things can and do affect individual workers and in turn impact business results. With too little sleep, stress, conflicts, and constant work demands, they neglect their whole-person needs and wind up in a very bad place. Even some of the most successful producers are neglecting critical areas of their lives and heading for burnout, hopelessness, and major setbacks.

I recently coached a woman I'll call Emily, who worked for an international consulting corporation and had experienced great professional success. Despite her successful 20-plus-year career, she was exhausted by the nonstop pace of her demanding role and wrestling with problems with her health and at home.

As we began our coaching engagement, we found that one of her biggest struggles was her inability to set boundaries. She felt a constant need to please others while trying to do a job three people would find overwhelming. Nonstop emails and instant messaging to colleagues continued into the late hours most evenings, with a barrage of follow-up emails that consistently greeted her at 5:45 a.m. every day. She used weekends and vacations to catch up on work.

So, we explored her mission, her values, her life purpose, and her vision of the future she wanted. She charted a plan that set clear boundaries, allowed for time off, and still kept appropriate focus on her work. As we identified the needs of the whole-person (financial, physical, emotional, intellectual, and spiritual), along with her core values in each of her roles (professional, family, and personal), she then determined her top priorities and the percentage of time she could allocate to each important area of her life.

Coaching enabled her to recover from a path toward burnout, ruined health, and weakened relationships. She was able to change behaviors and create new habits and weekly rituals that fulfilled all the dimensions of the whole-person.

Adopting Rituals to Serve the Whole-Person

The major work of the world is not done by geniuses. It is done by ordinary people, with balance in their lives, who have learned to work in an extraordinary manner.
—Gordon B. Hinckley, inspirational religious leader,
educator, and author

Once you set your whole-person goals, you'll need to block out time on your calendar for achieving them. Transformation usually requires lots of repetition: one exercise session won't do you much good, so you need to make time for an organized sequence of activities that will change your life. I call these activities *rituals* because they are programmed and repeated. Adopting certain rituals will help you fill your whole-person needs more easily.

Your whole-person plan might include rituals like these:

1. Over the next three to five years, I will schedule . . .
2. Over the next two years . . .
3. On a yearly basis . . .
4. On a quarterly basis . . .
5. On a monthly basis . . .
6. On a weekly basis . . .
7. On a daily basis . . .

You will always have more good ideas than you have time, resources, or capacity to execute. Keep it simple, narrow the focus, and don't try to do too much at once. Your ability to consistently carry out a few rituals will grow.

Emma had a 16-year-old daughter. That statement alone should explain what Emma was dealing with when it came to coaching the whole-person. She had an emotional need: how to connect with a daughter who thought that her mother was unavailable and disconnected.

"I have two summers left with my daughter before she moves out," Emma explained to me. "I am running out of time to connect with her. What can I do?"

I introduced Emma to the Learner/Judger mindset, and we discussed how she could begin to connect better with her daughter in a nonjudgmental way.

I brainstormed some options with Emma. She wanted her daughter to give less time and attention to her phone and social media. She wanted to find an opportunity to connect with her in a safe, uninterrupted environment. After some discussion, Emma settled on a service project in Mexico, helping to build a school.

As part of a team, Emma and her daughter mixed cement, sawed beams, drove nails, and painted, doing a different job each day. But they also participated in certain daily rituals. Each morning began with worship. At breakfast, they met with the children who would attend the school and got to know them. Each evening, the team gathered to talk about what they had learned from the experience.

These rituals brought clearly to their minds their reasons for being there—to give to little children something they could not achieve for themselves. It was an emotional and spiritual awakening for Emma's daughter and for her mother.

In the end, Emma and her daughter genuinely connected through this service project. "Our kids are raised not understanding what they have and how blessed they are. It was eye-opening for my daughter and myself," she shared. "My daughter saw kids without shoes, without access to an abundance of food, sleeping on the floor; she realized she has everything at her disposal. She saw children who were joyful, happy, and content, even though they had nothing."

Service helped Emma's daughter rethink her own life situation and become more humble and grateful as she found meaning outside of herself. Emma also became more connected and humbled by the experience.

Here are some coaching questions that lead to productive rituals:

- "Do you have a clear whole-person plan for the next one to five years?"
- "Does your plan include those family, friends, and colleagues who matter most to you?"
- "Do you have clear rituals in mind to support your plan?"
- "Why are the rituals important to you and others?"
- "What will the rituals do to help you remember those things that are most important?"
- "What rituals will you commit to?"
- "Who will help hold you accountable to execute your plan?"
- "Who else needs to be involved in this effort?"
- "When will you start?"
- "How can I help?"

Partnering for Accountability ━━━━━━

The most creative and productive work comes when people freely make commitments to one another, not when the boss tells them what to do.

—Jim Collins, business management author, consultant, and lecturer

Goals are great. Action is even better. One key to turning a commitment into action is to have a coach as an accountability partner: someone you can report to who will hold you to your commitments.

For about a year, I had the opportunity to be a coaching accountability partner for Parker, an entrepreneur and president of a very successful and profitable startup business. He was highly motivated, intelligent, and a great visionary. He had a very strong work ethic, but he still needed someone to help him stay true to his plan.

We put together a coaching plan for Parker to work on his personal and professional goals in all five whole-person areas: financial, physical, social/emotional, intellectual, and spiritual, with an emphasis on his key relationships and career success.

The plan also included guidelines for me as Parker's peer accountability coach:

- Be his "guide on the side" consistently each week
- Help him stay consistently on track with his rituals
- Listen and maintain ongoing support, accountability, and confidentiality
- Mentor him to solve big problems and overcome big challenges
- Help him stay focused on the right leadership mindset, behaviors, and performance results
- Role-play crucial conversations with others so he could build relationships of trust
- Challenge and support him in modeling the values he believed in
- Help review and track his success measures and help him adapt the plan as needed

Parker was a conscientious individual with every intention to stay true to his goals, but he told me that his goals always stayed at the forefront of his mind because he knew I would call, check in, and challenge him. He made real progress because he had a plan and knew there was going to be ongoing support and accountability.

Here are some questions to ask in your role as a peer accountability coaching partner:

- "What do you want to accomplish with your coaching agenda?"
- "What would you like to achieve this year?"

- "What are the most important personal whole-person issues for us to discuss? Why?"
- "What are the most important team and organization whole-person issues for us to discuss? Why?"
- "Who are your key stakeholders and influencers? What are their needs? What matters most to them?"
- "How will you measure success with your key stakeholders? Who will determine that?"
- "What would you like to be different? Why will that matter to your key stakeholders? To you?"
- "What do you expect to be different 3, 6, 9, or 12 months from now? One, two, or three years from now?"
- "Where are you now with your whole-person issues? Where do you need to be in the future?"
- "What barriers or challenges might get in your way of achieving these goals?"
- "What ongoing rituals will you commit to?"
- "How can I best hold you accountable on your journey?"
- "If you're not on track, what are you doing to get back on track?"
- "What will you do [topic area] and by when?"
- "How would you like to celebrate key wins or milestones?"
- "What time, systems, support, processes, information, training, or resources do you need?"
- "How can I best support you and hold you accountable going forward?"

PRACTICE: YOUR COACHING PLAYBOOK

Here I offer suggestions about how to approach each of the five whole-person need areas in coaching conversations that lead to greater levels of engagement. Following are questions for whole-person planning:

1. *Financial (money/budgets/resources):* "How do you generate more income, revenue, and cash? How do you better budget and manage your expenses? How are you doing with all the basic hygiene factor needs of food, clothing, housing? Write down one or two things you will do in the financial area to improve and get better."

2. *Body (health/wellness):* "How is your health? How are you renewing yourself physically? The healthier you are physically, the more engaged you will be and the better you will perform. Write down one or two things you will do in the physical area to improve and get better."

3. *Heart (social and emotional health/relationships):* "How can you become more engaged, supportive, kind, respectful, optimistic, positive, and hopeful? How well do you maintain your relationships at work with your boss, co-workers, teams, peers, stakeholders, customers, partners, etc.? What key personal or family relationships, friendships, or community networks do you need to maintain or develop? How can you genuinely connect in uplifting, loving, and mutually respectful relationships? Write down one or two things you will do to improve and get better in the social/emotional area."

4. *Mind (education/professional experiences/career development):* "How are you staying awake mentally? How do you feel about the state of your skills and knowledge? What new education, training, learning, skills, and capabilities do you need to develop to improve your performance? Write down one or two things you will do to develop in the educational and professional development area."

5. *Spirit (meaning/purpose/service/contribution):* "How will you cultivate a life that gives real meaning and purpose? How can you move beyond yourself and connect to the overall purpose and contribution of your organization? How can you be inspired and motivated by a cause, sense of purpose, service, principles, values, and contribution yet to be fulfilled? Write down one or two things you will do to develop the spiritual area."

The following coaching questions are a guide to your own whole-person planning, and then use them to help someone else do whole-person planning as well. This holistic approach to life can be game changing!

Determining Purpose and Motivation

1. THE WHY:

Why are your goals so critical to achieve?

What's your reason and driving motives?

Define my motive:
- Consecration
- Sacrifice
- Commitments
- Covenant

2. THE WHAT:

Define your most important goals to achieve:

Vision—5–10 years?
Strategy—2–5 years?
Important goal this year?

Focus & clarity?
Analyze & plan
- Years
- Quarters
- Months
- Weeks

3. THE HOW:

Define what strategies or path you'll take.

How will you achieve your goals?
What strategies?
What actions?
What behaviors?

Define my action plan:
- Disciplined thought
- Disciplined choices
- Disciplined actions

4. THE WHEN:

When will you achieve your goals, objectives, and targets?

A High	B Medium	C Low
Must be done	Should be done	Could be done

Achievement milestones:
- Define an X to Y
- Set a finish line (date)
- Clear measures

5. THE WHO:

Who will hold you accountable?

Who will help you?

Who is all in?

My board

1. Health coach
2. Financial advisor
3. Spouse/counseling
4. Professional mentor
5. Comm/religious/service

Accountability!
My board of directors:
- Ongoing personal check-in?
  - Past, present, future
  - Celebrate successes
  - Clear the path

Individual Whole-Person Examples

What are your individual needs, opportunities, and goals? How can you design a fulfilled life as a whole-person?

1. FINANCIAL	2. HEALTH	3. RELATIONSHIPS	4. PROFESSIONAL	5. PURPOSE

1. Self-reliance 2. Increasing income 3. Budgeting 4. Spending habits 5. Savings 6. Debt reduction 7. Investments 8. Business acumen 9. Financial planning 10. Tax strategies 11. Entrepreneurship 12. Financial partners	1. Work-life balance 2. Health, wellness 3. Exercise, recreation 4. Nutrition, diet, eating habits 5. Nutritional supplements 6. Sleep 7. Physical renewal 8. Meditation, yoga 9. Stress reduction	1. Social connections 2. Partner, spouse 3. Significant other 4. Family relationships 5. Family dinners 6. Friends and colleagues 7. Partnerships 8. Community service 9. Social networks 10. Travel/hobbies	1. Academic/school 2. Online training 3. Study abroad, internships 4. Trade-skill training 5. Professional development 6. Work experiences 7. Professional networking 8. Associations 9. Certifications	1. Time in nature 2. Journaling, reading 3. Meditation, prayer 4. Religious worship 5. Honoring family/ancestors 6. Volunteerism 7. Advocacy and service groups 8. Community, public service 9. Gov't service organizations

Individual Whole-Person Planning

What are your individual needs, opportunities, and goals? How can you design a fulfilled life as a *whole-person?*

1. FINANCIAL	2. HEALTH	3. RELATIONSHIPS	4. PROFESSIONAL	5. PURPOSE
GOALS/ACTIONS	GOALS/ACTIONS	GOALS/ACTIONS	GOALS/ACTIONS	GOALS/ACTIONS

III Coaching the Organization

15

Coaching the 7 Core Factors for Organizational Change

In all my years as a leader at Frito Lay and PepsiCo, I have found that building trust with my team and in our culture was the single greatest thing that I could do to improve performance.
—Al Carey, former president, PepsiCo North America

In this part of the book, we go beyond helping individuals change, to helping entire leadership teams and organizations learn and align to better serve their customers, better compete in the marketplace, and better serve its mission, vision, and ultimate purpose in society.

Of course, no one coaches an organization. You're still coaching people, but now we're talking about coaching senior executive leaders and teams and others who have general leadership, management, and often global responsibilities.

As a coach practitioner who has practiced in over 35 countries for approximately three decades, I have found that my favorite work is developing senior leaders and executive teams; helping them to set clear visions, values, strategies, and goals with aligned roles and structure for their organizations; and coaching them in a way that brings simplicity to their executive teams. Arthur W. Jones from Procter & Gamble famously stated, "All organizations are perfectly aligned to get the results they get." The trick is to design and align the organization to the desired results that are wanted. Executive coaches can play an essential role in that design and alignment.

Organizational coaching offers the executive team the opportunity to gain direction, clarity, focus, and alignment. Learning and change with leaders begins with the strategical level, then the operational level, and ultimately the team and tactical levels. This means coaching can be extremely useful at all levels. I believe a critical role with the executive and leadership team is a partnership with human resources or talent management, helping to build internal leaders who can become coaches, thus building a coaching culture across the organization. Internal leader-coaches can help individuals and teams everywhere to align and cascade vision, values, strategy, and goals to each business unit and function at every level.

Introducing the 7 Core Factors for Organizational Change

All organizational learning and change is dynamic and takes time to implement. It doesn't happen overnight and will not happen overnight; it requires top-level sponsorship and ongoing discipline to follow what I call the *7 Core Factors for Organizational Change*. Having worked with thousands of organizations across the world—corporate, government, education, and nonprofit—I have found that coaching leaders to answer 7 Core Factor questions can work well at any level, in any industry, and in any culture, *if* the leaders, sponsors, and internal coaches fully commit to the process. Success hinges on intensive coaching and ongoing follow-up. This process is not about simply teaching or training. It is an ongoing sustainability process that requires follow-up, accountability, ratification, engagement checkpoints, and ongoing coaching.

The 7 Core Factor questions are asked first at the strategic level and then at the operational levels, and then at the tactical and team levels. We will begin to uncover and help design and align around the following organizational coaching areas:

1. "Why does our organization exist? Who do we serve?"
2. "What are the cultural values, beliefs, and norms?"
3. "Where is our organization going strategically?"
4. "What are the critical and focused goals to be achieved?"
5. "What are the right roles, structure, and process to execute strategic goals and objectives?"

6. "Who will execute our critical goals? Do we have the right talent in the right seats on the bus?"
7. "How will we reward and recognize our talent if goals are achieved?"

Every executive team, division or business unit, and front-line team should be coached to clearly answer and align to these same simple questions. It is often said that the simple questions are the hardest to answer: they can be challenging, profound, paradoxical, and sometimes painful. But these 7 Core questions will help every team in the organization deal with the same challenges of clarity, focus, alignment, and ownership at all levels.

Figure 15.1 maps the design and implementation of the coaching process that I have used for decades with hundreds of CEOs and thousands of executive teams all over the world. This map can be used with any leadership team in any organization—corporate, government, education, or nonprofit.

Coaching with the 7 Core Questions ━━━

1. Rediscover Why—Why Do We Exist? Who Do We Serve? What Are Our Mission, Vision, and Core Values?

> *All organizations start with Why, but only the great ones keep their Why clear year after year.*
> *—Simon Sinek, British American author, motivational speaker, and organizational consultant*

First, start with clearly defining your "why." Why does this organization or team exist? What is the shared purpose and mission of the organization? Highly effective organizations understand their "why"— they know their customers and their markets and have a compelling vision of a desired future state.

Whom do we serve? Without loyal and satisfied customers, a business cannot survive. People at every level must understand their mission, purpose, and vision. They have to clearly identify their core values, norms, and beliefs. The culture must be one of respect, valuing diversity, inclusion, honesty, accountability, and transparency. People must also know the why and how they serve their customers. Managing budgets, increasing profits, and growing revenue are vital to organizational success; however, if they are gained without adding real value to customers through positive, loyal experiences, then that growth will not be sustainable. A great coach helps to define a clear strategic direction and gets the organization aligned to execute on what is most important in ways that offer significant, unique value to its key customers in ways that are sustainable in both the short and long terms.

Coaches add tremendous value in helping leaders, teams, and people at all levels develop awareness around their shared mission, purpose, vision, and values with questions such as:

- "Do your organization and your team have a clear mission and purpose?"
- "Is the mission statement posted where everyone can read and understand it?"
- "Is your mission and purpose shared at all levels?"
- "Does everyone in the organization understand why you exist, who you serve, and how you go to market to best serve your customers?"
- "Does your team understand how it contributes and how it is aligned to serve the overall organizational mission and purpose?"
- "How can leaders/managers help communicate and reinforce your overall purpose and mission?"

2. Rediscover Where—Where Will We Compete? What Is Our Unique, Competitive Strategy?

The essence of a great strategy is choosing what to do and what not to do.

—*Michael Porter, department head of strategy, Harvard Business School*

The "where" is about vision and strategy. Great organizations and teams have a clear and compelling vision over five to ten years that describes what success will look like in the future. They also have a competitive strategy with a clear path and plan to dominate, compete, and win in their marketplace over a one- to five-year timeframe. Due to limited resources, and with a need for focus, the strategic plan also clarifies where they will choose not to compete. As Jack Welch, the former chairman and CEO of General Electric, reminds all leaders, "Control your own destiny, or someone else will" and "If you don't have a competitive advantage, don't compete."

Coaches help leaders define their uniqueness. They discover how to innovate and differentiate themselves more clearly from their competitors and gain a unique competitive advantage. What does this organization do that no one else does? How will it competitively serve markets and customers, and offer unique products, services, or technologies?

Coaches can help define a clear, shared vision and strategy for future success by asking questions such as:

- "Do your organization and your team have a clear vision of their desired future state over the next 5 to 10 years?"
- "Have you written a compelling vision statement?"
- "Do you have a clear picture of where you will compete and where you will not compete?"
- "Is your vision and strategy shared at all levels?"
- "How will you help all levels of the organization share your vision and strategy?"
- "Do you have a rigorous, open, transparent, annual strategic planning process to review vision and strategy? Do you hold people accountable, annually or quarterly, for planning, formulating, and adapting strategy in an ongoing way?"

3. Rediscover What—What Are Our Narrowly Focused, Most Important Goals?

You can have many goals. But some goals are more wildly important than others—they must be achieved, or nothing else matters.
—*Jim Stuart, former FranklinCovey execution consultant*

"What" are you going to achieve in terms of clearly defined goals? Performance goals draw a clear line: this is what your individuals, teams, and overall organization must achieve, or nothing else matters. The path to achieve goals starts by setting stretch goals that are both achievable and narrowly focused. Those goals must be influenceable, narrowly focused, specific, and measurable. Goals must be stated in a format that is SMART: specific, measurable, actionable, realistic, and time bound. Execution is impossible without clear measures and a clear time frame that tell you when you have succeeded.

All high-performing organizations, teams, and individuals have shared performance goals with objectives and clear measures of success. The key is to align those goals with clear, measurable objectives by those who have the power and delegated authority to execute them.

Coaches can help question and define performance expectations, standards of excellence, and goal achievement. Ask the following questions to help gain goal clarity and alignment:

- "Are your organizational goals for this timeframe aligned with your overall vision, mission, and strategy?"
- "Are your organizational goals realistic, specific, and measurable?"
- "What are the most important or strategic goals that you must achieve?"
- "Have you narrowed down those goals to the one, two, or at most three that can be achieved with excellence?"
- "Are these organizational goals widely shared and supported with a clear business case for being the most important?"
- "Are they compelling and motivating?"
- "Do these goals have a clear, objective, and valid lag measure of success that can be measured and tracked accurately every month?"
- "Are they achievable?"
- "Do you have the right structure and roles defined to execute these goals?"
- "Does the team have at least 80% influence on these goals?"

4. Rediscover How—How Will We Execute Our Key Goals? What Are the Key Weekly Actions to Help Drive Our Goals to Success?

> *Don't tell people how to do things; tell them what to do and let them surprise you with their results.*
> —*George S. Patton, US Army General*

The "how" is also about the values you live by. Execution is not just about hitting targets: it's about respectful, collaborative, supportive communication within teams and across the organization with other groups. What are the organization's shared values? Goals are often missed not because people don't know their jobs, but because they don't know how to cooperate and play as good teammates. Furthermore, does the "how" include helping people to develop themselves? Will they become more skillful and more capable, and create an environment of continuous improvement?

The "how" is the process and the weekly actions you follow to achieve your goals. Once goals are defined, execution depends on taking the right actions, empowering people to experiment, and following up regularly and frequently to find out what is working. Teams decide what methods to follow and check in with each other at least weekly or even daily to help track their success. I say "weekly or daily" because goals that aren't revisited more than once a week tend to get lost in the urgency of the daily work. If a person or a team is focused on actions that happen one or two times monthly, it's way too late to drive the monthly goal or objective. The team and the individual players need weekly and daily frequency of action to proactively move the goal forward toward completion.

Coaches can help with execution by reinforcing the weekly or daily action-step process and the right values required to sustain an effective culture for goal achievement. Coaches can ask the following questions to help align the right weekly actions that drive goal attainment:

- "Do your organization and your team have clear core values?"
- "What are the organization's core values and beliefs?"
- "Are the core values understood and shared clearly at all levels across the organization?"
- "Are you achieving your goals in ways that build a high-trust, collaborative, respectful culture?"
- "What will it take to achieve your most strategically important goals—the fewest number of goals that must be achieved with excellence?"
- "What will be your action-step process for aligning every team and individual to those few key goals? Can the team influence these actions at least 80% each and every week?"
- "What are the weekly or daily actions that must be performed with consistency by the players or by the team?"
- "Do your performance reviews address performance results on key goals?"

- "Are job performance and career development linked to overall talent and performance management processes?"
- "How can you help improve the overall performance-based culture and a high-trust goal execution process?"
- "Do you systematically review how you are doing by living the values?"
- "Are the core values linked to clearly defined behavioral norms and standards of conduct?"
- "How can you improve as an organization by achieving performance results while living your values?"

5. Rediscover When—Goal Execution: The Right Roles, Structure, and Process

I have been impressed with the urgency of doing. Knowing is not enough. We must apply. Being willing is not enough. We must do.
—*Leonardo da Vinci, Italian painter, inventor, scientist, sculptor, musician, and writer*

The "when" is about the timeframe needed to execute goals. It is all about shared team performance and accountability. It's about how often the team reviews and openly communicates their scoreboard, determines whether they are winning or losing, and determines the right actions for success. Is there a weekly accountability session? Is there an established time frame to come together and discuss how things are going, learn from successes and failure, and create a culture of engagement and accountability? If so, "when?"

My graduate school professor at Columbia University, Dr. Victoria Marsick, is a world-class consultant and practitioner in the field of adult learning, training, and action-learning. She would often say, "Performance will dramatically improve when you take time to reflect on action, examine performance, question underlying assumptions, and get the group asking questions about how to get better." Team and individual accountability is critical for improvement in learning agility, innovation, sharing of best practices, and ongoing improvement.

Coaches can offer great insights to help reinforce the right actions and behaviors, performance management processes, talent development, talent promotion, feedback, and recognition. Ask the following to help drive the right talent development roles, responsibilities, and structure:

- "Does your organization support a formal performance management system to improve talent and employee development?"
- "Are all leaders equipped with the skills and process needed to conduct effective performance coaching conversations with individuals *and* teams?"
- "Does the performance management process effectively assess and improve performance, values, and development?"
- "How does the performance management process effectively help develop team members' knowledge, skills, abilities, and motivation?"
- "How is the performance management process driving the right, acceptable behaviors and values?"
- "How does information get communicated frequently and shared most effectively at all organizational levels?"
- "How do you and your team hold each other accountable weekly to performance goals and targets?"
- "How does your team connect and effectively communicate weekly? What is most effective? What is least effective?"
- "How can leaders and managers help improve the overall talent and performance management process?"

6. Rediscover Who—Your Talent: Identify the Right People, in the Right Seats

If you pick the right people and give them the opportunity to spread their wings, then you almost don't have to manage them.
—Jack Welch, former chairman and CEO of General Electric

The "who" is about your talent and your leaders. Who has what roles and responsibilities? Each team must have an accountable leader supported by team members who share the same goal and are rewarded to achieve it. Coaches can help clearly define the "who": who is responsible for getting the work done? Who is responsible for supporting the team? Who can produce the resources needed? Who can remove obstacles? And who can leverage the strength needed to produce great performance and results?

Coaches can help ask questions to reinforce clear talent development roles and responsibilities for all team members:

- "Does your organization have a clear organization chart and structure that clearly defines all the roles and responsibilities?"
- "What roles and responsibilities are needed in the team to be most effective?"
- "Are you currently clear on your roles and responsibilities?"
- "Is team talent structured in a way that they can best leverage their unique strengths, gifts, and talents?"
- "Are all individual contributors and team members recognized and rewarded to act in ways that position people to work and maximize their strengths, gifts, and talents?"
- "How can leaders help improve the roles, responsibilities, and strengths of their people and teams?"

7. Rediscover the Motivation—Recognizing and Rewarding Talent

You are not here merely to make a living. You are here to enable the world to live more amply, with greater vision, with a finer spirit of hope and achievement. You are here to enrich the world, and you impoverish yourself if you forget the errand.
—Woodrow Wilson, *former US president, statesman, lawyer, politician, and president of Princeton University*

Psychologist and philosopher William James said, "The deepest principle in human nature is the craving to feel appreciated and valued." Every organization and team should be aligned to reward and recognize great performance (the "what") and values (the "how"). Both are critical for sustained success.

Making time to coach your team members shows that you value them. Coaching helps people be more self-aware and perform better, but it's also a signal that the organization cares about them and wants to invest in them.

Coaching can change negatives to positives. You cannot ignore bad performance or poor behaviors, or you encourage them. Don't store up a bunch of bad feedback and criticism in a bag and then unload it on people. Give people helpful feedback as soon as possible. Make it accurate, objective, and observable—not personal. All coaching is to help people to get better, to learn, and to move forward—not to shame or to punish. When it comes to giving feedback, make sure every encounter has a happy ending—be respectful and helpful, not hurtful.

Both business performance and adherence to values should be equally assessed, weighed, and rewarded. Give ongoing feedback and course correction to ensure that you are building a positive, motivating, trusting, and safe culture. Your role as a coach is to stimulate positive emotions in people to get them to engage in achieving the right goal and doing it right.

Finally, make sure team members understand that positive feedback, recognition, and rewards are all about achievement of the big picture. As the organization wins, so does the team, and so does the individual.

Coaching the organization can help align rewards and recognition to performance standards. The key is how to move from standard to breakthrough performance. Ask the following questions to help reward and recognize talent:

- "Have you successfully aligned rewards and recognition incentives for all people to drive the right performance goals and the right values and behaviors?"
- "Does your performance evaluation process help drive the right behaviors, values, and performance objectives?"
- "Does the performance evaluation process effectively link compensation and recognition to drive the right strategy, goals, and culture?"
- "Do you feel that rewards and recognition are driving the right kind of behavior and results?"
- "What could you do to get better alignment of both performance (the "what") and values (the "how")?"
- "Do you offer performance management reviews and rewards across all teams and departments in a fair and equitable way? Do you reward and recognize top performance?"
- "How can you be better align and empower your people to achieve the right results and model the right culture and values through your compensation, recognition, and rewards for your employees?"

***

Every team and organization can dramatically improve performance and results by thinking through these 7 Core Factors questions. Review of these seven questions should not be conducted only once or twice a year. They should not just be printed or showcased on a plaque on the company wall. People need to hold ongoing, dynamic, real-time coaching conversations and offer feedback to continually reinforce and align with the answers to these critical questions. Otherwise, over time, the organization will start to drift, disengage, and become demotivated.

PRACTICE: YOUR COACHING PLAYBOOK

Leader-coaches must take time to understand and engage time with other leaders, managers, and people at all organizational levels in exploring these questions. If possible, remember to start first at the senior or strategic level, then move to the business unit or operational level, and then to the tactical or team level as you design for clarity, focus, alignment, and accountability at each level of your organization:

1. *Why:* "Why do we exist? Who do we serve? What are our mission, vision, and values?"
2. *Where:* "Where will we compete? What is our unique, competitive strategy?" "What is our path and plan?"
3. *What:* "What are our narrowly focused, most important goals?"
4. *How:* "How do we execute the right actions and behaviors?"
5. *When:* "What is the timeframe for achieving our goals with excellence?"
6. *Who:* "Who are the right people? Are they in the right seats?"
7. *Systems:* "How do we recognize, reward, and develop talent?"

Ask yourself, in relation to the 7 Core Factors:

1. Where can our organization get better focus and alignment?
2. Where do we have great alignment, commitment, and buy-in?
3. Where are we clear, focused, and aligned?
4. Where are we unclear, unfocused, and misaligned?
5. Where do we need better sponsorship, engagement, and support?
6. Where can we help coach and offer better support and accountability?

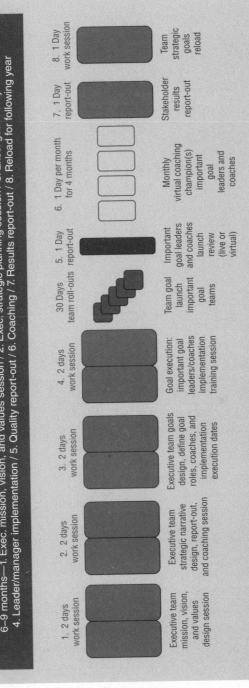

The 7 Core Factors for building successful organizational change

6–9 months—1. Exec. mission, vision, and values session / 2. Exec. strategic planning session / 3. Exec. goal clarity session / 4. Leader/manager implementation / 5. Quality report-out / 6. Coaching / 7. Results report-out / 8. Reload for following year

| 1. 2 days work session | 2. 2 days work session | 3. 2 days work session | 4. 2 days work session | 30 Days team roll-outs | 5. 1 Day report-out | 6. 1 Day per month for 4 months | 7. 1 Day report-out | 8. 1 Day work session |

Executive team mission, vision, and values design session

Executive team strategic narrative design, report-out, and coaching session

Executive team goals design, define goal roles, coaches, and implementation execution dates

Goal execution: important goal leaders/coaches implementation training session

Team goal launch important goal teams

Important goal leaders and coaches launch review (live or virtual)

Monthly virtual coaching champion(s) important goal leaders and coaches

Stakeholder results report-out

Team strategic goals reload

Figure 15.1 The timeline and process for implementing the 7 Core Factors

16 Coaching Across the Globe

Our ability to reach unity in diversity will be the beauty and the test of our civilization.
—Mahatma Gandhi, Indian lawyer, politician, writer, and social activist

In 1987, I traveled to London, England, to participate for two semesters in a study-abroad program at Brigham Young University's London Center for International Studies. It was an amazing learning opportunity. For a few short months, I had the opportunity to study international business, politics, history, culture, art, and music and, of course, go to a lot of plays and symphonies and eat a lot of foods that were new to me.

This cross-cultural experience changed me. I was initially planning to major in business marketing but immediately changed to international relations and business upon my return to the United States.

After my trip to London, I wanted deeply to engage with the diverse and exciting peoples around the globe. Upon graduation, I went back to Europe for three months, traveling throughout Scandinavia, Western and Eastern Europe, Israel, and Egypt. The diversity of civilizations I encountered was inspiring and exhilarating.

Additionally, after I spent eight years with the Covey Leadership organization, the BYU Kennedy Center for International Studies offered me a one-year teaching professorship position at South China University of Technology in Guangzhou, China. Most of my travels had been in Europe and the Americas. Now the whole new world of Asia opened to me. I greatly enjoyed the history, people, culture, and food of Asia as I worked with the bright college students there. I also had the opportunity to design, instruct, and coach high-potential leaders for a year in a Chinese high-potential management program that I developed at the Nike Corporation in Guangzhou, China.

While working as an external consultant at Nike, I came across the work of well-known psychologist Dr. Geert Hofstede, formerly of IBM and professor of anthropology and international management at Maastricht University.

I found Hofstede's framework useful for coaching across cultures, starting with Chinese leaders and then across Europe, Australia, New Zealand, and back to the United States. Later, when I was at Columbia University, I adapted Hofstede's work successfully in the conflict-resolution and mediation classes that I taught during my graduate school internship at the United Nations in New York City. One of my favorite quotes was given to me by my wife Cynthia upon my graduation from Columbia University and upon finishing my work at the United Nations. The quote is from Senator William Fulbright and states, "We live in a world of diversity. The legitimate, realistic aim of international education is neither to convert not to indoctrinate, but rather to encourage empathy and understanding between cultures." Throughout my academic and professional career, I have enjoyed studying and practicing how to lead, work, and coach effectively in a multicultural world in over 35 countries and counting.

Coaching and Global Diversity

If we cannot now end our differences, at least we can help make the world safe for diversity.
—John F. Kennedy, former US president

Organizations are recognizing that while workforces are becoming more diverse, so are marketplaces, customers, and stakeholders. In an increasingly global economy with persisting cultural differences between nations, no universal management method exists that can be considered valid everywhere. For any company that deals in international business and global commerce, understanding and leveraging cultural diversity is imperative. Even companies that only deal locally or nationally can benefit from understanding the nuances across a diverse global marketplace.

I am hopeful that there's no going back to the old days of isolation, fear, and protectionism. There are only exciting and new diverse and innovative frontiers ahead. I like to say that with an increase in globalization, the world of work is becoming smaller and smaller. With international trade and global outsourcing, as well as advances in technology, communication, and travel, the world is truly open for business 24 hours a day every day of the year.

This reality means the competition to attract, retain, and engage global talent has never been more intense and competitive. There is a war for recruiting, developing, leveraging, and keeping the best talent. Thus, it makes sense that organizations are embracing global diversity and inclusion not only in trade and commerce but also in leveraging a diverse talent pool.

Can you coach people to adopt a global mindset? Can you effectively engage a diverse, multicultural talent pool? Do you possess global self-awareness? Do you value diversity and inclusion? Hopefully, you can say yes to each of these questions. If not, keep open and practicing.

Leaders who understand the significance of these skills can connect more effectively with others, understand and respect different worldviews, and improve learning, innovation, collaboration, and results. Coaches who demonstrate cross-cultural intelligence can build trust and rapport with others far more quickly and easily than those who ignore cross-cultural issues and the unconscious bias that exists within all people.

However, engaging diversity is not simple. Like an iceberg, the elements of culture are often both visible and invisible. Figure 16.1 displays both sides of culture and diversity.

While race, gender, work style, language, and behavioral norms are easy enough to see on the surface, coaches must be aware of the many attitudes that are not so perceptible. Religious values, national sensitivities, life experiences, orientation, and diverse attitudes and perceptions toward life need careful study and empathy, which are less visible beneath the surface.

Therefore, managing global diversity requires a long-term commitment to coaching about handling differences across cultures. Business issues such as strategy, goals, values, leadership philosophy, and talent management can present minefields. Diversity touches nearly everything: recruitment, development, business transactions, partnerships, and relationships.

One example of a successful diversity and inclusion initiative with coaching at its heart is GlaxoSmithKline's (GSK) Accelerating Difference program. The aim of the diversity and inclusion program is to promote more women to senior levels within the organization

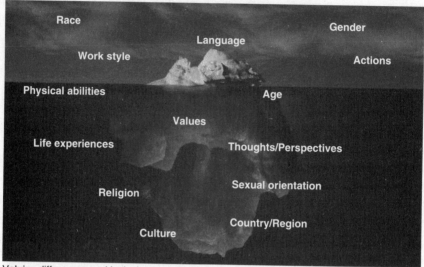

The Diversity Iceberg
It's what we see AND cannot see

Race

Gender

Language

Work style

Actions

Physical abilities

Age

Values

Life experiences

Thoughts/Perspectives

Sexual orientation

Religion

Country/Region

Culture

Valuing differences and inclusion is about engaging *all* employees to be the best they can be!

Figure 16.1 Understanding culture and diversity

through coaching, mentorship, and open dialogue. Approximately 46% of 2013 participants have been promoted by at least one level, compared to 26% of women and 27% of men at the same grades across the organization.

Participants were also 76% more likely to stay at the organization, and they improved in manager effectiveness and overall engagement scores more than three times faster than the control group. This is just one of many examples of how coaching for diversity can support professional growth, organizational development, and overall success of the enterprise.

Recognizing Cultural Diversity

It is never too late to give up your prejudices.
—*Henry David Thoreau, American essayist,
poet, and philosopher*

I felt the world getting much smaller when I taught an executive leadership development course at an offsite retreat in Denmark that included global leaders from Europe and Asia. I was able to coach several of them on their 360-degree feedback and help co-create action plans to be more effective and build trust across cultures. One leader I coached was from Denmark and was a key operations leader with an international retail firm. Responsible for global operations, he often visited his colleagues at manufacturing plants in Thailand. While there, he met with the local leaders, managers, and team members, fielding issues such as poor on-time delivery of products, operating process breakdowns, and quality and cost issues.

While coaching the leader in Denmark, I became aware that his strong, direct leadership style was based on individualism, being honest and direct, supporting low power distance to challenge ideas from everywhere, a value for equality of both masculinity and femininity, and a high level of certainty and value for risk. When this great Danish leader was working with his colleagues in Thailand, he confided in me, "I am stepping on cultural land mines everywhere! They don't get me, and I don't get them. It's like communicating with strangers! It is very frustrating because I think we have agreement when I am open, direct, and transparent on their operational issues. I am sharing facts openly and publically with the entire team. I could not be more honest and transparent about our issues. But then nothing ever seems to change." This manager was clearly struggling with his cross-cultural awareness. He had failed to adapt his communication and management style to a different culture in Asia.

The Asian culture of his colleagues tended to value collectivism and teamwork, high power distance and respect for the leader, indirect communication in which they would "save face" and not embarrass a leader in front of the leader's people, and uncertainty avoidance where risk was low, decisions took consensus and group input, and final decisions came from authority at the top. Their approach to leadership was radically different from his. His colleagues in Thailand were loyal and protective of each other, and they considered his factual, open, direct communication to be rude and somewhat arrogant and insensitive—particularly when he seemed harsh and judgmental in front of the entire team.

The results were awful. The company went through four CEOs in four years. It lost 25% of its market share in two years. It did not have a clear vision or strategy for growth. There was no transparency or integrity, and a complete inability to communicate about how to get better. Essentially, there was a toxic relationship between Denmark and Thailand, with suspicion, mistrust, and plenty of blame to go around. It was very unhealthy.

My coaching client wanted a healthy company with a healthy, trusting, two-way relationship between the two global offices, so he needed a new plan.

We discussed the research on cultural diversity from Geert Hofstede. We talked about the differences between a Judger and a Learner mindset, and the choice to change even if it meant leaving some old ways behind. He realized that he needed to support his colleagues and to stop diminishing and judging them harshly in public settings. In our conversations, he outlined four key goals to try to build cross-cultural trust and to turn things around:

1. Show better loyalty and respect for his Thailand leader and team.
2. Clarify his intent and take the time to listen better first, clarify issues, and express support with affirmation and loyalty to the leader and team.
3. Allow his Thailand leader to "save face" and share difficult data in a respectful, indirect, and open way, even using confidential one-on-one communications with the leader to get his buy-in, support, and respect for the process of desired changes. After sharing the data, he could offer resources and support to improve the processes and communication breakdowns. He began to look for ways to lead and engage his Asian counterparts without a spirit of guilt, blame, judgment, and defensiveness.
4. Leave each conversation by clarifying what was expected, what everyone had agreed to, and how each side would be accountable to improve and get better over time.

Coaching Across Diverse Cultures

> When we're talking about diversity, it's not a box to check. It is a reality that should be deeply felt and held and valued by all of us.
> —Ava DuVernay, American filmmaker and film distributor

Business today is often global, and success requires self-awareness and cross-cultural intelligence regarding the nuances of diverse cultural values, behaviors, and customs, which requires more learning agility and personal responsibility in adapting to those differences. Every organization has a unique culture, just as every nation state has a diverse culture. In his study of cultural dimensions in 53 cultures and 20 languages for over three decades, Geert Hofstede examined global norms, values, and styles of doing business and came up with five key elements and questions that can help any leader-coach effectively work and navigate across almost any global context. Answering these questions can help greatly increase any leader-coach's cross-cultural intelligence and effectiveness. Hofstede's five key dimensions of cross-cultural differences are defined next.

1. Power Distance: Low vs. High Power

This refers to the degree to which the people in a society or culture accept differences in power, status, rank, office, or leadership levels or positions among themselves. A high-power-distance style of leadership and management is top-down, with more formal levels of approvals and decision-making. For example, people in a high-power-distance society tend to be more hierarchical and autocratic, and display dictatorial control from the top. In low-power-distant societies, they have a strong preference for flat organizational structures with more trusting, open, transparent communication; open, upward feedback; role equality; and participatory decision-making and empowerment are encouraged at all organizational levels.

According to Hofstede, if you are interacting with someone in a high-power-distance culture (e.g. South East Asia, Japan, China, India, the Middle East, Russia, or Eastern Europe), that person would likely prefer to be in a hierarchy and be directed, ordered, and guided through a task. This person may tend to:

- Be less willing to ask questions or give direct feedback upward in meetings, especially when more senior members are present
- Be more subtle or indirect when expressing disagreement
- Be respectful of authority and less willing to debate issues in public forums
- Prefer that certain things be avoided and left unsaid

On the other hand, a low-power-distance organization is shared within a flatter, more empowered structure with less hierarchy (e.g.

the United States, Canada, United Kingdom, Scandinavia, and Australia). Delegation and empowerment are expected, and when everyone is affected by a decision, they likely have the chance to provide input and feedback. These people tend to:

- Be more forthright and direct about asking questions, criticizing ideas, or giving honest upward feedback to others
- Be less subtle, more open, and transparent when expressing disagreement
- Be more willing to directly debate issues openly at meetings
- Get to the point more directly and quickly

Key coaching questions: Does this society or organization tend to have high-power-distance or a low-power-distance culture, behaviors, and communication style?

2. Individualism vs. Collectivism

Individualism refers to a social structure and culture that place a high degree of importance on personal freedoms, individual expression, and personal interests. A collectivism culture focuses more on the needs and interests of the collective society, group, or team.

For example, in high-individualism cultures, they tend to be focused on the person's needs, success, personal fulfillment, individual rights and freedoms, autonomy, pleasure, and well-being. "I" is more important that the "we" or the group (e.g. the United States, Canada, United Kingdom, Scandinavia, and Australia).

In contrast, collectivism's focus is on the group people belong to, and the interests and success of the society, group, or team is more important that satisfying the individual's rights and needs. The needs of the overall state, or organizational interests, tend to outweigh any individual needs and concerns. However, with a collectivism mindset, the state and organization must seek to take care of the individual's needs. The individual's duty is to respect the overall society or group membership. In a collectivist society (e.g. Russia, Eastern Europe, China, South East Asia, India, and the Middle East), people are very loyal to one another and more communal, socialistic, caretaking, and responsible for each other. Individuals in such a culture tend to:

- Require more input from others before taking action
- Subordinate individual rights to that of the state or government
- Offer fewer personal opinions and be more cautious in expressing disagreement
- Have more appreciation and respect for protocols in society and the organization or the nation state

What does this element look like in business? In high-individualism cultures, individual accomplishments are encouraged. Individual rewards are expected for hard work, individual productivity is high, and individual ideas are encouraged and transparently shared openly. If you are doing business in a high-collectivism culture, hierarchy, harmony, respect, and equality are crucial. Ideas that would disrupt harmony and respect are suppressed. Direct or negative feedback in public is very impolite and inappropriate, and unquestioning loyalty is expected from individuals and groups.

Key coaching questions: Does this culture or organization tend to be more individualistic or more inclined to support collective views and behaviors for the greater good of society, organization, and group success?

3. Masculinity and Femininity

This section refers to the degree to which a culture is based on values that emphasize masculine and feminine traits. In masculine-oriented societies, the roles of men and women rarely overlap; gender roles are clearly differentiated. Masculine cultures are intended for men to lead and women to follow: people admire the achievement and accomplishment of men. They value male independence, aggressiveness, dominance, and assertiveness. Women tend to receive less pay and work in lower-level supporting roles and jobs.

If you are doing business in a high-masculine country or culture, you need to recognize that gender, title, ego, power, status, and money outweigh other considerations. Examples of masculine-oriented societies include Latin and South America, Southeast Asia, China, India, the Middle East, Russia, and Eastern European countries.

In a feminine culture, there is value for equality in work and social status among men and women, including role equality; equal opportunity in education, pay, and work; interdependence; and little or no glass ceiling. Neither men nor women are seen to be better than each other, but are viewed as equal in capability, skill, and experience. Both sexes are recognized for their work and accepted in the workplace and in society. The emphasis is not on being assertive, but rather on cooperating, equality, and establishing good relationships. Examples of feminine-oriented societies include the United States, Canada, United Kingdom, Scandinavia, Western Europe, and Australia.

If you are conducting business in a high-feminine culture, you need to understand that relationships matter, equality for all matters, and success is often found through empathic listening, mutual understanding and respect, negotiation, and collaboration. In addition, it is important to value and promote flexibility with an emphasis on work-life balance and accommodation to gender differences.

Key coaching questions: How does this culture view the roles of men and women? Does this culture or organization tend to have masculine dominance, aggressiveness, and male-dominated characteristics and behaviors? Or does this culture or organization tend to value men and women equally in terms of pay, role responsibilities, professional and career advancement opportunities, decision-making opportunities, and social status? Is there a lot of overlap between male and female roles in a more collaborative, fair, and empathic culture?

4. Decision-Making Capability: Certainty Avoidance (High Risk) vs. Uncertainty Avoidance (Low Risk)

This element refers to the degree to which the culture is willing to make or comfortable with making absolute or certain decisions that require taking risks. In both cases, life is uncertain and full of risks and unpredictable events.

Certainty avoidance (where risk is accepted) focuses more on trust, comfort, and lower levels of structure and controls. Life is meant to take risks, tolerance and valuing of differences is essential, conflict can be managed constructively, and there should be as few rules and laws as possible. These countries and cultures tend to embrace more risk and to be more relaxed, laid back, flexible, adaptable, and open to ideas and change. They prefer rapid decision-making and quick results and place great importance on flexibility and initiative. They value speed over thoroughness. Their motto may be: take it easy, and take it one day at a time.

When doing business in a certainty-avoidance culture, expect to see overall openness; extending of trust; and a desire for innovation, failure, course correction, and speed to market. In this culture, too much structure is unwelcomed, and titles are not as important as the ability to adapt to new circumstances and situations. Certainty-avoidance countries include: United States, England, India, China, and Singapore.

Uncertainty-avoidance cultures (where risk is low and not tolerated) are more fear-based and micromanagement oriented. Life is seen as dangerous, uncertain, and full of risks that must be controlled externally and internally. These cultures seek predictable results and control over their future. They spend significant time on background checks, policies, rules, and research. They establish proper procedures before starting a project. They value thoroughness over speed. This culture feels more comfortable with written laws, rules and regulations, lots of policies and procedures, and high accountability and oversight; and has a high need for structure, accountability measures, and negative consequences and threats to help reduce uncertainty and risk. Stability in this society comes from lots of safeguards, accountability, and oversight. Uncertainty-avoidance countries include Italy, Korea, Mexico, Belgium, and Russia.

Doing business in an uncertainty-avoidance cultures means being clear, direct, and concise about expectations, roles, and responsibilities. There are also many cultural structures, policies, and rules that must be followed.

Key coaching questions: How does this culture or organization view its comfort or tolerance for failures, mistakes, the unknown, or taking calculated risks? Does this culture avoid risks based on fear of the unknown? Is this culture comfortable with taking calculated risks and potential failure? Is this a highly engaged culture of trust, innovation, collaboration, partnering, openness, and transparency?

5. Long-Term and Short-Term Orientation

This section refers to the degree to which the culture or society emphasizes the long-term future and values thrift, frugality, and persistence. A long-term orientation looks for incremental improvements and strong relationships, rather than breakthroughs, so they are comfortably patient and slow to make decisions. This cultural style desires to be modest, uses more indirect communication, and wants to learn from other countries. Elements of perseverance, savings, and education are highly valued. In business, long-term cultures seek market share; investment in real, sustainable growth; and long-term profits. Norms and values are all relative and depend on the situation. Long-term-oriented cultures include Japan, China, Germany, Russia, Netherlands, France, Italy, and Sweden.

A short-term orientation emphasizes respect for tradition, national pride, strong social obligations, and saving face. People are more direct and make quicker decisions, and the culture tends to be more principle-based, religious, and nationalistic. The culture supports individualism, personal values, personal convictions, and individual rights. Individuals must proactively sell themselves to be taken seriously, and flattery is always appreciated. Short-term-oriented cultures also seek quick gains and efficient procedures, and like to take shortcuts through formal structures. Businesses seek quarterly profits, short-term cost controls, and immediate bottom-line results. Norms and values are absolute. Short-term-oriented cultures include Egypt, Nigeria, Australia, Mexico, the United States, Israel, India, and Great Britain.

Key coaching questions: How does this culture or organization value a long-term approach that is based on modesty, frugality, indirect communication, strong relationships, and being comfortable with patience and calculated decisions and actions? How well does the culture or organization value and respect individualism, individual rights, selling yourself, and looking at short-term, shortcut ways to act and make efficient decisions?

Coaching with Global and Cross-Cultural Intelligence

Geert Hofstede's comprehensive cross-cultural work from over three decades of research worldwide has offered an easy-to-use framework and global context to improve any leader-coach's mindset, skill set, and tool set to be more culturally intelligent (Hofstede 2010). Being effective across cultures as a global coach requires empathy, respect, self-awareness, and social awareness.

I recognize that many cultural values are stable and enduring. However, with the unprecedented change throughout the world with the speed of innovation, technological advancements, international education, changes in the global economy, political change and reform, democratization of nation states, and social advancements, the world is becoming increasingly flat, more engaged, and more connected.

Leader-coaches must be less insular, self-centered, and ethnocentric, and able to effectively and fully engage in a diverse, interdependent, dynamically changing world. Engaging global talent effectively is one of the biggest opportunities for competing in a global economy. Due to vast differences across cultures, all nation states, organizations, teams, and individuals must become more interculturally intelligent and agile with regard to global learning and development. Leader-coaches must have the social, emotional, and global cultural awareness, skills, and capability to operate effectively in global networks that often supersede nation-state borders and are open for business 24 hours a day, 7 days a week, 365 days a year.

Understanding and applying Hofstede's five key cultural dimensions will equip leader-coaches to be empathic, inclusive, respectful, and effective as they navigate diverse values, norms, beliefs, and behaviors. Using Hofstede's five elements is essential for any external or internal coach who seeks to be effective either across the world or in a local culture that desires to create a more interdependent, diverse, inclusive, and effective value-based organization.

PRACTICE: YOUR COACHING PLAYBOOK

To support ongoing diversity and inclusion development in your organization, you may find the following exercises helpful.

Develop a clear set of global values and cross-cultural expectations based on mutual respect, responsibility, empathy, access, opportunity, and inclusion. Take into account the cultural diversity issues discussed in this chapter. Remember, diversity and inclusion are talent readiness, talent engagement, and leadership pipeline imperatives.

As a leader-coach, you can help increase diversity and multicultural awareness and global practices through:

1. Establishing common organizational values, laws, and policies consistent with mutual respect, dignity, and equality; and valuing embracing differences, championing diversity, global

experiences, cross-cultural exchanges, improved awareness training, and inclusivity

2. Ongoing training about global and multicultural awareness, diversity and inclusion, and unconscious bias

3. Promoting mentorship, sponsorship, and access for diverse populations with key senior leaders, with advancement opportunities

4. Offering leadership development, coaching, and mentoring access with senior executives

5. Offering diverse groups to promote social networking and develop professional communities, such as: women's groups, Hispanic groups, African American groups, LGBTQ-plus groups, and various ethnic and religious groups.

6. Offering equal pay and advancement opportunities, with global job rotation and cross-cultural work assignments

7. Encouraging breakthrough thinking, innovation, creativity, and being open to ideas from all people at all levels

8. Championing equal employment opportunity laws, diversity and inclusion policies and procedures, and anti-discrimination policies

Reference

Hofstede, Geert. (2010). *Cultures and Organizations: Intercultural Cooperation and Its Importance for Survival*, 3rd ed. McGraw-Hill.

17 Putting It All Together

I hope this book has been a very practical and useful resource to help you on your path to becoming a great leader, manager, team member, business partner, and, most important, coach! Also, I hope you are able to use these leadership and coaching tools at work and at the personal and family level. You now have tools to help you ask better questions, listen more empathically, challenge mindsets and behaviors, respond positively, and, above all, change for the better and help invest in the great talent of all those around you.

The question is, what are you going to do about it?

Making It Stick

The secret of your success is determined by your daily agenda. It all comes down to what you do today.
—*John C. Maxwell,* New York Times *best-selling author*

A Blessing-White study found that 75% of all managers have been through some type of coach training. Does this mean 75% of all internal leaders or managers are effectively coaching their employees on a regular basis? No. Why? Because the coaches' development training didn't stick. The training was static and offered as an event, not as part of an ongoing development effort. Coach training needs to be dynamic, with ongoing application and practice, follow-up implementation and tools, peer coaching accountability, and sustained support so that reflection, sharing, action-learning, and improvement happen over time.

Certainly, the need for coaching is critical, and opportunities for leaders to become great coaches are abundant. But like most training, it won't stick if participants don't find it easy to adopt and apply and don't have ongoing reinforcement.

We all know what to do; we simply don't do it. Or, we haven't put in place a rigorous coaching process and structure that demands ongoing practice, the use of ongoing tools, reflection, and peer accountability and support.

Change is hard and uncomfortable. Charles Duhigg, reporter for the *New York Times* and author of *The Power of Habit: Why We Do What We Do in Life and Business,* explained in an interview with *Harvard Business Review* that habits are formed neurologically (Duhigg 2012). He explained that a habit has three components:

1. A trigger for a new behavior
2. A routine behavior (the habit itself)
3. A reward to ensure our brain neurology encodes this positive recognition pattern for the future

Instead of focusing on the second component—the habit itself—Duhigg argues that we should focus on the trigger (the stimulus or the cue) and the reward (the response or compensation for the action).

Our behaviors originate in the prefrontal cortex, a relatively new addition to the brain. But for a behavior to become habitual, it needs to move into the basal ganglia, the oldest parts of the brain, located near the center of the skull. The basal ganglia don't require thinking or decision-making; this is where our habits become automatic. Conscious decisions occur in the prefrontal cortex. To get to the basal ganglia, where we act out of natural habit, we need to rely on (cues) the emotional trigger and (rewards) the reinforcement or compensation. A cue could be a ritual, a time of day, a place, the presence of other people, or an emotional connection. A reward is an emotional or physical compensation for the habit.

If it sounds too difficult, Duhigg hopes to inspire you by reminding you that things you do every day without thinking were once not so common. About 100 years ago, no one (except perhaps the upper class) brushed their teeth—until the owner of a toothpaste company decided to make brushing teeth a habit. How? By creating a cue, a ritual, and reward.

The cue was to make people uncomfortable about that filmy feeling on their teeth, by advertising that the film was a bad thing. The routine was brushing every day. But the reward? What reward would make people come back for more? Surprisingly, it was not healthy teeth or whiter teeth. It was the tingly, fresh, minty feeling!

Back in 1915, Pepsodent added ingredients to toothpaste that made the mouth tingle. People became addicted to the feeling! The tingling sensation was a great reward, and it became associated with cleanliness. Duhigg reports that within five years of Pepsodent's new advertising campaign, half of America was brushing every day. That is the brain science behind the behavioral change via habits.

If you want to make a habit, you need to determine what cues and rewards to adopt. This is an important principle for coaches. Duhigg explains, "Good managers understand the importance of habits, and they think about it. Bad managers pretend like organizational habits don't exist. And so, when habits emerge, they end up being distortive or toxic."

If you want habits to stick, pick your cue, pick your behavior, and pick your reward.

Practice: Your Coaching Playbook ━━━

At the end of most of the chapters in this book, you found an activity called "Practice: Your Coaching Playbook." In the world of sports, a playbook is a coach's tool that contains *plays*, or strategies and action plans for different situations. These activities are to help you apply what you've learned in each chapter.

Following, for your convenience, is the entire playbook. If you work through the playbook, choosing the plays that can become habitual for you, you'll become an effective coach to others. And you'll help to transform yourself along the way!

PRACTICE: YOUR COACHING PLAYBOOK: THE SIMPSON 3DS COACHING MODEL: THE "HOW TO" OF COACHING

Consider an issue that has become a challenge in your team or organization. Either alone or with your team, take the time to practice the following coaching phases with their interrelated powerful coaching questions:

1. *Diagnose:* What is the coaching agenda?
2. *Design:* What matters most?
3. *Deliver:* What actions will be done?

PRACTICE: YOUR COACHING PLAYBOOK: COACHING FROM THE INSIDE-OUT

Based on what you've learned in this chapter, grade your own mindset. On a scale from 1 (low) to 10 (high), how positive and optimistic is your mindset? Where do you fall short? Are you a victim of what fate or circumstance has dealt you, or fixed in an unproductive narrative? Do you have it within yourself to grow, improve, and change your narrative? Can you help others discover their own effective stories? As a leader, in what ways can you begin to improve your mindset and your team's mindset? Check yourself against the following questions.

Mindset Check List

1. Do you have positive inner thoughts and messages for yourself with good intent or motive?
2. Are you acting with integrity and in alignment with your deepest motives, values, and beliefs?
3. Are you assuming and looking for good intentions in others?
4. Are you acting toward others with genuine care, respect, and mutual benefit?
5. How can you catch others doing something right?
6. How will you make time to connect with others in honest and open communication?
7. How will you actively listen, show respect, and fully understand the viewpoints of others?

PRACTICE: YOUR COACHING PLAYBOOK: COACHING WITH A MINDSET OF ABUNDANCE

As you seek to coach other in more abundant ways, use the following abundance questions to help frame your ongoing coaching conversations:

1. "Who are great examples for you of people who operate in abundant, win-win ways?"
2. "What are the key benefits of living and leading others with abundance?"
3. "In what ways can you choose to be more abundant in your personal and work life?"

4. "How can you reward those around you who choose to act abundantly?"
5. "With whom do you need to practicing being more abundant?"
6. "In what ways can you be generous today? This week? This month? This year?"

PRACTICE: YOUR COACHING PLAYBOOK: COACHING WITH AUTHENTICITY

Think about those people—leaders at work, teachers, coaches, mentors, instructors, trainers, family members, friends—who made and continue to make a difference in your life. They believed in you. They trusted you. They brought out the very best in you.

Now it's your turn to do the same:

1. What is your vision? How and where can you best make a difference?
2. What is your unique contribution?
3. Whom are you going to help and inspire?
4. What lives are you going to seek to influence for good?
5. When do you plan to do this?
6. What actions will you take to make this a reality?
7. Who else needs to be involved?

PRACTICE: YOUR COACHING PLAYBOOK: KNOWING WHEN TO COACH

Hold a practice coaching session in which you strive to follow the key principles in this chapter. Invite someone you trust to be coached, and explain to them the key elements outlined in this practice session. Remember to:

1. Care about the person you're coaching.
2. Ask questions that support their agenda, not yours.
3. Clearly identify the topic of the conversation.
4. Be courageous in the moment.
5. Ask coaching questions that were highlighted in this chapter.
6. Bring all conversations to focused actions.

PRACTICE: YOUR COACHING PLAYBOOK: SETTING PRIORITIES

Here is a list of questions you might ask while coaching people toward setting their most important priorities, vision, and clarity of purpose:

1. "How meaningful is your work?"
2. "What is your mission, vision, values, strategy, or goals?"
3. "What roles do you have in carrying out your most important goals?"
4. "Who are your most important relationships (customers, partners, stakeholders)?"
5. "How can you be more effective with your time and key priorities?"
6. "What do you want to start doing more of?"
7. "What should you continue doing that is working well?"
8. "What is distracting you from achieving your key goals more effectively?"
9. "What low-leverage, nonessential activities should you stop doing?"
10. "What do you want to stop or let go of?"
11. "What urgencies are you caught up in that are really not that important?"
12. "Where can you delegate nonessential or low-value-added activities?"
13. "How can you intentionally give more time to your key priorities?"
14. "What are you committing to do differently?"
15. "What will be your most effective next steps?"

PRACTICE: YOUR COACHING PLAYBOOK: ASKING THE RIGHT QUESTIONS

Hold a practice coaching session in which you strive to follow the key elements of asking the right questions, in the right way, at the right time. Invite someone you trust to be coached, and explain to them that it is a practice session. Remember to:

1. Express appreciation and respect to the person you're coaching.
2. Ask questions that support their agenda, not yours.

3. Clearly identify the topic of the conversation. Practice the 3Ds!
4. Be courageous and transparent about any key issues or opportunities of focus in the moment.
5. Ask good coaching questions to clearly summarize issues.
6. Help the participant narrow the focus on key actions and next steps.

PRACTICE: YOUR COACHING PLAYBOOK: GROWING BY SETTING SMART GOALS

Think of a time when you achieved a goal that you set for yourself, your team, or your organization. Think of a time when you failed to reach a goal. What made the difference between your success and your failure?

Have there been times where you've set lofty and inspiring goals, and then lost commitment or focus on the goals? What happened? How can you avoid those problems in the future?

How can you help hold others accountable and committed to achieving their most important goals and objectives?

Can you improve performance and accountability by holding regular follow-up check-ins and ongoing performance conversations?

What are your most important goals for the immediate future? Are they SMART goals?

As you begin to design and align your goal-planning process, here's a way to write your SMART goals to ensure that they align across your organizational structure to the business unit or division level, the team level, and ultimately the individual level. Make sure your individual and team goals are aligned, up to the higher-level goals at the division and organization levels:

1. Organizational goals (strategic level):

   _____

   _____

   _____

2. Business unit/division/department goals (operational level):

   _____

   _____

   _____

3. Team goals (tactical level):

_____

_____

_____

4. Individual goals (personal level):

_____

_____

_____

PRACTICE: YOUR COACHING PLAYBOOK: LISTENING WITH EMPATHY

In the Broadway musical *Hamilton*, Alexander Hamilton talks with Aaron Burr, who advises him, "talk less, smile more." Here's a coaching challenge: During the next week, pick one conversation where you talk less and listen more. In fact, make a concerted effort to talk less than the person you are talking to. Instead of talking, pause and reflect on what is being said, and listen. Instead of inserting or commenting, just listen. Instead of inserting ideas, overpowering, and dominating, simply listen. At the end of the week, take a moment to note: When were you successful in practicing empathy and when could you get better?

1. How did the other person respond to me when they noticed they had my complete attention?
2. How did I feel during the conversation? Was it hard to remain silent? Did it feel awkward?
3. Did I learn anything that I might otherwise have missed by talking?
4. What were the benefits of practicing empathy?
5. What barriers or challenge get in the way of me becoming a better listener?
6. What was the hardest part?
7. What was the easiest part?
8. Did others give any positive feedback—either verbal or nonverbal—due to practice with empathic communication?

PRACTICE: YOUR COACHING PLAYBOOK: COACHING AND FEEDBACK

Experiment with discussing feedback. Choose someone you trust to practice with. Here are some sample coaching questions you can use in end-of-year reviews, debriefing 360-degree feedback, planning conversations, and other ongoing conversations involving feedback:

1. "What was your initial reaction to your feedback?"
2. "What were your greatest strengths in your feedback?"
3. "What surprised you most?"
4. "What areas would you like to target for improvement?"
5. "What themes or issues emerged for you to pay close attention to?"
6. "Where are you most motivated to get better?"
7. "What short-term actions will you take based on your feedback?"
8. "What was your biggest success this past year?"
9. "What was the best decision you made this year?"
10. "What was the biggest risk you took?"
11. "What surprised you the most?"
12. "What do you want to keep working on?"
13. "What do you never want to do again?"
14. "What mistake did you learn the most from?"
15. "What is your biggest takeaway lesson from this last year?"
16. "Did you improve any relationships this year?"
17. "Did you eliminate any distractions this year?"
18. "What is the best compliment you received this year?"
19. "What compliment did you not receive about something that should have been validated?"
20. "Reflecting over the past year, are there any other key issues, items, areas, or relationships that you would like to discuss?"

YOUR COACHING PLAYBOOK: COACHING FOR ENGAGEMENT

1. Do you have the right people on the bus? If not, who needs to be eased out of position or placed into another position? How and where will you find the right people?
2. Who appears to be disengaging? Do you know why? What is your plan for re-engaging this person?
3. Experiment with putting your team members into the Skill-Will Matrix. Who has high skill and high will? Who has high skill and low will? And so on. What will you do about the results?

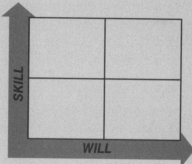

YOUR COACHING PLAYBOOK: COACHING FOR CONTRIBUTION

PRACTICE: The following activity cannot be done in a few minutes or in a day. Sustainable change is often a process of self-discovery and illumination that will sometimes come quickly, but may require long contemplation and planning, and change in behaviors and actions over time.

Consider two or three of the primary roles in your life where you would like to make change or a significant contribution, and ask yourself the following:

1. What changes do I need to make that would be beneficial to me and others?
2. What unmet needs or big opportunities do I see for change?
3. Why is change so important to me and others?

4. What is my bold vision for change?
5. What are the benefits of making these changes?
6. What are the costs of not changing?
7. What have I always loved doing? How can doing those things contribute to the world or those around me?
8. Where could I be an agent for change or make a significant difference?
9. What would make my life more meaningful, joyful, and fully engaged?
10. What inner need must I satisfy in order to feel like I'm making a contribution?
11. Does the need or the opportunity for change tap into my passion and excitement?
12. What values, beliefs, or principles are most important to me to advance or pursue?
13. Do my values and conscience inspire me to take action and become involved?
14. Do I possess the right skills, talent, and resources to make the contribution I want to make?
15. What does my desired future success or contribution look like?

PRACTICE: YOUR COACHING PLAYBOOK: COACHING THE WHOLE-PERSON

Here I offer suggestions about how to approach each of the five whole-person need areas in coaching conversations that lead to greater levels of engagement. Following are questions for whole-person planning:

1. *Financial (money/budgets/resources):* "How do you generate more income, revenue, and cash? How do you better budget and manage your expenses? How are you doing with all the basic hygiene factor needs of food, clothing, housing? Write down one or two things you will do in the financial area to improve and get better."

2. *Body (health/wellness):* "How is your health? How are you renewing yourself physically? The healthier you are physically, the more engaged you will be and the better you will perform. Write down one or two things you will do in the physical area to improve and get better."

3. *Heart (social and emotional health/relationships):* "How can you become more engaged, supportive, kind, respectful, optimistic, positive, and hopeful? How well do you maintain your relationships at work with your boss, co-workers, teams, peers, stakeholders, customers, partners, etc.? What key personal or family relationships, friendships, or community networks do you need to maintain or develop? How can you genuinely connect in uplifting, loving, and mutually respectful relationships? Write down one or two things you will do to improve and get better in the social/emotional area."

4. *Mind (education/professional experiences/career development):* "How are you staying awake mentally? How do you feel about the state of your skills and knowledge? What new education, training, learning, skills, and capabilities do you need to develop to improve your performance? Write down one or two things you will do to develop in the educational and professional development area."

5. *Spirit (meaning/purpose/service/contribution):* "How will you cultivate a life that gives real meaning and purpose? How can you move beyond yourself and connect to the overall purpose and contribution of your organization? How can you be inspired and motivated by a cause, sense of purpose, service, principles, values, and contribution yet to be fulfilled? Write down one or two things you will do to develop the spiritual area."

The following coaching questions are a guide to your own whole-person planning, and then use them to help someone else do whole-person planning as well. This holistic approach to life can be game changing!

Determining Purpose and Motivation

1. THE WHY:

Why are your goals so critical to achieve?

What's your reason and driving motives?

Define my motive:
- Consecration
- Sacrifice
- Commitments
- Covenant

2. THE WHAT:

Define your most important goals to achieve:

Vision—5–10 years?
Strategy—2–5 years?
Important goal this year?

Focus & clarity?
Analyze & plan
- Years
- Quarters
- Months
- Weeks

3. THE HOW:

Define what strategies or path you'll take.

How will you achieve your goals?
What strategies?
What actions?
What behaviors?

Define my action plan:
- Disciplined thought
- Disciplined choices
- Disciplined actions

4. THE WHEN:

When will you achieve your goals, objectives, and targets?

A	B	C
High	Medium	Low
Must be done	Should be done	Could be done

Achievement milestones:
- Define an X to Y
- Set a finish line (date)
- Clear measures

5. THE WHO:

Who will hold you accountable?

Who will help you?

Who is all in?

My board

1. Health coach
2. Financial advisor
3. Spouse/counseling
4. Professional mentor
5. Comm/religious/service

Accountability!
My board of directors:
- Ongoing personal check-in?
- Past, present, future
- Celebrate successes
- Clear the path

Individual Whole-Person Examples

What are your individual needs, opportunities, and goals? How can you design a fulfilled life as a whole-person?

1. FINANCIAL

1. Self-reliance
2. Increasing income
3. Budgeting
4. Spending habits
5. Savings
6. Debt reduction
7. Investments
8. Business acumen
9. Financial planning
10. Tax strategies
11. Entrepreneurship
12. Financial partners

2. HEALTH

1. Work-life balance
2. Health, wellness
3. Exercise, recreation
4. Nutrition, diet, eating habits
5. Nutritional supplements
6. Sleep
7. Physical renewal
8. Meditation, yoga
9. Stress reduction

3. RELATIONSHIPS

1. Social connections
2. Partner, spouse
3. Significant other
4. Family relationships
5. Family dinners
6. Friends and colleagues
7. Partnerships
8. Community service
9. Social networks
10. Travel/hobbies

4. PROFESSIONAL

1. Academic/school
2. Online training
3. Study abroad, internships
4. Trade-skill training
5. Professional development
6. Work experiences
7. Professional networking
8. Associations
9. Certifications

5. PURPOSE

1. Time in nature
2. Journaling, reading
3. Meditation, prayer
4. Religious worship
5. Honoring family/ ancestors
6. Volunteerism
7. Advocacy and service groups
8. Community, public service
9. Gov't service organizations

Individual Whole-Person Planning

What are your individual needs, opportunities, and goals? How can you design a fulfilled life as a *whole-person*?

1. FINANCIAL	2. HEALTH	3. RELATIONSHIPS	4. PROFESSIONAL	5. PURPOSE
GOALS/ACTIONS	GOALS/ACTIONS	GOALS/ACTIONS	GOALS/ACTIONS	GOALS/ACTIONS

PRACTICE: YOUR COACHING PLAYBOOK: COACHING THE 7 CORE FACTORS FOR ORGANIZATIONAL CHANGE

Leader-coaches must take time to understand and engage time with other leaders, managers, and people at all organizational levels in exploring these questions. If possible, remember to start first at the senior or strategic level, then move to the business unit or operational level, and then to the tactical or team level as you design for clarity, focus, alignment, and accountability at each level of your organization:

1. *Why:* "Why do we exist? Who do we serve? What are our mission, vision, and values?"
2. *Where:* "Where will we compete? What is our unique, competitive strategy?" "What is our path and plan?"
3. *What:* "What are our narrowly focused, most important goals?"
4. *How:* "How do we execute the right actions and behaviors?"
5. *When:* "What is the timeframe for achieving our goals with excellence?"
6. *Who:* "Who are the right people? Are they in the right seats?"
7. *Systems:* "How do we recognize, reward, and develop talent?"

Ask yourself, in relation to the 7 Core Factors:

1. Where can our organization get better focus and alignment?
2. Where do we have great alignment, commitment, and buy-in?
3. Where are we clear, focused, and aligned?
4. Where are we unclear, unfocused, and misaligned?
5. Where do we need better sponsorship, engagement, and support?
6. Where can we help coach and offer better support and accountability?

PRACTICE: YOUR COACHING PLAYBOOK: COACHING ACROSS THE GLOBE

To support ongoing diversity and inclusion development in your organization, you may find the following exercises helpful.

Develop a clear set of global values and cross-cultural expectations based on mutual respect, responsibility, empathy, access, opportunity, and inclusion. Take into account the cultural diversity issues discussed in this chapter. Remember, diversity and inclusion are talent readiness, talent engagement, and leadership pipeline imperatives.

As a leader-coach, you can help increase diversity and multicultural awareness and global practices through:

1. Establishing common organizational values, laws, and policies consistent with mutual respect, dignity, and equality; and valuing embracing differences, championing diversity, global experiences, cross-cultural exchanges, improved awareness training, and inclusivity
2. Ongoing training about global and multicultural awareness, diversity and inclusion, and unconscious bias
3. Promoting mentorship, sponsorship, and access for diverse populations with key senior leaders, with advancement opportunities
4. Offering leadership development, coaching, and mentoring access with senior executives
5. Offering diverse groups to promote social networking and develop professional communities, such as: women's groups, Hispanic groups, African American groups, LGBTQ-plus groups, and various ethnic and religious groups.
6. Offering equal pay and advancement opportunities, with global job rotation and cross-cultural work assignments
7. Encouraging breakthrough thinking, innovation, creativity, and being open to ideas from all people at all levels
8. Championing equal employment opportunity laws, diversity and inclusion policies and procedures, and anti-discrimination policies

Reference

Duhigg, Charles. (2012). Habits: Why we do what we do. Interview. *Harvard Business Review*.

Acknowledgments

I would like to start by thanking all those who made this book possible. I've had a fantastic team of writers, editors, contributors, and champions who challenged me to write a follow-up to my two previous coaching books, *Unlocking Potential and Talent Unleashed*. I believe all books are challenging to write. Fortunately, I've been surrounded by intelligent people encouraging me to uncover the right topics based on my coaching experiences with top global leaders, with a focus on sharing practical insights in an applicable way. Thanks to the many coaching clients whom I've learned so much from, those willing to be interviewed, those offering book endorsements, and the many other people who helped along the way. This book would not have happened without the ongoing support of John Wiley's publishing and editorial team. They helped push and prod me along given my intense and crazy domestic and international client work and never-ending travel schedule. Thanks to those who managed book design, formatting, copy editing, graphic design, marketing, promotions, and a million other publishing details. The team includes: Richard Narramore, Vicki Adang, Victoria Anllo, and Dawn Kilgore. Many thanks to the brilliant writing and editing from Dr. Breck England, and the interviews and terrific writing from Alicia Cunningham. Many thanks to my wife Cynthia and our boys Zachary, Luke, Jacob, and McKay. Behind every man is a wife and family helping to coach him up to greater levels of success. Thanks for their ongoing love, support, and examples to me and each of their desires to make meaningful contributions to our family and society.

Professionally, I am grateful for my FranklinCovey colleagues and the many amazing clients I have the privilege of partnering with. There are so many across the US and the world to mention. I've had several examples and mentors in coaching, leadership development, brain science, and human development, including Dr. Terrence E. Maltbia, director of Columbia University's Executive Coaching Certification Program. I was a part of his second Cohort Group in New York City in 2008. We've co-facilitated a number of FranklinCovey-Columbia University Global Coaching Certification Programs. Aside from Dr. Maltbia's genius and humility, he's been great mentor, advocate, and role model. I'm thankful to my friend Dr. Marshall Goldsmith. Over the years, I've appreciated Marshall's honest, direct, practical approach to coaching, free from new-age fluff and complex academic jargon. Thanks to Dr. Daniel Goleman's brilliance on social and emotional intelligence and David Rock's work in brain sciences, overcoming biases, and neuro-leadership. Thanks to my dear friend Dr. Marilee Adams of the Inquiry Institute and her insights in learner-judger mindsets and her curiosity in asking powerful, timely, and provocative coaching questions. Lastly, I am indebted to the late Dr. Stephen R. Covey and his son Stephen MR Covey, who both have had such a profound and positive impact on my life. They are master teachers who model what they teach and who have engaged the world to apply principle-centered and character-based leadership and build high trust individuals, teams, and organizational cultures. I've been blessed to have been taught, tutored, and mentored by so many great roles models who have shaped my life's work to "influence the influential" in people, teams, and in organizations throughout the world. It's a joy to be on this coaching journey. In closing, I echo what my friend Dr. Marshall Goldsmith is famous for stating: "Life Is Good!"

About the Author

Michael K. Simpson is one of the world's preeminent executive coaches, leadership thought leaders, and organizational development consultants and advisors to top leaders and teams globally. He is a distinguished author of eight leadership and coaching books, an engaging keynote speaker, and a practitioner who has held senior executive positions and served on numerous boards of directors. As a coaching and leadership development thought leader, Michael has spent 30 years, in over 35 countries, helping leaders and teams drive vision, strategic direction, goal execution, accountability, and a high trust culture. For over 20 years, Michael has been the Managing Director of Executive Coaching and a Global Consultant with FranklinCovey's Strategy Execution, Leadership, and Trust Practices. As a facilitator, teacher, and keynote speaker, he was on the faculty for three years at Covey's Executive Leadership Summit, teaching with Dr. Stephen Covey, Dr. Ram Charan, and Dr. Mette Norgaard. Michael also taught and coached senior government leaders for three years at the US Department of Defense's senior executive Vanguard Leadership Program in Washington, DC. Michael has conducted thousands of executive offsite leadership retreats and offered executive coaching to senior leaders and teams in top organizations, including: General Electric, PepsiCo, Frito-Lay, Marriott, Hilton, Coca-Cola, IBM, Hewlett Packard, Xerox, Lilly, Baxter, Amgen, Sunovion, Johnson & Johnson, Nike, HSBC Bank, OCBC Bank, Bank of Islam, John Deere, Whirlpool, TE Connectivity, ExxonMobil, Chevron, Shell, Petronas, United Nations, NASA, NATO, Los Alamos National Labs, US Nuclear Regulatory Commission, US Department of Homeland Security/ICE, US Army, US Navy, US Air Force, US Marines, and US Coast Guard.

Michael was a Principal Consultant in the Strategy and Organizational Change Practice for PricewaterhouseCoopers in New York City. He was a Senior Consultant in the Change Management Division for Ernst & Young in Washington, DC. He was Vice President of Sales and Marketing for two leading technology companies, Mediconnect Global and America To Go. Michael is CEO of Simpson Executive Coaching, and CEO of Impact International Education (IIE) in China, in partnership with Franklin-Covey-International. He leads 7 Habits and Leader in Me educational leadership and educational technology for Chinese children, teens, college students, leaders, and parents throughout mainland China.

Michael is a certified executive coach and partner with Columbia University's Executive Coaching Certification Program and Columbia Coaching Learning Association (CCLA). He is a fellow and thought leader with Harvard University's Institute of Coaching (IOC) in partnership with McLean Hospital and Harvard Medical School.

Michael brings a strong academic background to his practical business experience. He has been an adjunct professor at Columbia College's School of Business; a visiting professor for one year at South China University of Technology in Guangzhou, China. He has been a guest lecturer at Hong Kong University, University of Malaysia, Northwestern's Kellogg Business School, BYU's Marriott Business School, Kennedy's School of International Studies, and Utah State University's E-MBA Program. Michael has authored the following books: Powerful Leadership Through Coaching; Unlocking Potential; Talent Unleashed; Ready, Aim, Excel, with Dr. Marshall Goldsmith and Dr. Ken Blanchard; Your Seeds of Greatness; and The Execution-focused Leader, with Pricewaterhouse-Coopers. Michael has a master's degree in Organizational Behavior from Columbia University, and a bachelor's degree from the Kennedy Center for International Studies from Brigham Young University.

When he's not busy traveling, speaking, teaching, coaching, or consulting, Michael enjoys traveling, snow skiing, mountain biking, hiking, and spending time with his family in the beautiful Wasatch Mountains of Utah.

Contact Michael K. Simpson

Do you want to book Michael for your next offsite leadership retreat, keynote presentation, or for one-on-one executive and team coaching, or coaches certification?

For information on booking Michael K. Simpson for one-on-one or team executive coaching, coaches training and certification, keynote speaking engagements, vision and strategic planning, and leadership development training or leadership retreats, contact by phone: 435-602-9031, email: msimpson@ebacs.net, or web: www.simpsonexecutivecoaching.com.

Do you want to purchase group orders of books?

For bulk purchases and book orders *for Powerful Leadership Through Coaching*, contact www.simpsonexecutivecoaching.com.

Index

NOTE: Page references in *italics* refer to figures.